"Owing to his expertise after decades of research in Turkey during the Greco-Roman and Christian eras, Mark Fairchild was invited to collaborate with the Turkish marine archaeologist Mustafa Şahin, who in 2015 discovered and has been excavating the underwater church found in a lake by ancient Nicaea. This discovery is thought to be the very church where the Council of Nicaea was held in AD 325, and Fairchild artfully guides the reader through the early written sources that inform about the church and provides a fascinating treatment of the architectural remains. This book is a major contribution that sheds light on the early chapters of church history, and is written in an engaging style."

James K. Hoffmeier, professor emeritus of Near Eastern archaeology at Trinity Evangelical Divinity School

"This is an excellent study of the recent archaeological discovery of an underwater basilica at the site of Nicaea in modern northwestern Turkey. The real strength of the book is integrative: Dr. Fairchild adeptly weaves history and archaeology to help the reader understand the importance of Nicaea in the early history of the church. Dr. Fairchild's work is masterful in demonstrating how archaeology sheds light on this most critical site in antiquity. This book is a good read for anyone interested in Nicaea as an early setting for the development of Christian theology."

John D. Currid, professor of Old Testament at Reformed Theological Seminary, Dallas

"Mark Fairchild invites readers not only to explore an important archaeological site but also to enter into the circumstances and challenges Christians faced in Nicaea and its environs for the centuries leading up to one of the most significant landmark moments in the articulation of Christian theology. Readers of this book will come away with a deep appreciation for the legacy of the Christians of the first three centuries after Christ's death and resurrection, as well as a thorough immersion into the challenges of archaeological work and the interpretation of its findings."

David A. deSilva, Trustees' Distinguished Professor of New Testament and Greek at Ashland Theological Seminary and author of *Honor, Patronage, Kinship, and Purity*

"This book is a wonderfully readable overview of the archaeology and history of the underwater basilica of Nicaea. It is simultaneously an accessible introduction to the history and archaeology of early Christianity in the years following the Constantinian shift. Good for students and scholars alike, *The Underwater Basilica of Nicaea* draws readers into the world of Christianity in the fourth century by addressing the major scholarly questions about the basilica, including whether it might have been the original meeting place of the First Ecumenical Council. Few books on the archaeology of early Christianity are this readable and accessible!"

Jordan J. Ryan, associate professor of New Testament at Wheaton College and author of *From the Passion to the Church of the Holy Sepulchre*

"Building on the historical and archaeological records, Fairchild sets out an insightful case for the site of Nicaea's Council. Readers are drawn to sift the tantalizing evidence for themselves as Fairchild gathers it from ruins below Lake Iznik and the remnants of the Church's earliest records. Exploring the re-use of the site as a converted Roman temple, Fairchild explores its Christian conversion into a martyrion and later church. He gives readers a detailed look at the development of this early Christian basilica and its possible role as the site where the young faith hammered out her orthodox creed and convictions. A thought-provoking read for scholars and students alike."

David Maltsberger, retired professor of Biblical studies at Wayland Baptist University in Plainview, Texas

"This volume represents the culmination of Mark Fairchild's two decades of field work in Turkey exploring sites of value for Christian origins. Here he draws on collaboration experience with archaeologist Mustafa Şahin, adding a chorus of voices from primary and secondary sources to comment authoritatively on the recently discovered underwater basilica of Nicaea. Calculating from available data, the author determines that the basilica likely was constructed as a martyrion in the fourth century following the liberating Edict of Milan and entertains the question of the significance of the site for the first and most famous ecumenical council that took place in this corner of the ancient Mediterranean world."

John T. Noble, assistant director of the Franciscan Leadership Institute and chair of the theology department at Marian University

"As the 1700-year anniversary of the Nicene Creed approaches, Mark Fairchild delivers a volume that opens up the material culture of fourth-century Nicaea. In this work with the feel of 'notes from the field,' Fairchild guides the reader to the heart of Nicaea (Iznik) itself and to an enigmatic underwater structure on Lake Iznik whose origin and function remain unanswered. Fairchild's expertise and close investigation of the submerged Nicene basilica attempts some answers to its presenting questions: what is the origin of this structure? Was it dedicated to a pagan god or a Christian martyr? And—most pressing for Nicene believers—did this basilica host the gathering of bishops in AD 325? Drawing on his decades of archaeological research in the 'cradle of Christianity' (eastern Turkey) and focusing on worship structures and inscriptions, Fairchild assembles his argument and, in the process, delivers the book's true value for students of Nicaea in AD 325: building out in the reader's imagination Nicaea's geographical milieu, giving it color and dimensionality beyond doctrinal and ecclesiological texts."

Stefana Dan Laing, associate professor of divinity at Beeson Divinity School at Samford University

MARK R. FAIRCHILD

THE UNDERWATER BASILICA OF NICAEA

ARCHAEOLOGY IN THE BIRTHPLACE OF CHRISTIAN THEOLOGY

An imprint of InterVarsity Press
Downers Grove, Illinois

InterVarsity Press
P.O. Box 1400 | Downers Grove, IL 60515-1426
ivpress.com | email@ivpress.com

©2024 by Mark Robin Fairchild

All rights reserved. No part of this book may be reproduced in any form without written permission from InterVarsity Press.

InterVarsity Press® is the publishing division of InterVarsity Christian Fellowship/USA®. For more information, visit intervarsity.org.

All Scripture quotations, unless otherwise indicated, are taken from The Holy Bible, New International Version®, NIV®. Copyright © 1973, 1978, 1984, 2011 by Biblica, Inc.™ Used by permission of Zondervan. All rights reserved worldwide. www.zondervan.com. The "NIV" and "New International Version" are trademarks registered in the United States Patent and Trademark Office by Biblica, Inc.™

The publisher cannot verify the accuracy or functionality of website URLs used in this book beyond the date of publication.

Cover design: David Fassett
Interior design: Daniel van Loon

ISBN 978-1-5140-1067-9 (print) | ISBN 978-1-5140-1068-6 (digital)

Printed in the United States of America ♾

Library of Congress Cataloging-in-Publication Data
Names: Fairchild, Mark R., author.
Title: The underwater basilica of Nicaea : archaeology in the birthplace of Christian theology / Mark R. Fairchild.
Description: Downers Grove, IL : IVP Academic, [2024] | Includes bibliographical references and index.
Identifiers: LCCN 2024014599 (print) | LCCN 2024014600 (ebook) | ISBN 9781514010679 (paperback) | ISBN 9781514010686 (ebook)
Subjects: LCSH: Christian antiquities–Turkey–Iznik Lake. | Basilicas–Turkey–Iznik Lake. | Excavations (Archaeology)–Turkey–Iznik Lake. | Nicaea (Turkey)–Buildings, structures, etc. | Nicaea (Turkey)–Church history. | Iznik Lake (Turkey)–Antiquities. | BISAC: RELIGION / Antiquities & Archaeology | RELIGION / Christian Church / History
Classification: LCC DS156.N5 F35 2024 (print) | LCC DS156.N5 (ebook) | DDC 939/.313–dc23/eng/20240513
LC record available at https://lccn.loc.gov/2024014599
LC ebook record available at https://lccn.loc.gov/2024014600

31 30 29 28 27 26 25 24 | 13 12 11 10 9 8 7 6 5 4 3 2 1

DEDICATION

This volume is dedicated to my wife, beautiful in every way,

Darlene Annette (Marsh) Fairchild,

who has blessed me with four children;

they have inspired us with their talents, minds and spirits:

Peter, Hannah, Ennea, and Malina.

CONTENTS

Acknowledgments .... *ix*

Introduction *1*

CHAPTER 1 | HISTORY OF NICAEA AND CHRISTIAN BEGINNINGS IN BITHYNIA | 11

A Brief History of Nicaea *11*

Christian Beginnings in Nicaea *15*

Trajan, Pliny the Younger, and the Christians in Bithynia *19*

Early Martyrs from Nicaea *25*

The Testimony of Early Christian Tombs in Phrygia and Bithynia *27*

Neophytos, the Martyr of Nicaea *35*

The First Council at Nicaea *40*

Summary *47*

CHAPTER 2 | THE EARLIEST CHRISTIAN PLACES OF WORSHIP | 49

Christianity Prior to Constantine—an Underground Movement *49*

The Earliest Churches Following the Edict of Milan—AD 313 .... *56*

Imperial Edicts Regarding Christianity and the Pagan Temples *60*

When Were Temples Converted into Churches? *64*

Summary *67*

CHAPTER 3 | THE DISCOVERY, EXCAVATION, AND RESEARCH OF THE UNDERWATER BASILICA | 69

Discovery and Research *69*

How Was the Basilica Submerged? *74*

Other Ancient Remains and Byzantine Churches in Nicaea *80*

Summary *92*

CHAPTER 4 | WAS THE UNDERWATER BASILICA ORIGINALLY A CONVERTED PAGAN TEMPLE? | 94

The Temple Theory *94*

Support for the Theory *96*

Evaluation of the Theory *99*
Summary *112*

CHAPTER 5 | WAS THE UNDERWATER BASILICA A MARTYRION? | 114

Was the Basilica a Martyrion Built to Commemorate Neophytos? *114*
The Nicaea Basilica and the Early Christian Martyrions in Rough Cilicia *121*
Is the Sarcophagus of Neophytos in the Iznik Museum? *131*
Summary *134*

CHAPTER 6 | WAS THE UNDERWATER BASILICA THE PLACE OF THE FIRST COUNCIL OF NICAEA? | 136

Is the Underwater Basilica the Place Where the First Council of Nicaea Met? *136*
Was the Underwater Basilica Originally Constructed of Wood? *141*
Summary *150*

CHAPTER 7 | THE LEGACY OF NICAEA | 152

CHAPTER 8 | CONCLUSION | 161

Glossary *165*
Bibliography *167*
Image Credits *175*
General Index *179*

ACKNOWLEDGMENTS

THIS VOLUME COULD NOT HAVE BEEN WRITTEN without the patient and loving support of my wife, Darlene, who spent countless days home alone in Indiana while I was trudging through the brush and climbing heights in search of the ancient cities of Anatolia. Our long-suffering children have endured many weeks during summertime without their father. I wish now that I could reclaim the time. As the apostle said, "Buy back the time for the days are evil."

A number of others have been instrumental in offering assistance, for whom I am deeply indebted. Mustafa Şahin's offer to have me collaborate with him on the research at Nicaea was the beginning of a wonderful professional relationship, and his friendship has been a blessing to me. Süha Cura, Şahin's grad student and assistant director of the excavation, has been particularly helpful. The students, faculty, and rector of Uludağ University, Prof. Dr. Ahmet Saim Kılavuz, have been gracious in all of my meetings and associations on campus. Dr. Bülent Şenay, professor of history of religion and culture at Uludağ, has given me opportunities to address students and faculty at the university. These have been wonderful opportunities to engage in stimulating discussions.

Of course, I cannot neglect to thank my own Huntington University, which has encouraged my research in Turkiye and provided me with a sabbatical to work on this project in Nicaea. In particular, I want to thank President Sherilyn Emberton, Academic Dean Luke Fetters, and the chair of the department of Christian Thought and Practice, Dr. Karen Jones. Our students, faculty, and staff have blessed me more than I can say. Our library staff, especially Noelle Keller and Randy Neuman, have been tremendous in helping me track down needed resources.

I would be remiss not to mention my friends at Tutku Educational Travel in Izmir. Their support and assistance for all my travel arrangements over the past twenty years has been immense. The President of Tutku, Levent Oral, has been a personal friend and consultant for years. The cartography skills of Cuneyt Oral and Burhan Oral are well displayed with the excellent maps in this book. The staff has demonstrated excellence in arranging most of my flights and accommodations, and Tutku's guides have contributed many excellent insights.

My travels throughout Turkiye have taken me to every corner of the country and I have made friends with more people than I can list here. Most of them will never see this book, but in small ways they have contributed to its contents. I wish I could thank them in person, but I will never see many of them again.

Glen Thompson, Professor Emeritus at Asia Lutheran Seminary, offered many helpful insights on an early draft of the manuscript. Likewise, two anonymous outside readers contributed greatly to the structure of the volume. Throughout the process, it has been a delight to work with Rachel Hastings, my IVP Academic editor, whose perceptive suggestions added much clarity to this volume.

Finally, support from a Fulbright Senior Research Grant for the 2021–2022 year, coupled with the sabbatical from Huntington University, made it possible to spend several months in Turkiye to amass much of the research that has made this volume possible. The director and staff of the Turkish Fulbright Commission have gone overboard to help with problems and issues related to the logistics of living in Turkiye.

INTRODUCTION

IN 2014 A SUBMERGED STRUCTURE was discovered near the eastern shore of Lake Iznik in modern-day Iznik, Turkey. While most Western Christians today may be unfamiliar with Iznik, they certainly will recognize the city's ancient name—Nicaea. This structure had gone unnoticed for centuries, but as water levels began dropping in the lake, aerial photography revealed a shocking discovery. This was no ordinary civic structure. The nave, aisles, and the apse pointing east suggested that this building was a basilica church (see plate 1).

Figure I.1. Map of ancient Anatolia, Macedonia, and Greece

The location of the structure evoked a great deal of interest. Nicaea was the site of the First Ecumenical Council, where Christians from across the Mediterranean world gathered together to debate issues that threatened to divide the church into factions. The first and arguably the most important ecumenical council for the Christian faith took place on the shores of Nicaea in 325, called by the newly converted emperor Constantine in the early fourth century. Over the next 450 years, seven of these councils convened in western Anatolia (modern Turkey) to unite the church. The first and the last of these met in Nicaea. These councils were so important that the brightest and best early Christian theologians and leaders traveled upward of a thousand miles to attend these meetings. In spite of the difficulties of ancient travel, hundreds made the journey.

Although several Byzantine churches have been discovered in Iznik, the meeting place, or church, of the council has never been discovered. News of the discovery quickly spread throughout the archaeological world and the media seized on the story. The attention brought about a swift response from Turkish authorities, who quickly appointed a director of excavations and a team of archaeologists. Work on the project commenced in 2015.

Authorities at the Iznik Museum and the Turkish Ministry of Culture and Tourism assigned the task of investigating the structure to Professor Mustafa Şahin. I first became involved with the project in 2017 when Professor Şahin asked me to collaborate with him on research for the structure. I had been doing research in Turkey over the past twenty years and had traveled to over four hundred ancient sites dating back to the Greek, Roman, and Byzantine periods. A large number of these sites had churches constructed during the Byzantine period. My work in eastern Turkey involved work in some of the earliest basilica churches. In 2018 we jointly published a preliminary report on the work for the *Biblical Archaeology Review.*[1] In 2022, Huntington University gave me a sabbatical, which coincided with a Fulbright Senior Research Grant I received for the 2021–2022 year. During that time, I spent six months in Turkey working on the structure and historical sources related to it.

[1]Mustafa Şahin and Mark R. Fairchild, "Nicea's Underwater Basilica," *BAR* 44, no. 6 (November–December 2018): 30-37, 61.

The selection of Professor Şahin to conduct research at the site was a prudent choice. He received his PhD from Atatürk University in Erzurum and received his first academic appointment in 1997 at Selçuk University in Konya. In 2002, he founded Turkey's first Department of Underwater Archaeology, at Selçuk University. In 2005 Şahin took a position at Uludağ University in Bursa, where he promptly established the university's first Department of Archaeology. The department has grown significantly since then, and he is currently the chair of the Archaeology Department as well as the director of the Mosaic Research Center at Uludağ University.

Uludağ University is one of Turkey's major universities, with over 74,000 students studying at the Bursa campus. Its proximity to the underwater basilica, located sixty miles southwest of Iznik, makes it feasible for undergraduate and graduate archaeological students to participate in the dig. Work at the site has continued since 2015, with interruptions in 2020 and 2021 due to the Covid pandemic. In 2022, a new museum was opened in Iznik near the Yenişehir Gate, displaying many of the artifacts from the underwater excavations. Plans for the future include an underwater museum constructed above the ruins once excavations are completed. The year 2025 will mark the seventeen hundredth anniversary of the Council of Nicaea, and the city of Iznik is preparing celebrations to mark the event.

Nineteen hundred years ago, Christianity was negotiating its way through a hostile environment.[2] From the last years of the first century until the first years of the fourth century, Christianity was deemed an illegal religion by the Roman state. Christians were misunderstood, mistrusted, and mistreated.[3] At times and in places the persecutions were so intense that Christians were martyred for no other reason than for their faith in Christ. Unknown thousands of Christians were slaughtered in cities throughout the empire and the properties of Christians were

[2]Cf. Jonathan Hill, "Christians in a Hostile World," in *The Crucible of Christianity: The Forging of a World Faith* (Oxford: Lion Hudson, 2010), 108-29.

[3]Caecilius Natalis, a character created by Marcus Minucius Felix, reflects the suspicions of the pagans toward the Christians: "Why do they never speak in the open, why do they always assemble in stealth? It must be that whatever it is they worship and suppress is deserving either of punishment or of shame." *Octavius* 10.2. Cited in G. Clark, *The Octavius of Marcus Minucius Felix* (New York: Paulist, 1974), 66.

seized.[4] The Christian communities in Anatolia bore the brunt of the persecutions. The Christian community became an underground movement, operating discreetly in the villages, towns, and countryside. Nonetheless, the Christian message spread throughout the empire.

Following a period of some 250 years of sporadic but intense persecution, Constantine, the first Christian Roman emperor, called the council to reconcile and unify the church. It is not known exactly how Christianity came to the imperial palace. Constantine's mother, Helena, converted to the faith shortly after her son ascended to the throne and there is little doubt that she had an impact on Constantine embracing the faith. However, Eusebius cites the defining moment in 312, prior to the battle of the Milvian Bridge.[5] There, Constantine saw a sign in the sky (or experienced a vision) of the chi-rho, the first two letters of the name Christ. This was taken as a sign from God, and Constantine had the symbol painted on his troops' shields. Constantine won the battle and promptly converted to Christianity. Shortly thereafter, in 313, Constantine and Licinius (corulers of the Western and Eastern Roman Empire) issued the Edict of Milan, making Christianity a legitimate religion in the empire and returning property that was previously seized to the Christians.

After Licinius was killed in 324 and the empire was united under Constantine, the emperor attempted to resolve theological disputes emerging within the church. The First Council of Nicaea convened in 325 to unify the church and to settle theological issues that threatened to divide the Christian faith. Never before had there been a gathering of bishops and theologians from across the then-known Christian world for worship,

---

[4]Candida Moss significantly minimized the extent of the early Christian persecutions and the number of Christians martyred. She claimed that Christians were persecuted for no more than twelve years and that the early Christian reports were largely fictional accounts. See *The Myth of Persecution: How Early Christians Invented a Story of Martyrdom* (New York: Harper Collins, 2013). In his review of the book, Paul Maier claimed, "The most indisputable fact from the church's past is that Christians were indeed tortured and martyred in the early years of the faith. To question this is to share in the crude folly of Holocaust-deniers today." Paul L. Maier, "The Myth of Persecution: A Provocative Title, an Overdone Thesis," *CRJ* 36, no. 6 (2013): 1. Likewise, Clayton Croy responds "this is a deeply flawed book, a work of revisionist history. . . . While conservative Christian rhetoric is sometimes guilty of excesses, this book swings hard in the opposite direction, revising history and denying much of the evidence for early Christian persecution." N. Clayton Croy, review of *The Myth of Persecution*, by Candida Moss, *Review of Biblical Literature* 10 (2013).

[5]Eusebius, *Life of Constantine* 1.28-30.

fellowship, and debate. The name of the ancient city at that time was Nicaea, and it was here that members of churches from across the Mediterranean world were invited to debate the issue of Arianism, as well as other issues. The well-known Nicaean Creed became a theological cornerstone of orthodoxy as a result of this council. In the years that followed, six more councils were called to address issues. All of these met in western Turkey, with the last of these in Nicaea in 787. Together, these constitute the Seven Ecumenical Councils, which most denominations accept as defining moments in Christian history.

Today, Iznik is a small town located in northwestern Turkey. The city has a population of around 15,000 people and is located around sixty miles southeast of Istanbul, on the other side of the Sea of Marmara. Driving around the sea from Istanbul, the trip involves around 130 miles. Bursa, the fourth largest city in Turkey with over two million people, is sixty miles to the southwest. Lake Iznik (ancient Ascania) is a freshwater lake that borders the city on the west. The lake measures around twenty miles in length (east to west) and six miles in width, and covers 115 square miles, a little less than Yellowstone Lake in Wyoming.

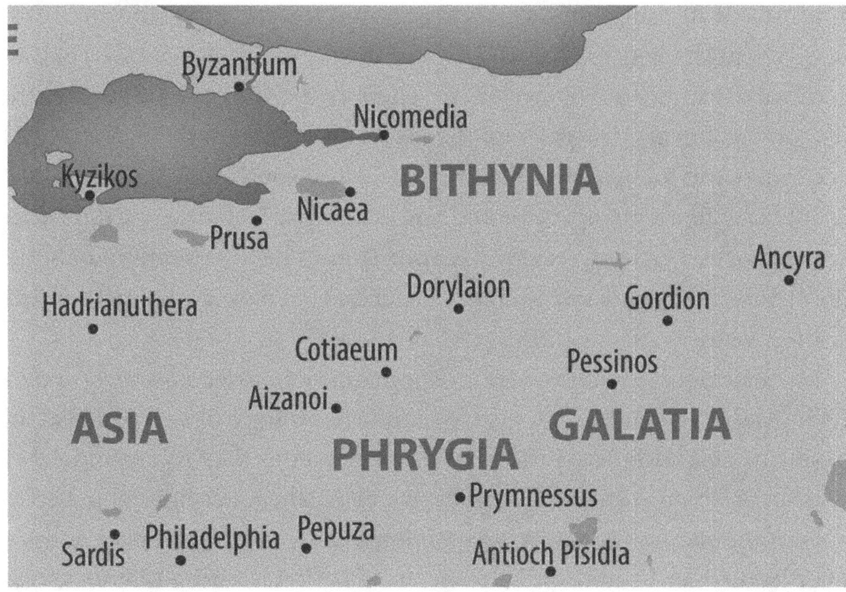

Figure I.2. Map of Roman provinces of Bithynia and Phrygia

The city of Iznik is well-known in Turkey as a center for the production of ceramics. From the fifteenth to the seventeenth century, the pottery and porcelains produced at Iznik were of the highest quality and decorated some of the most important Ottoman structures in Turkey and the Ottoman Empire. Early Iznik pottery was inspired by Chinese porcelain and combined Ottoman patterns with Chinese blue and white designs. Iznik tiles can be found in the Topkapı Palace, the Sultan Ahmed Mosque (Blue Mosque), Istanbul's Süleymaniye Mosque, and numerous other structures in cities throughout Turkey and abroad. The Blue Mosque alone contains over twenty thousand Iznik tiles. Early Iznik pottery can be found in museums across the world.

The ceramic industry is still vibrant in Iznik. The Iznik Foundation carries on the Iznik ceramic cultural heritage through training, education, and research. Numerous workshops throughout the city continue the ceramic production using the same high quality quartz materials (known as fritware) as in the past. The ground quartz fritware was a technological advance, unknown outside of China, that produced porcelain with improved durability and enhanced glaze colors.

Iznik retains many of the ruins from the past. The city is encircled by a massive wall containing over one hundred towers, many of which are in excellent shape (see plate 2). Three of the four city gates located in the cardinal directions are likewise in excellent shape. The gates on the north (Istanbul Gate) and the gates on the east (Lefke Gate) have been recently excavated and are wonderfully preserved. The southern gate (Yenişehir Gate) is currently being excavated and is likewise well preserved. Inside the walls the ruins of several Byzantine churches are scattered about the city. A well-preserved Roman theater has been excavated within the last few years.

The Fulbright grant gave me an opportunity to research source materials regarding Nicaea, the history and archaeology of early Christian basilicas, and early martyrions in Anatolia, as well as to examine the seasons of excavations at the underwater basilica. Additionally, I was able to interact with faculty and students at Uludağ University and to offer lectures at Uludağ and elsewhere in Turkey. During that time my research focused on three questions: First, was the underwater structure originally a temple dedicated to Apollo? This theory has been pursued by Professor Şahin and has been promoted in a number of publications.[6] Second, was the underwater structure a martyrion memorializing a Nicaean martyr? A Nicaean tradition holds that a young man named Neophytos was executed at the beginning of the fourth century and that the basilica was constructed to mark the spot of his execution. And third, was the underwater structure a basilica where the historic Council of Nicaea took place? The place of the council has vexed scholars and some have suggested that a church did not exist in Nicaea at the time of the council. The answers to all three of these questions could prove to be yes. Alternately, the answers to all three of these questions could be no. This volume will assess the strengths and weaknesses of these issues.

The book begins with a brief history of Nicaea and the surrounding region of Bithynia. This historical survey begins with the origin of the city of Nicaea and its development up through the early Byzantine period. Additionally, I summarize the origin of Christianity in the region and describe the struggle of the Christian communities through the years of sporadic and somewhat intense persecutions until the Edict of Milan. The Christians in this region and neighboring Phrygia expressed their faith in discreet ways, particularly through funerary inscriptions, with the result that Christianity expanded greatly throughout the area.

The second chapter describes the discovery of the underwater basilica and the subsequent excavation of the site. Earthquakes over the last seventeen hundred years have changed the shoreline of Lake Iznik and the basilica now lies underwater a short distance from the beach. The North Anatolian Fault, running through Iznik, is very active and cataclysmic seismic activity has damaged the ancient city over the years. This chapter includes a brief survey of the many ancient churches and structures in Iznik.

[6]M. Şahin, "İznik Gölü Bazilika KalıntısıSualtı Yüzey Araştirmasi—2015," *TINA Denizcilik Arkeoloji Dergisi* 4 (2015): 32-51; M. Şahin, "İznik Gölü Bazilika Kazılari—2016," *TINA Denizcilik Arkeolojisi Dergisi* 6 (2016): 64-79; M. Şahin, "Nikaia'nın Kayıp Apollon Tapınaği," *Bursa'da Zaman* (July 2017): 52-53; M. Şahin, "Hava Fotoğrafları ve Arkeoloji Biliminde Yeni Bir Keşif: İznik Gölü Bazilikasi," *Yüksek Öğretim Dergisi* (Nov. 2018): 79-81; M. Şahin, "Neue Forschungen und Ausgrabungen in Der Basilica des İznik Sees," in *Imperial Residence and Site of Councils: The Metropolitan Region of Nicaea/Nicomedia*, vol. 96, *Asia Minor Studien*, Imperial Residence and Site of Councils (Bonn: Rudolf Habelt, 2020), 93-106; M. Şahin, "Underwater Excavation at the Basilica Church in İznik Lake—2019," *IJEGEO* 9 no. 2 (2022): 70-80.

At the beginning of the fourth century, two edicts reversed the previous policies of the Roman state and gave Christianity legal status throughout the empire. Property that had previously been seized from the Christians was returned and Christianity emerged from an underground movement to become a licit religion in the Mediterranean. I propose that the underwater basilica was one of the earliest basilicas constructed after Constantine solidified his position on the throne. This change brought about sweeping changes in the empire. Over the next three hundred years Christianity began to dominate the religious landscape, and slowly the pagan cults receded from public sphere. As the pagan temples were abandoned, many of the temples were repurposed for Christian use. The third chapter describes this development and explains how the ancient sanctuaries were converted into basilica churches.

In the fourth chapter I tackle the issue regarding the origin of the submerged structure. The director of excavations, Professor Şahin, has argued that the building originated as a second-century temple dedicated to Apollo. Professor Şahin has given me access to his research, the excavation data, and photographs of the excavation. Many of Şahin's photos appear in this volume. He has been a wonderful friend, colleague, and an example of scholarly cooperation. The excavation team has likewise been extraordinarily helpful with their assistance. This book would not be possible without the collaboration of Professor Şahin and his team.

Here, I describe the temple theory in detail and present several pieces of evidence that support the theory. A temple dedicated to Apollo is mentioned in a seventh-century document called the *Chronicon Paschale*. The *Chronicon*, written by an anonymous cleric in Constantinople, documented events from the time of Adam up to the seventh century. Among the many items listed, the document briefly mentioned an Apollonion that was constructed outside the walls of Nicaea during the fourth year of the Emperor Commodus (AD 183). Small column drums in the atrium are thought to come from columns of the temple along with an architectural piece outside of the temple that may be a portion of the pediment. An external wall on the perimeter of the basilica may be part of a temenos wall. A well in the atrium could be the location of a sacred spring, common to Apollo temples.

The fifth chapter examines the question whether the basilica was a martyrion, and if so, for whom? The location of the basilica and the presence of numerous tombs in and around the basilica suggests that the structure was originally built as such. A martyrion is an ancient church constructed not only for worship, but also to remember and commemorate the life of a Christian saint who was killed during the 250 years prior to the time of Constantine. Although the names of most of these martyrs have been lost, there were thousands of unknown Christians executed during this time.

In this chapter, I compare the submerged structure at Nicaea with a number of known martyrions in an area of southeast Turkey, known as Rough Cilicia. Christianity arrived early in this area, even before the three missions reported in the Acts of the Apostles. Some of the earliest post–Edict of Milan churches can be found here, and several of them were dedicated to early martyrs from the area. A comparison of these martyria with the underwater structure in Nicaea illustrates the role of the cult of the saints in early Christianity. This chapter also illustrates how the remains of the saints were incorporated into these early churches.

Christian traditions regarding the saints have evolved over the centuries. In most instances legends have grown up, describing miraculous works of the saint and logically improbable events. Nevertheless, the names of many martyrs have persisted, even if the stories surrounding them have changed. The Nicaean traditions connect the name of Neophytos with this basilica. The traditions are from the late tenth century, causing one to wonder if they accurately tell the story of Neophytos or are traditions that have no basis in historical fact.

The penultimate chapter deals with the most important issue. Was this basilica the place where the First Council of Nicaea met? Archaeological evidence suggests that the masonry structure underwater at Nicaea dates to the late fourth century. If this data is correct, it would rule out the possibility of this being the place of the council. However, we have to contend with several facts that need to be explained. First, several tombs have been found inside of the basilica. Some of these are underneath the walls of the masonry structure. The tombs preceded the masonry church. What does this imply? Second, excavators believe there was a floor some eighteen or more inches below the masonry basilica. This floor was either wooden (and no longer visible) or earthen. And finally, a large number of nails have been discovered in the excavations. All of this leads us to the question, Was the masonry basilica constructed over an earlier structure?

The volume concludes with a short chapter on the legacy of Nicaea. For seventeen hundred years churches of all denominations have looked back on this event and have celebrated a time when the universal church was able to arrive at a consensus on an important theological issue. Unfortunately, over the years, the Christian community has splintered over issues of much less significance. Catholic, Protestant, and Orthodox believers still retain a common bond in our faith. We may never agree on all the theological aspects of the Christian faith. Paul himself referred to the "mystery" of the faith more than twenty times. Despite our differences, the findings in Lake Iznik harken back to a foundational time when the early church leaders were intentional in resolving issues while maintaining the unity of the faith. The council that convened at this site was only the first of Seven Ecumenical Councils, yet it was the most important. Nicaea was a beginning. It was a beginning of Christian theology with an imperial endorsement. It was a beginning for the faith as it emerged from the secrecy of an underground movement and became an unabashedly professed belief. It was an important beginning for what was later to become the most widely embraced faith in the world.

CHAPTER ONE

HISTORY OF NICAEA AND CHRISTIAN BEGINNINGS IN BITHYNIA

A BRIEF HISTORY OF NICAEA

The Sangarius River (known as the Sakarya today) is the third longest river in Turkey. It flows a mere fifteen miles to the east of Iznik. Portions of an ancient road leading to Nicaea and a Roman bridge crossing the Sangarius can be seen today. According to the myth, the river god Sangarius and the indigenous Anatolian goddess Cybele gave birth to the Nenaid nymph, Nikaia. Nikaia was associated with the springs and lake at Nicaea. She was a devoted follower of Artemis, the Greek manifestation of Cybele. Nonnus, a fifth-century AD epic poet, claims that the city Nicaea was named after Nikaia. According to the myth, the god Dionysus fell in love with Nikaia, but she rejected him. Nevertheless, Dionysus schemed to rape Nikaia, and he impregnated her. Nikaia gave birth to a daughter, Telete. As the story goes, the site at Nicaea was founded by Dionysus and named after his lover Nikaia: "And the god built a city of fine stone beside the tipplers' lake, Nikaia, city of Victory, which he named after the nymph."[1] Telete was destined to follow Dionysus and became involved in the ritual dances and initiation rites for the Bacchic mysteries.

Myths aside, excavations have revealed that the site of Nicaea was first occupied around 2500 BC. Much later in time, a Hellenistic tradition claimed that the city was founded by men from the army of Alexander the Great who had come from another Nicaea, a town near Thermopylae in central Greece. These men named their settlement after their former

[1]Nonnus, *Dionysiaca* 16.1-405.

Figure 1.1. Roman bridge crossing the Sangarius River near Osmaneli

home. Perhaps more trustworthy is the testimony of Sephanus of Byzantium, who claimed that the site was colonized by Bottiaeans (in ancient Macedonia) as early as the seventh century BC and that the place was called Ankore. After Alexander's conquests, in 316 BC Antigonus Monophthalmus established a city at this place and named it after himself, Antigoneia. Following the battle of Ipsus in 301 BC, Lysimachus gained control of the city, reestablished it, and named it after his wife, Nicaea.

After Lysimachus's death in 281 BC, Nicaea was taken by Nicomedes I, and the city functioned as the capital of the kingdom of Bithynia until the capital was moved to Nicomedia in 265 BC. The city was strategically located on trade routes, and throughout the third century the town flourished and was often the residence of the kings of Bithynia. Near the end of the second century BC, Rome started intruding into Anatolia and Bithynia. When Nicomedes IV was made king in 94 BC, he was little more than a Roman pawn. The king of Pontus, Mithridates VI, attempted to overthrow Nicomedes, and in 88 BC Mithridates had eighty thousand Roman settlers executed in several western Anatolian cities. This sparked the First Mithridatic War from 88 to 84. A second war with Mithridates was fought from 83 to 81, at which time a treaty was signed. Finally, when Nicomedes IV died in 74 BC, he offered Bithynia to the Romans and the Senate promptly made Bithynia a province, naming Nicaea as its capital. This prompted Mithridates VI to launch the Third Mithridatic War, lasting from 73 to 63 BC. Rome crushed Mithridates in the war and abolished any further threats from the Pontic king.[2]

Strabo provided a description of the city at the beginning of the first century.[3] He referred to it as the metropolis of Bithynia, located on Ascania Lake and surrounded by a large and fertile plain. Coins minted in Nicaea confirm that it was given the coveted title of metropolis.[4] Strabo asserted that the city was quadrangular in shape with streets intersecting at right angles according to the Hippodamian city plans. The city's perimeter was sixteen stadia (around two miles). At Strabo's time, the city had four gates, one in each direction, and they were all visible from the gymnasium located in the center of the city. Based on the ruins in the city today, Strabo's description seems quite accurate.

The city prospered throughout the Roman imperial period. Augustus significantly added to the city's infrastructure, and during the reign of Claudius, Nicaea became the chief city of Bithynia. Vespasian constructed large triumphal arches in the north at the Istanbul Gate, in the east at the Lefke Gate, and in the south at the Yenişehir Gate. Nicomedia, located forty miles to the north, also vied for prominence in Bithynia, and at one time or another each city became the capital of the province. In 110 Pliny the Younger was appointed governor (Praetorian Legate) of Bithynia and Pontus. During that time Pliny was faced with the question of what to do with Bithynian residents that had been identified as Christians. From a letter that he wrote to the Emperor Trajan, it is evident that Christianity had made great gains throughout the region. More of this will be discussed below.

In 123 the Emperor Hadrian visited the city, and Nicaea maintained its prominent position from the late imperial period through the Byzantine

---

[2]Cf. the well-written volume by Adrienne Mayor, *The Poison King: The Life and Legend of Mithridates, Rome's Deadliest Enemy* (Princeton, NJ: Princeton University Press, 2010).

[3]Strabo, *Geography* 12.4.7.

[4]A "metropolis" was the "mother city" of a province, an honor implying the significance of the city. The metropolis was usually the seat of the governing authorities.

period. The senator and historian Dio Cassius was born and raised in Nicaea in the middle of the second century before moving to Italy after his father's death, around 180. He later returned to Anatolia when he was appointed curator of Pergamon and Smyrna.

By the early third century, the walls from the Hellenistic period were in a serious state of disrepair. They offered little resistance to the Goths, who swept down from the north in 258 and wiped out the cities of Bithynia and the surrounding areas. The residents of Nicaea fled before the Goths and returned to find their city burned and destroyed. The residents rebuilt the city and its walls. The new city walls were attached to the triumphal arches constructed earlier by Vespasian, and the project was completed under the reign of Claudius Gothicus (268–270). The new city walls were three miles in length, around thirteen feet thick, and roughly thirty feet in height.

The Emperor Constantine had a palace constructed on the lake, and the First and Seventh Ecumenical Councils were held in Nicaea in 325 and 787. The Nicene Creed, one of the first and most important doctrinal statements by the Christian church, was formulated at the First Ecumenical Council. Here 250 to 318 bishops from across the Mediterranean gathered together in Constantine's palace to discuss, debate, and agree on some of the primary Christian beliefs. This will be described in more detail later.

As early as the late seventh century the Muslim caliphs began their incursions into Anatolia. The Taurus Mountains in southeast Anatolia slowed the Muslim advances until the ninth century, when renewed attempts to conquer the Byzantine Empire succeeded, in part because of civil war within the empire. The crushing defeat of the Byzantine forces at the battle of Manzikert in 1071 by the Seljuk Turks opened the bulk of Anatolia to Seljuk control. In 1078 the governor of Nicaea, Nikephoros III Botaneiates, seized control of Constantinople with the assistance of Turkish mercenaries and was made emperor over the declining Byzantine Empire.[5] Upon leaving Nicaea, Nikephoros left the city, along with Cyzicus, Nicomedia, Chalcedon, and Chrysopolis, to the control of the Muslim

[5]Clive Foss, *Nicaea: A Byzantine Capital and Its Praises* (Brookline, MA: Hellenic College, 1996), 35-38.

Suleyman ibn Qutalmish in exchange for his assistance in gaining the Byzantine throne. Suleyman made Nicaea the capital of his newly enlarged state (the Sultanate of Rum).[6] The fall of the Byzantine Empire and Constantinople was completed centuries later in 1453 when the Ottoman army led by Sultan Mehmed II breached the walls and conquered the city.[7]

Figure 1.2. Masonry jutting out into Lake Iznik, north of the submerged basilica

CHRISTIAN BEGINNINGS IN NICAEA

There are no concrete traditions detailing how Christianity was first established in Nicaea or Bithynia. However, the Acts of the Apostles might offer a few clues. On Paul's so-called second mission with Silas and Timothy (Acts 16), it is reported that Paul wanted to enter Asia (most probably Ephesus), but the Holy Spirit forbade him from doing so. Consequently, the apostle turned north and was trying to enter Bithynia. But again, the Spirit prevented him from entering Bithynia. Lying in the

[6]Foss, *Nicaea*, 41-42.

[7]Cf. An engaging volume on the conquest is Roger Crowley's *1453: The Holy War for Constantinople and the Clash of Islam and the West* (New York: Hyperion, 2005).

south of Bithynia, Nicaea was the major city that attracted the attention of Paul. Twice frustrated, Paul and his companions came to Troas (Alexandria Troas) and received a vision bidding him to sail to Europe.

On his next mission, after strengthening the churches in Galatia and Phrygia, Paul quickly made his way to Ephesus (Acts 18). There he spent the next three years, the longest period of time he spent in one city on any of his journeys. During that time Paul taught at the school (or lecture hall)[8] of Tyrannus.[9] Students from this school not only learned the gospel, but also traveled to the neighboring regions to share the faith. Acts 19:10 described the results of this ministry: "so that all the Jews and Greeks who lived in Asia heard the word of the Lord." Since Paul had designs on evangelizing Bithynia on his earlier mission, it is plausible that Paul's disciples were also sent to Nicaea and Bithynia during this time.

Another possibility is that the apostle Peter may have spent time in Bithynia. The first epistle of Peter is addressed to residents of Pontus, Cappadocia, Galatia, Asia, and Bithynia. Although the epistle never explicitly states that Peter visited these regions, it seems probable that he did. The apostles typically wrote their letters to Christian communities that they had personally established or supervised. It is known that Peter came to Rome sometime in the latter half of the first century, but there is little known about his travels until his arrival in Rome. When Paul wrote his letter to the Romans around AD 58, Paul greeted twenty-five people by name and several others in the church at Rome. However, Peter was not one of them. This would be strange if Peter was there at the time. Eusebius, following 1 Peter 1:1, assumed that Peter visited Bithynia along with Pontus, Galatia, Cappadocia, and Asia.[10] Likewise Epiphanius and

[8]Schools for Jews were in the synagogue; however schools for Gentiles were in the gymnasium. The expression "school of Tyrannus" suggests that Tyrannus was the owner of this location and that this place was not in the gymnasium. Wealthy people often had villas that included lecture halls. Sometimes these were large dining rooms where lectures accompanied the meals. Some of the slope houses excavated by the Austrians in Ephesus contain such lecture halls. The fact that Paul taught in the lecture hall for two years indicates that Tyrannus was a convert or sympathizer.

[9]The Ephesus Museum in Selçuk displays an inscribed stele found in the harbor. The stele contains the names of many wealthy citizens of Ephesus who contributed money for harbor construction projects. The Tyrannus family is mentioned twice on the stele. Another inscription mentioning the Tyrannus family currently resides in the collection located in the foundations of the temple of Domitian.

[10]Eusebius, *Ecclesiastical History* 3.1.2, 3.4.2.

Jerome believed Peter was in the area.[11] According to Epiphanius, "Paul even reached Spain, and Peter often visited Pontus and Bithynia."

Peter's familiarity with the region and the Christian community's troubles in the area are manifest in the first epistle.[12] All five chapters of the letter describe the afflictions and persecutions of those who confessed faith in Christ. Achtemeier notes that the policy in Rome during the early imperial period was such that the emperors were revered as divine only after their death. "In the provinces, however, particularly Asia Minor, it was another matter. All of the emperors mentioned above had divine honors paid to them."[13] Christians who refused to participate in the imperial cult experienced levels of persecution that ranged from verbal harassment to economic sanctions, to physical abuse or death. Those who administered the abuse were local administrators and citizens. "A challenge to the emperor cult in those provinces was not only a challenge to Roman rule, it was a challenge to the social fabric itself, and constituted a threat to unravel the cultural continuity such cultic activity provided. Pressure to conform therefore would be greater from the local indigenous authorities than from the Roman overlords."[14]

The text is sprinkled with statements that display the troubles the Christian community was experiencing: "you may have had to suffer grief in all kinds of trials" (1 Pet 1:6), "refined by fire" (1 Pet 1:7), "rejected by humans" (1 Pet 2:4), "suffer for what is right" (1 Pet 3:14), "the fiery ordeal that has come on you" (1 Pet 4:12), "if you suffer as a Christian" (1 Pet 4:16), "those who suffer according to God's will" (1 Pet 4:19), "the same kinds of sufferings" (1 Pet 5:9). The Christians were being falsely slandered: "though they accuse you of doing wrong" (1 Pet 2:12) and "those who speak maliciously against your good behavior" (1 Pet 3:16) and were being intimidated: "do not fear their threats" (1 Pet 3:14). Charges were brought against the Christians in legal proceedings:

---

[11]Epiphanius, *Panarion* 27.6.6; Jerome, *On Illustrious Men* 1.

[12]Per Achtemeier, "It is evident that the author of 1 Peter knows that the readers suffer the disfavor of, indeed persecution by, those who do not share the Christian faith." Paul Achtemeier, *1 Peter: A Commentary on First Peter* (Philadelphia: Fortress, 1996), 23.

[13]Achtemeier, *1 Peter*, 27. Achtemeier's earlier reference was to temples that were built in Asia to Augustus, Tiberius, Claudius, Vespasian, Titus, Domitian, and Trajan.

[14]Achtemeier, *1 Peter*, 28.

"Submit yourselves for the Lord's sake to every human authority: whether to the emperor, as the supreme authority, or to governors, who are sent by him to punish those who do wrong and to commend those who do right" (1 Pet 2:13-14), and the Christians were instructed to be ready to make a defense (ἀπολογία—a legal term used to describe a response to charges) to those who slandered and challenged them (1 Pet 3:15-16).

If it is accepted that Peter or one of Paul's disciples spent time in these regions, where did they go and where were the early Christian communities established? This is largely guesswork. However, based on the patterns of Christian evangelists, one can posit some educated guesses. The early Christian evangelists typically targeted large and prominent cities within the Roman provinces. Nicaea was the chief city of Bithynia during the first century, and the city had a network of Roman roads that provided easy access from other large cities to Nicaea. From Cyzicos, a road traveled east to Nicaea. Another road from Pergamon led northeast to Nicaea. Roads coming from the west connected Ancyra and Sinope to Nicaea. And still other roads went north from Nicaea to Nicomedia and on to Byzantium.

The early Christian evangelists typically visited cities that had a Jewish presence. They shared the gospel message in the synagogues. An inscription found in an underground baptistry (or fountain) associated with the Koimesis church in Nicaea was inscribed with a menorah and Jewish Scripture. The piece was reused from elsewhere to frame the pool. This indicates that there was an early Jewish presence in the city.[15] The inscription cites Psalm 135. The piece was probably originally part of a synagogue, and the inscription was used for liturgical purposes (see plate 3).

Unfortunately, aside from the Bible, written sources tell us only a fraction of what we would like to know the early Christian communities in Anatolia. The earliest Christian community in Nicaea is even more obscure. The second century apocryphal writing Acts of Andrew may

[15]Alfons M. Schneider, *Die römischen und byzantinishchen Denkmäler von Iznik-Nicaea*, Istanbuler Forschungen, 16 (Berlin: Deutsches archäologisches Institut, 1943), 17, dates the inscription to the second century, but Steven Fine and Leonard Rutgers, "New Light on Judaism in Asia Minor During Late Antiquity: Two Recently Identified Inscribed Menorahs," *JSQ* 3 (1996): 17, suggest a date between the fourth and sixth centuries.

include local traditions of the apostle's visit to the city.[16] It claims that the apostle Andrew came to Nicaea, where he cast out seven demons, baptized the people of the city, and appointed a bishop (Callistus) to oversee the church.[17] Even if the details of the account are legendary, there is no reason to discount the presence of Andrew in the city. It would make no sense to describe such a visit if the residents of Nicaea had no recollection of Andrew. Pliny the Younger's correspondence with Trajan in the early second century also gives us some insight into the presence of Christian communities in Bithynia. The letters describe the governor's and emperor's policy for dealing with them. Pliny's letter indicates that the number of Christians in the province was considerable, and that the Christian faith had spread to the cities, towns, and farms and had permeated all steps of society from the nobility to the peasants and slaves.

TRAJAN, PLINY THE YOUNGER, AND THE CHRISTIANS IN BITHYNIA

The book of Revelation in clear, thinly veiled terminology, described the social, economic, and physical persecutions suffered by Christians in seven cities of western Anatolia during the reign of Domitian. Of course, the troubles of the Christians were not isolated to those cities, but were troubles experienced in Christian communities throughout the region. The ruthless tyrant was disliked not only by the Christians, but by most of the powerful senatorial families. After the autocrat was assassinated in AD 96, the Senate declared *damnatio memoriae*, and his memory was stricken from the public records and inscriptions.

Following the tempestuous years of Domitian, the question was, What would be the policies of the emperors that followed Domitian? Following Domitian's assassination, the Senate promptly named Nerva as the emperor. Nerva ruled for only sixteen months before passing away of natural causes. The Roman historians Tacitus and Suetonius regarded him as a

---

[16]Schneemelcher dates the Acts of Andrew as early as AD 150, though additions and revisions followed in the years thereafter. Wilhelm, Schneemelcher, ed., *New Testament Apocrypha*, vol. 2, *Writings Related to the Apostles; Apocalypses and Related Subjects*, rev. ed. (Louisville, KY: Westminster John Knox, 1989), 115.

[17]Acts of Andrew 6. The Acts of Andrew is preserved in several versions. The details of Andrew's ministry in Nicaea are recorded in the *Narratio*.

good and fair emperor. Eusebius, the Christian historian, did not have much to say about Nerva, primarily because his term was short. But it could be inferred from Eusebius's brief comments that Christians were treated well. Those who were exiled were permitted to return, and their property was restored.[18]

When Trajan followed Nerva in AD 98, the imperial policy toward Christians seems to have been a resumption of Domitian's program, although it appears that he less aggressively pursued followers of the faith. Still, Trajan was intolerant of the Christians, and he regenerated the program of persecuting members of the new faith. Trajan interpreted the Christians' obstinate refusal to participate in the imperial cult as an act of treason.

The early Christian Ignatius was a disciple of the apostle John and was appointed minister of the church in Syrian Antioch near the end of the first century. Following Trajan's ascension to the imperial throne and his conquest of Dacia, Trajan set his sights on the conquest of the Parthian kingdom. At the same time, the emperor had designs on subduing the intractable Christians. While at Antioch, Trajan had Ignatius brought before him for questioning. Following Ignatius's refusal to worship the Roman pagan deities, Trajan ordered that Ignatius be bound and sent to Rome for execution.

Accompanied by ten soldiers, Ignatius sailed to Smyrna, where he met Polycarp, a fellow disciple of John, and other leaders of churches in Asia. From there, Ignatius wrote letters to the churches in Ephesus, Magnesia, and Tralles. The journey continued to Troas, where Ignatius wrote additional letters to the churches at Philadelphia and Smyrna, as well as a letter to Polycarp. Before departing from Asia, Ignatius also wrote a letter to the Christian community in Rome. The *Martyrium Ignatii*, a document purportedly written by two of Ignatius's companions on the journey to Rome, detailed the travel to Rome and the martyrdom sometime around AD 110. The authenticity of the document is disputed, but the account probably roughly followed the route taken on the journey and documented Ignatius's encounters with church leaders along the way.

---

[18]Eusebius, *Ecclesiastical History* 3.20.10-11.

One of Trajan's friends and advisers, Pliny the Younger, stealthily maneuvered his way through the difficult years of Domitian's reign and rose in rank through a number of civil offices. Pliny, the nephew of the Roman statesman Pliny the Elder, was named consul in AD 100.[19] Ten years later in 110 Trajan appointed Pliny to govern the provinces of Bithynia and Pontus.[20] Bithynia and Pontus previously were two separate provinces along the southern coast of the Black Sea. Now they were combined. Bithynia was more populated and was more Romanized, while Pontus was more rugged and mountainous. The Pontic population largely maintained their traditional lifestyles.

One of Pliny's chief tasks was to set in order the financial matters of some of Bithynia's cities. Nicomedia was the capital of Bithynia at that time and Pliny governed from Nicomedia. As it was the second city of the province, Pliny had several dealings with Nicaea and the city was frequently mentioned in his letters. The province of Bithynia abutted the province of Asia, and Pliny's term as governor was closely connected to the time and places of Ignatius's letters to the churches in Asia. Even though Pliny never mentioned Ignatius by name, he was no doubt familiar with the developments in the province to the south of Bithynia.

As a newly appointed governor, Pliny was made aware of the growing Christian population in the region. And he was aware that from the time of Domitian the imperial policy required that all citizens embrace the Roman gods as well as participate in support of the imperial cult. He also knew that, according to earlier precedent, Christian defiance of these policies was punishable with death. Even though Pliny was somewhat aware of Trajan's policies regarding the treatment of Christians, he was unsure of how these policies applied to specific individuals. Should the nobility be subject to the same application of the policy as peasants? How should Roman citizens, or young children be dealt with? What about

---

[19]Robert Louis Wilken, *The Christians as the Romans Saw Them* (New Haven, CT: Yale University Press, 2003), 4-6. Pliny learned the political arts of compromise, flattery, and silence.

[20]Pliny's powers and responsibilities are debated. His official title, *legatus Augusti pro praetore*, was typical for senior provincial governors. As Hicks notes, his "legal powers and position would have been parallel to most governors of major provinces." See Benjamin Hicks, "Pliny the Younger and the Role of the Governor in Imperial Communication" (paper from the 109th Annual Meeting of the Classical Association of the Middle West and South, Iowa City, 2013), 3-4.

those who apostatized? Should they be punished or forgiven? Pliny knew practically nothing about the Christians and their faith.[21] Nevertheless, Pliny began to implement the policies as he understood them from the previous practices going back to the time of Domitian and the earlier years of Trajan's rule. Meanwhile, Pliny wrote to Trajan describing his dealings with Christians while asking for guidance from the emperor. From what Pliny says in his correspondence, it is clear that persecutions of the Christians continued from the time of Domitian through the reign of Trajan, even if the rule of Nerva provided a brief respite from the trouble.

Several of Pliny's letters to the emperor have survived, but *Epistula* 10.96 is indispensable for understanding how the Roman governors and the emperor dealt with Christians at the beginning of the second century. Among Pliny's collection of letters, we also have Trajan's response (*Epistula* 10.97) which affirmed Pliny's actions, but also cautioned Pliny not to ambitiously seek out the Christians. There was a danger that anonymous accusations might come from personal animosity and thus disrupt the public order.

At the outset of his letter, Pliny acknowledged that he had never participated in the trials of Christians. However, when Christians were brought before him, Pliny prosecuted them and executed those who were found guilty. It is clear from Pliny's correspondence that there had been an established Roman policy for dealing with Christians. It is not clear how far back in time this policy can be traced but it seems reasonable to assume that the policy took shape during Domitian's reign and continued through Trajan's reign as emperor. The book of Revelation offers somewhat vague details, often couched in symbolic terminology, that give us a glimpse of what transpired during that time.

Pliny took it for granted that the mere confession of the Christian faith was a crime deserving of death. Pliny even asked whether or not apostate Christians who had given up the faith as many as twenty years earlier should be punished. Pliny questioned Trajan whether or not young Christian children should be given mercy. All of this reflects a severe and coldhearted posture that had been established toward Christians in the

---

[21]Richard Carrier, "The Prospect of a Christian Interpolation in Tacitus, 'Annals' 15.44," *Vigiliae Christianae* 68, no. 3 (2014): 266-67.

years leading up to the time when Pliny took office. After his interrogations Pliny acknowledged that these Christians committed no crimes. The apostates who were questioned maintained that the Christians bound themselves with an oath not to commit crimes, not to steal, not to commit adultery, and not to lie. Pliny took this testimony to be true, yet he still believed that Christians should be punished, not because they posed a threat to Roman rule, but simply because of their obstinate refusal to follow the will of the emperor.

Those who had been accused of being Christians but denied that they ever were had to prove their denial by praying to the gods and worshiping their images. In addition, they had to worship an image of the emperor, and they were required to curse Christ. Pliny was aware that Christians may be coerced into worshiping idols, but true Christians would not go so far as to curse Christ. Those people who lied and apostatized were released. For those who confessed that they had been Christians, Pliny offered an opportunity to deny their faith. He claimed that he questioned them a second and third time threatening them with death. Those who persisted in maintaining their faith were executed. Pliny was unsure of how to deal with those who renounced their faith. His question was, Should they be punished for their past participation in this cult?

Through his actions Pliny came to realize the breadth of the problem. He recounted that the disease (as he called it) had spread to persons of all ages, sexes, and social classes. He realized that the faith had spread throughout the cities, villages, and countryside. Pliny was concerned about the large numbers involved in the faith and wrote to Trajan asking him for advice regarding how he should proceed. Pliny suspended the proceedings against the Christians until he heard back from Trajan.

Trajan's response affirmed Pliny's actions. However, Trajan continued by indicating that Pliny should not aggressively pursue the issue by going about looking for Christians. Nevertheless, Trajan stated that Christians who were denounced and found guilty should be punished as Pliny had done. Trajan also indicated that anyone who abandoned the faith should be given mercy and a pardon.

This correspondence between Pliny and Trajan is important not only for insights into what was happening in Bithynia and Pontus, but these letters also give us a glimpse into what was happening elsewhere in the Roman Empire. When Pliny took office in Bithynia, he was familiar with the Roman practice of persecuting and executing Christians. However, Pliny did not know how this practice was to operate in his domain. Pliny had questions about prosecuting young Christians, the Christian nobility, and those who apostatized. By the end of the first century Christianity had sunk deep roots into Asia Minor, Bithynia, Galatia, Cappadocia, and Pontus. The first epistle of Peter was addressed to Christians in these regions (1 Peter 1:1). All five chapters in the letter addressed the problems of Christian persecutions in those provinces and offered advice regarding the Christian response. Pliny mentioned that the faith had spread to all steps of society and was prevalent in the cities as well as in the countryside. With the large number of Christians who represented all levels of society in the province, Pliny was asking Trajan, How far do we go with the intimidation and persecution of these people?

Other letters of Pliny may also refer to the presence of Christians in Bithynia, although the word *Christian* is lacking in these letters. In *Epistula* 10.33 Pliny wrote to Trajan asking permission to establish an association for firemen. The city of Nicomedia had suffered a devastating fire that destroyed two public buildings and several private homes while the people stood by helplessly. Pliny requested Trajan's consent to create a small fireman's association not to exceed 150 people, while guaranteeing that the association would not engage in subversive activities. The Romans were cautious of all associations, fearing that these groups might be involved in surreptitious and seditious activity against the empire. Christian gatherings in particular were looked on with great suspicion. At that time Christianity was a clandestine movement, operating discreetly in society. The Christians refused to venerate the Roman gods, refused to participate in the imperial temples, and secretly met in private homes. There was a concern that groups would use religion as a cover for subversive activities.

Trajan's response (*Epistula* 10.34) was to refuse Pliny's request to establish an association of firemen. Trajan replied that these cities (referring to Nicomedia and Nicaea) were notorious for creating disturbances through factions like these. Trajan's fear was that they would become a secret brotherhood (*hetaeria*). The Latin term *hetaeria* was used with negative connotations and may be translated "cabals" or "conspirators." The same term was also used in Pliny's above-mentioned letter regarding Christians (*Epistula* 10.96.7). There Pliny claimed that the Christians stopped gathering together after he issued an edict banning the existence of secret brotherhoods (*hetaerias*). Thus, it appears that Trajan's reference to secret brotherhoods in 10.34 was concerned, at least in part, with Christian congregations.[22] It is also possible that the persons who were condemned in yet another letter (*Epistula* 10.31) and whose sentences were terminated or reduced to lesser punishments were Christians. Pliny stated that they were currently living respectable and peaceful lives.

EARLY MARTYRS FROM NICAEA

Late traditions and hagiographies offer sketchy details for several martyrs in Nicaea and the area. Scholars agree that the details of the lives, trials, and executions of these martyrs were embellished over the centuries until the hagiographies were recorded. Miraculous legends were commonly associated with the accounts surrounding their lives and executions. This was a common development with the apocryphal writings that were written in the centuries following the apostolic period. Yet, it does not follow that these traditions were entirely bereft of any historical content. At a minimum, it can be assumed that the people in some of these accounts were real people who were martyred for their faith. The early Christian communities remembered the names of those who kept the faith and died when so many others apostatized in the face of death.[23]

[22] Nikos Giannakopoulis, "Groups and Associations in Bithynia and Pontus: Interaction with Prominent Statesmen and Provincial Governors," in *Sencer Şahin Anısına Yazılar* (Istanbul: Kuzgun Yayınevi, 2016), 375n68.

[23] It is not surprising that most of these accounts were unwritten. Only about 10 percent of the population was literate during that period. This was a period where oral traditions were passed down from one generation to the next. A common assumption among people today is that oral traditions have a short shelf life. However, at a time when written materials were scarce, memories were more sharp and more enduring. People who have no recourse to draw on written materials have stronger memories than those dependent on the written word. Memories are like muscles; the more they are used, the stronger they become.

It makes no sense to imagine that these accounts were mere fictions, and that the stories of the actual martyrs were forgotten. Instead, we must assume that the names of the martyrs and the places of their martyrdoms were accurately remembered, even if some details of their lives and deaths were created by later Christians. Here we note several of these traditions.

A thirteenth-century basilica was built in Nicaea by Theodore II for the martyr Tryphon. This church was built on an earlier small martyrion commemorating Tryphon.[24] Earlier hagiographical accounts refer to the martyrdom of Tryphon in Nicaea during the persecutions of Decius (249–251). According to these traditions, Tryphon was a devout Christian from Lampsacus (Campsada—modern Lapseki) on the Bithynian side of the Hellespont. He was brought before the governor in Nicaea. After refusing to apostatize Tryphon was tortured and executed.[25] Procopius of Caesarea claims that the Emperor Justinian built or restored an expensive and well-built sanctuary to the martyr Tryphon on a street named Palargos in Constantinople. This was probably after the relics of the saint were moved to Constantinople. Raymond Janin lists seven churches built in Constantinople during the Byzantine period dedicated to Saint Tryphon.[26] An inscription from Cyprus, dated between 400 and 600, mentioned Saint Tryphon, and another inscription found at Ezine, near Alexandrian Troas, recorded a vow made by the nearby villages and people to Saint Tryphon. The inscription is dated between the fifth and eighth centuries. The broad, multiple attestation of Tryphon lends credence to his martyrdom.

Several Christian traditions mention individuals executed during the persecutions of Diocletian (303–311). On February 23, 303, Diocletian issued a decree outlawing Christianity and ordered that the new church at Nicomedia be destroyed and the Christian Scriptures burned. After

---

[24]This basilica is described in more detail in the next chapter.

[25]Foss, *Nicaea*, 6, citing the *Encomium to the City of Nicaea* written by Theodore II Laskaris (1254–1258). An earlier tradition is preserved by Theodoric of Fleury in 1005. Theodoric wrote that Tryphon was martyred along with his companion Respicius. For the Latin text, see Thierry [Theodoric] de Fleury, ed., "Acta Martyrum," *Analecta Bollandiana* 27 (1908): 7-10, 15, 28. A Greek text was published by Franchi de Cavallieri, *Hagiographica,* Studi e Testi 19 (Rome: Biblioteca Apostolica Vaticana, 1908).

[26]R. Janin, *La geographie ecclesiasatique de l'Empire Byzantin. Premiere Partie: Le siege de Constantinople et le Partiarcat Oecumenique*, tome III (Paris: Les eglises et les monasteres 2, 1969), 488-90.

the decree was posted, a Christian named Eutius tore it down and was promptly arrested, tortured, and burned alive before the citizens of Nicomedia. Three more edicts restricting or banning Christianity were issued in the following years. The edicts were not uniformly enforced throughout the empire, particularly in the west, but Asia Minor was harshly impacted by the persecutions. Since Nicomedia was the eastern capital of the Roman Empire and the resident palace of Diocletian, the persecutions in Nicomedia and Nicaea were the most intense.

During this time, Nicaean traditions cite the martyrdoms of Eustathios, Thespesius, and Anatolius, who were from the city of Gangra, but were martyred in Nicaea. The three were supposedly baptized by Anthimus of Nicomedia, who himself was among the supposed twenty thousand martyrs in Nicomedia during the reign of Diocletian. The martyrological traditions also mention the physician Diomedes of Tarsus, who traveled around Anatolia preaching the gospel. When he arrived in Nicaea during the time of Diocletian, he was arrested and passed away shortly before he was brought to trial. Likewise, Theodote, a pious widow, and her sons were natives of Nicaea. When they were arrested during the reign of Diocletian, her young son Evodus defended the faith of his mother and brothers, whereupon he was beaten mercilessly. Theodote and her children were burned alive. A short time later, Antonia was arrested under the Emperor Maximian and refused to renounce her faith. She was drowned after she was thrown into the lake in a sack. Finally, the story of Neophytos should be noted here as well. Neophytos is thought to be the martyr associated with the underwater basilica. His story will be discussed later.

THE TESTIMONY OF EARLY CHRISTIAN TOMBS IN PHRYGIA AND BITHYNIA

The persecution of Christians extended from the first century until the early fourth century when the Edict of Milan, issued in 313, acknowledged Christianity as a legal religion within the Roman Empire. Up until that point Christians were subject to abuse, harassment, the seizure of property, persecution, and death at the hands of local officials who acted on imperial policies handed down by the emperors. The persecutions and executions varied from place to place and from time to time. At times, emperors and local officials disregarded earlier policies and paid little attention to the Christians. In some areas, local officials silently brushed off the edicts of the emperors in order to avoid embittering the population. At other times, however, the persecutions were intense, particularly in the western regions of Anatolia. Throughout those years, the Christian communities operated discreetly as underground movements, knowing that at any moment the persecutions could return. Indeed, the Christian writings during that period speak of thousands of martyrs who died during the sporadic periods when property was seized, beatings were administered, and Christians were killed.

While the persecutions muted the testimony of many Christians, the memory of numerous Christians was recorded on the tombstones of others. As Ramsay MacMullen asserts, "Anyone who wants to acquaint himself with the religious life of the empire, whatever literary sources he may also find useful, must really begin and end with inscriptions."[27] Several Christian funerary inscriptions have been found in Bithynia and nearby Phrygia that can be dated within the first three centuries.[28] It is remarkable that we have as many of these funerary inscriptions as we do, given the fact that the expression of the Christian faith on a tombstone would endanger the family and friends who were still living. We can assume that the vast bulk of the martyr's burials were done secretly, sometimes in unmarked graves and at other times in tombs with nondescript headstones. Yet, the number of Christian funerary inscriptions that have survived bear testimony of a large Christian community in the region. These inscriptions were tombstones (grave steles), which bore the names of the deceased and included sundry details of the person's life, including family members (see plate 4). Written before the Edict of Milan, during the turbulent and precarious times of the Antonine and Severan dynasties (or even earlier), these funerary inscriptions were evidence that

---

[27]Ramsay MacMullen, *Christianizing the Roman Empire, A.D. 100–400* (New Haven, CT: Yale University Press, 1984), 102.

[28]The number and early date (prior to the Edict of Milan) of these explicit Christian funerary inscriptions in this area is noteworthy and far exceeds the number found elsewhere in the Mediterranean realm.

the sporadic persecutions levied against the Christian communities did not suppress the witness and testimony of the growing church.

These inscriptions often included crosses, Christian symbols, or expressions that identified the deceased and their families as Christians. Some of these tombstones lacked the explicit term *Christian* but still bore cryptic emblems that fellow Christians would recognize. The letter *chi* could be turned so that the *X* would stand upright, representing the cross. William Tabbernee identified five funerary inscriptions, lacking any explicit Christian expression, that display bread imprinted with a small, discreet cross sitting on a table.[29] While unknown to others, Christians could quickly identify the Communion table. These are all dated to the early third century. Scholars are less certain of a few examples of *tau* and *upsilon* that are inscribed like a cross.

The prospect of persecution restrained most Christians from more overt expressions on their tombstones. Many inscriptions invoked the so-called Eumeneian Formula.[30] This was an imprecation condemning anyone who vandalized or sought to reuse the tomb. The expression ΕΣΤΑΙ ΑΥΤΩ ΠΡΟΣ ΤΟΝ ΘΕΟΝ ("he will be subject to God") or a close variant concluded these inscriptions.[31] The singular use of God (rather than gods) was a cryptic reference to monotheism and was used primarily by Christians, although Jewish use is also known. As Tabbernee notes, "It is significant that they were only prepared to reveal their Christianity through relatively ambiguous terms and phrases."[32]

The sarcophagus of Markos Iulios Eugenios well illustrates the precarious situation of Christians just prior to the Edict of Milan. The extensive inscription on his sarcophagus explained that Eugenios, son of a nobleman from Kouessa, served with distinction as a soldier in Pisidia. The emperor, Maximinios Daza, realizing that many of his troops were Christians, issued a decree commanding officers to offer sacrifices to the

---

[29]William Tabbernee, *Montanist Inscriptions and Testimonia: Epigraphic Sources Illustrating the History of Montanism*, PMS 16 (Macon, GA: Mercer University Press, 1997), 62-86.

[30]Paul McKechnie, "Eumeneia (Işıklı) and the Eumeneian Formula," in *Christianizing Asia Minor: Conversion, Communities, and Social Change in the Pre-Constantinian Era* (Cambridge: Cambridge University Press, 2019), 210-31. See also Tabbernee, *Montanist Inscriptions and Testimonia*, 144-46.

[31]At least four of these are currently in the museum at Hierapolis (Pamukkale).

[32]Tabbernee, *Montanist Inscriptions and Testimonia*, 145.

Roman gods and prohibiting Christians from being discharged from the military. As the sarcophagus records, "When an order had been issued in the time of Maximinos that the Christians were to sacrifice and were not to be released from military service and having endured, repeatedly, very many tortures when Diogenes was governor, I hastened to leave the service, keeping the faith of the Christians."[33] The inscription goes on to explain that Eugenios was appointed bishop at Laodicea (Katakekaumene) for twenty-five years. He "rebuilt the entire church from its foundations" out of his own resources. The church had been destroyed earlier during the persecutions.[34] Maximinos rescinded the Edict of Toleration (Edict of Serdica) issued by Galerius in 311 and renewed the persecution of Christians. Eugenios survived the persecutions of Maximinos, who died in 313, and the Edict of Milan was issued a month later.

Eugenios's predecessor, however, was not so lucky. Another sarcophagus contained the remains of Severos, the bishop that preceded Eugenios at the church in Laodicea. Both of these sarcophagi were placed in the church. The inscription on this sarcophagus claimed that Severos "won the glorious prize of the Heavenly Father," an expression meaning that he was martyred.[35] The church was presumably destroyed at the time of Severos's martyrdom. The inscription also mentioned Eugenios along with Severos: "During their lifetime they held a hallowed name because of their stripes."[36]

Other funerary inscriptions speak of Christians who discreetly or more explicitly professed their faith over the centuries. H. S. Öztürk has published a number of recently discovered inscriptions in the region of Nicaea.[37] Among these, three funerary inscriptions bear the name Χρηστός.[38] Öztürk dates all of these between the first and second

[33]Translation in Tabbernee, *Montanist Inscriptions and Testimonia*, 428.

[34]Translation in Tabbernee, *Montanist Inscriptions and Testimonia*, 435.

[35]Translation in Tabbernee, *Montanist Inscriptions and Testimonia*, 440.

[36]Translation in Tabbernee, *Montanist Inscriptions and Testimonia*, 438.

[37]Hüseyin Sami Öztürk, "Nıkaıa'dan Yeni Yazıtlar V," *Cedrus* 3 (2015): 257-67.

[38]Env. No. 179, found near Hamidiye village in the Osmaneli district, states that Chrestos, son of Aristainetos, built this tomb for his father, mother and wife, Chreste. Env. No. 155, found at Keskin Village near Gölpazari, marked the tomb of Entrope, the daughter of Chrestos, who passed away at 19 years of age. Env. No. 186, found at Soğucakpinar near Osmaneli, simply states "Chrestos, son of Apollonius, lived 63 years." Öztürk, "Nıkaıa'dan Yeni Yazıtlar V," 258-63.

centuries. It is reasonable to think that these tombstones are those of early Christians.[39] The phonetic difference between Χρηστός and Χριστός was minuscule,[40] and several other Christian funerary inscriptions in this area used the term Χρηστός with the *eta*, rather than the *iota*.[41] Likewise, there is the well-known statement by Suetonius, who wrote about riots in Rome during the time of Claudius. Suetonius claimed that Jews were constantly rioting at the instigation of Chrestus. Although Suetonius wrote in Latin, he referred to Christ as "Chrestus," rather than "Christus."[42] Additionally, the Alexandrian codex *Sinaiticus* spelled Christian as *Chrestianos* in Acts 11:26, 26:28 and 1 Peter 4:16.[43]

Several undated inscriptions in the Nicaea Museum marked the tombs of early Christians in Nicaea. A funerary inscription with a chi-rho flanked by an alpha-omega marked the tomb of a mother and daughter who were martyred: "Aurelia Theodote Diogenes, who lived in Nicaea with her family, known for their wisdom, devoutly offered her life to God along with my sweet daughter Aurelia Polychronia who purchased her destiny. If anyone desecrates this tomb they will give an account to God on the day of judgment. Farewell, Passersby." Another tombstone, also with a chi-rho flanked by an alpha-omega, is located in the garden of the Nicaea Museum. The epitaph reads, "Here lies Aurelius Chrestos, builder of homes, friend of the common people. Having constructed this burial place myself for my wife Aurelius Sesbamapina and for our children and their wives and their children. If anyone despoils

---

[39]One possibility is that some of these inscriptions marked the tombs of unknown Christians who identified with the death of Christ, as did Saint Paul (Gal 2:20). The name Christ could have been used as a cloud of anonymity—a way of identifying the deceased as a Christian without being explicit, thus exposing the remaining Christian family.

[40]Pachoumi claims, "At this period the two forms Χρηστός and Χριστός are pronounced identically by pagans and Christians." Moreover, the Christian epigraphic monuments of Phrygia, including Christian funerary inscriptions, use both Χρηστός and Χριστός. Eleni Pachoumi, "An Invocation of Chrestos in Magic: The Question of the Orthographical Spelling of Chrestos and Interpretation Issues in PGM XIII.288-95," *Hermethena* 188 (2010): 32-33.

[41]A Christian named Chrestus was addressed in a letter from Narcissus of Neronias, cited by Eusebius of Caesarea. Eusebius, *Contra Marcellum* 1.4.39. See "Fragments of a Letter of Narcissus of Neronias to Chrestus, Euphronius and Eusebius," Fourth-Century Christianity, www.fourthcentury.com /fragment-of-a-letter-of-narcissus-of-neronias-to-chrestus-euphronius-and-eusebius/.

[42]Suetonius, *Claudius* 25.

[43]William L. Lane, "Social Perspectives on Roman Christianity During the Formative Years from Nero to Nerva: Romans, Hebrews, 1 Clement," in *Judaism and Christianity in First-Century Rome*, ed. K. P. Donfried and P. Richardson (Grand Rapids, MI: Eerdmans, 1998), 204-6.

Figure 1.3. Aurelia Theodote Diogenes funerary inscription, Nicaea Museum

this place, they will give an account to God." The Eumeneian imprecation at the end of both of these inscriptions supports dates prior to the early fourth century.

Other artifacts in the collection at Nicaea include a broken sarcophagus that bears the name Gaius Cassios Chrestos, who is described as a presbyter, high priest, and priest of Augustus. A funerary relief, topped with a cross, memorialized another person named Aurelius Chrestos, who is described as a skilled baker who lived near the tetrapylon. And yet another tombstone mentions Boteris, who built this memorial for Christians, including Camenes, a servant of God (see plate 5).

Some of the inscriptions from the nearby province of Phrygia bear veiled terminology that other Christians would recognize, but were not evident to those not familiar with the faith. An example of this is the inscription on the tomb of Aberkios of Hierapolis, dated to the end of the second century. The inscription, created while Aberkios was still alive, was loaded with Christian metaphors. Aberkios claimed that he was a "disciple of the holy shepherd" who "taught him the faithful scriptures." He described his travels to Rome, where he saw "the people who had a shining seal," and his journey across the Euphrates River where he had brothers everywhere, including Paul who traveled in his wagon. There a holy virgin took a fish (ἰχθύς) from the source and gave it to friends everywhere to eat. She had good wine (οἰνόν χρηστόν) and offered it with bread. The inscription concludes with a reference to Aberkios's good (χρηστή) hometown of Hierapolis. In addition to references to the Eucharist, the ichthus symbol, the church in Rome, and Paul, one can easily see that the terms χρηστόν and χρηστή were chosen as homonyms of Χριστός (Christ).[44]

Similar to the Aberkios funerary inscription, the tomb of Alexander, son of Antonius, shares common expressions. This tombstone from Brouzos in Phrygia is dated by the inscription to 216.[45] The inscription described the deceased as a "disciple of the Holy Shepherd." It also asserts that Alexander was a citizen of the chosen city and concludes with the Eumeneian Formula.

Figure 1.4. Aurelius Chrestos funerary inscription, Nicaea Museum

The early third century inscription of Telesphorus and Teimolaos, found at Hacıbeyli, Afyonkarahisar (Phrygia) is brief and more cryptic, but still clear. Concluding with the words "Grace. Before God, do no wrong," the chi for χάρις was drawn as a cross.[46] The tomb of Aurelius Trophimus, found at Apamea, is also dated to the early third century.[47] At the bottom of the tombs' inscription, an acrostic ΙΧΘΥΣ was spelled out. The word "fish" (*ichthus*) was used cryptically as an acrostic with each of the letters ΙΧΘΥΣ representing "Jesus Christ, God, Son, Savior."

Other Phrygian tombs were more brazen in their expression of the Christian faith. Elsa Gibson has cataloged twenty-nine Phrygian inscriptions with the expression "Christians for Christians," all of which

[44]*Inscriptiones Christianae Graecae* 1597; *Supplementum Epigraphicum Graecum* 30, 1479.

[45]Edouard Chiricat, "The 'Crypto-Christian' Inscriptions of Phrygia," in *Roman Phrygia* (Cambridge: Cambridge University Press, 2013), 206-9.

[46]*Inscriptiones Christianae Graecae* 1361; *Supplementum Epigraphicum Graecum* 15, 800.

[47]*Inscriptiones Christianae Graecae* 962; *Monumenta Asiae Minoris Antiquae* 6, 224.

are dated prior to Constantine.[48] This explicit identification of the deceased and their family exposed the living to the dangers of pre-Constantinian persecutions. One of these inscriptions is in the Garden of the Bursa Museum. The funerary monument was erected for an anonymous Christian described as "a lover of Christ." The top center of the panel has a cross flanked by palm leaves (see plate 6). The second line from the bottom contains the "Christians for Christians" phrase. William Ramsay believed that Christianity spread to northern Phrygia from Christian communities in Bithynia and that the remoteness of the region contributed to the bold Christian expressions on the tombstones.[49] Fewer Roman officials were present in those areas to prosecute the Christians for their faith. Remote or not, Christians even in this area were caught and executed.

Perhaps the most poignant are two martyr inscriptions. One is a broken inscription in the courtyard of the Kutahya Museum. Written at a time of great persecution and fear, the tombstone boldly displays a cross inside a wreath. Below the wreath are the words "Aurelius Trophimus [set this up] for his father Alexandros, a martyr. Christians for Christians" (see plate 7). In the Bursa Museum an ossuary, dated to the late third century, is inscribed with the words "Herein are the bones of Trophimos, the martyr."[50] The ossuary was found at Şuhut (ancient Synnada in Phrygia). Tabbernee connects this with the *Acta Sancti Trophimi*, which described the martyrdom of Trophimos from Synnada and two of his associates, Sabbatius and Dorymedon. The three were traveling through Antiocheia when a festival to Apollos was taking place. Trophimos tried to convert the people. However, they turned on the Christians, brought them before the authorities, and executed them. Sabbatius was executed at Antiocheia, while Trophimos and Dorymedon were executed at nearby Synnada.[51] The text claimed this happened during the reign of Probus (276–282). In spite of the obvious dangers,

---

[48]Elsa Gibson, *The "Christians for Christians" Inscriptions of Phrygia: Greek Texts, Translation and Commentary*, Harvard Theological Studies 32 (Missoula, MT: Scholars Press, 1978).

[49]William M. Ramsay, *The Letters to the Seven Churches of Asia and Their Place in the Plan of the Apocalypse*, 4th ed. (London: Hodder and Stoughton, 1904), 195.

[50]Translated in Tabbernee, *Montanist Inscriptions and Testimonia*, 236-40.

[51]Translated in Tabbernee, *Montanist Inscriptions and Testimonia*, 238-39.

many of the Phrygian and Bithynian Christians courageously proclaimed their faith in life and in death.

Four other Christians for Christians funerary inscriptions are currently located in the Kutahya Museum.[52] One of them, said to have been found at Üçyük, was dedicated to Eutychos by his wife Aurelia Kyrila and their children, all of whom were still living. Tabbernee states, "Consequently, the children, who are also still alive, have no hesitation in declaring publicly that their father was and that their mother is a Christian."[53] Only the bottom half of the inscription survives. The other three are better preserved, although the last one is missing the bottom. All of these are topped with wreaths surrounding large crosses. All four of these are dated between 290 and 310 (see plate 8).

NEOPHYTOS, THE MARTYR OF NICAEA

The story of Neophytos was preserved in the tenth-century Synaxarion of the Church of Constantinople (also known as the Menologion of Basil II, currently in the Vatican Library) and in the early eleventh-century Imperial Menologion from Byzantium, currently in the Walters Art Museum in Baltimore. These manuscripts were produced in Constantinople for the Byzantine Emperor Basil II and were used for liturgical purposes. The manuscripts are illustrated collections of the lives of the saints with accompanying Greek text. The texts offer brief summaries of the saints' lives and provide a small color painting depicting an event in the life of the saint. These were abbreviated versions of a collection by Symeon Metaphrastes from the tenth century.[54] They were designed as calendars for the Eastern Orthodox Church, arranged in order of the saints' celebrated feast day.[55]

The Vatican Menologion was created around fifty years earlier than the Walters manuscript (see plate 9). The two miniature illustrations in

[52]Tabbernee, *Montanist Inscriptions and Testimonia*, no. 41-44, pp. 267-84.

[53]Tabbernee, *Montanist Inscriptions and Testimonia*, 271.

[54]Nancy Patterson Sevcenko, "The Walters 'Imperial' Menologion," *Journal of the Walters Art Gallery* 51 (1993): 43-44.

[55]A third menologion is in Moscow's State Historical Museum, cod. 9. This also dates to the eleventh century and may have been a companion volume to the Walters manuscript. The Walters manuscript covers only the days of January, and the Moscow manuscript contains the month of March. The Vatican manuscript began with the ecclesiastical calendar in September and ends six months later in February.

the documents are remarkably similar, except for two notable differences. The Vatican Menologion depicts Neophytos's execution by the sword, while the Imperial Menologion in Baltimore has the executioner wielding a club. The text accompanying both manuscripts describe the execution with a sword. The Vatican Menologion also portrays the execution beside the lake. The manuscript depicts the executioner standing on green land, while Neophytos is depicted in the foreground, fallen and cowering partially on the land and partly in the blue waters of the lake. The Walters Menologion, on the other hand, has no blue water in the foreground. The text of the Walters Menologion is more extensive and detailed than the one at the Vatican. A summary of the Walters text follows.

The text began with a praise of the city of Nicaea, describing it as the site of the first council that spread orthodoxy to the whole world, a city with solid ramparts and a mild climate. However, the city's most illustrious claim to fame was the martyr Neophytos. Neophytos was born in Nicaea to Christian parents Theodore and Florence. Neophytos displayed great piety from his youth. After his baptism, he was sent to a teacher, and he increased in virtue and wisdom. At the age of nine, Neophytos began to train his fellow students in piety, and he urged them to follow God's will. He shared his food with his orphaned companions and miraculously provided them with water after he struck the city walls.

Early one morning Neophytos's mother came to his bed and observed a dove that descended from the sky and fluttered around his bed. The dove spoke to his mother and explained what Neophytos would do in the years to come. Overcome by the incident, his mother fell to the ground and expired. Soon his father and a large grieving crowd assembled. Neophytos began to pray and miraculously, his mother rose.

When he was ten, a dove seen by his mother led Neophytos to Mount Olympus (probably Mount Uludağ). There, he entered a cave occupied by a lion, which promptly left the cave. Neophytos spent the next five years in the cave, practicing virtues while an angel provided him with food. During that time, Neophytos received a revelation from God, and he briefly returned to Nicaea to distribute part of his parents' property to the poor.

During the reigns of Diocletian and Maximian, the emperors issued edicts commanding all their subjects to offer sacrifices to the pagan deities or to face death. During that time a governor of Bithynia named Decius ambitiously harassed and tortured the Christians in the area. Instructed by an angel, Neophytos left the mountain and traveled to Nicomedia to the residence of the governor. Neophytos strongly reproached the governor and insulted him before his family and officials.

Decius had Neophytos suspended in the air and beaten mercilessly. Then his servants poured vinegar and brine over his body. Neophytos continued to resist the governor. Thereafter, Decius had Neophytos locked in an oven for three days, which did him no harm, and threw him to the lions and bears. The beasts bowed down before Neophytos. Enraged, the governor had Neophytos brought before the tribunal and ordered a soldier to execute him with his sword. The Christians retrieved his body and buried it in a "chosen place." The date of Neophytos's martyrdom was AD 303, ten years before the Edict of Milan.

The text concludes with a prayer asking Neophytos to grant "our pious emperor" Basil II a victory over the barbarians (probably the Bulgarians). Each of the lives of the saints concludes with a similar prayer asking the saint to intercede on behalf of the emperor and appealing for an assortment of requests, such as victory over his enemies, health, long life, forgiveness of sins, and eternal life.

The late date of the Vatican and Walters menologia call into question the traditions of Neophytos. Those who produced the menologia had access to earlier sources. It is evident from the differences between the Vatican and the Walters menologia that their sources existed before the tenth century, but there is no mention of those sources in the texts. With the hundreds of saints honored in the pages of the menologia there must have been dozens of sources. However, over the years the two beautifully illustrated menologia were preserved, and the earlier texts disappeared. Thus today, the earliest remaining written traditions date to the tenth century.

The surviving texts offer a hagiographic description of Neophytos replete with mythological elements that make it difficult to assess the historical details of the saint. Clearly, very little (or next to nothing) can be known of his early life and miracles. Likewise, nothing is known of a governor named Decius in this area, although it should be added that little is known of the governors in Bithynia at this time. Nevertheless, the tradition of a Nicaean martyr named Neophytos is hard to dismiss.

What we do not know are (1) the persistence of oral traditions in a culture that was overwhelmingly illiterate rather than literate, and (2) the presence of written traditions that existed in the past and were available to those who wrote the documents that we currently possess. These earlier sources have not survived, and they are not acknowledged in the traditions that have survived in the present menologia. Ancient writers were not as concerned to document their sources as thoroughly as we do today. Some of the more educated and scholarly authors of the past would refer to the writings of others, but this was not a standardized procedure, particularly among the hagiographies. We simply do not know how well grounded their sources were and how they embellished them.

Perczel's comparison of Cyril's writings with Eusebius's illustrates the dichotomy of hagiography.

> Cyril blends hagiography with the scrupulous need of dating the events, in which he introduces an innovation to hagiography. As such, it is our unique source for the church history of the second half of the fifth, first half of the sixth century. On many ecclesiastic events it is our only source, and it is an important parallel source for secular events. It follows Eusebius also in two other important features. One is that it is entirely saturated with the miraculous; the other is that Cyril had first-hand access to official documents, presumably kept in the patriarchal archives of Jerusalem, and that he extensively used these documents, many of which are otherwise lost.[56]

Perczel concludes, "As to the usage of the text of Cyril as a historiographic source, although it should always be used with caution due to its highly polemical and apologetic character, it contains irreplaceable data worth considering."[57]

---

[56]István Perczel, "Hagiography as a Historiographic Genre: From Eusebius to Cyril of Scythopolis, and Eustratius of Constantinople," in *Christian Historiography Between Empires (4th–8th Centuries)*, Late Antique History and Religion 23 (Leuven: Peeters, 2021), 196-97.

[57]Perczel, "Hagiography as a Historiographic Genre," 198.

Eric Brook's thoughts are similar.[58] He asserts that there is real history to be found in the hagiographies, but they must be examined with a critical eye. Since the hagiographies share data that coincides with what is known about the period, scholars can assign a degree of probability.[59] Nevertheless, one must treat them first as historical representations. That is to say, they are representations of how the earlier Christian communities viewed those featured in them and celebrated their lives. Brook cautions us about what he calls a modern trend to bypass critical historiographic procedures in order to mine the hagiographies for authentic history. On the other hand, there is a tendency among many scholars to treat the hagiographies as works of literature, wrapped in untrustworthy legends.

Brook points to two major biases among scholars that come to play in the examination of hagiographies. The first is

> an all too common suspicion toward religion among modern intellectuals, so that the value of interpreting historical representation using hagiography may be dismissed due to the topic of holiness itself, perhaps its association with the miraculous, or simply because the subject matter itself is "religious" at all. The second bias, one generally shared by modern historians who are themselves "believers," concerns the reliability of the record due to the fact that hagiography seems closer to legend, folklore, and myth than to history proper.[60]

Brook is not suggesting that historians dispense with the accepted methods of historical research. "Instead, I am offering the notion that hagiographical sensibilities concerning matters such as representation could be used to inform contemporary historiographical discussions."[61]

In my mind, we need to be cautious of dismissing the later traditions without just cause. There can be no doubt that stories were embellished, and legends were added. But a healthy skepticism is better than a presupposed disbelief. The wholesale dismissal of traditions is unreasonable and reduces our understanding of the past to our contemporary standards of proof, even if the earlier writers held to different standards of historiography.

---

[58]Eric Brook, "Hagiography, Modern Historiography and Historical Representation," *Fides et Historia* 42, no. 2 (2010): 1-26.

[59]Brook, "Hagiography, Modern Historiography," 1.

[60]Brook, "Hagiography, Modern Historiography," 24.

[61]Brook, "Hagiography, Modern Historiography," 24.

At a minimum, I tend to believe that the names and the fact of the martyrdoms should generally be accepted. I find it hard to believe that the Christian communities would entirely forget the lives of those who provided the strongest testimony of their faith with their blood. Memories of such traumatic events persist, even if little more than a name survives. Thus, I submit that an individual named Neophytos was martyred in Nicaea and that a confrontation with civic or provincial authorities leading to Neophytos's execution is quite plausible.

The traditions of Neophytos's martyrdom with Nicaea are too strong to discount as an entirely fabricated account. Later we will discuss earlier authors who saw a sarcophagus of Neophytos (or portions of a sarcophagus) in the Koimesis basilica in Nicaea. Unfortunately, this basilica was destroyed in 1922. As is the case with many other accounts of the lives and deaths of martyrs, little more can be known than the names and places of their executions.

THE FIRST COUNCIL AT NICAEA

It will be helpful to summarize the circumstances that brought about the Council of Nicaea and to briefly note the details of the council itself. It is generally considered a turning point in the history of the Christian faith, not necessarily because of the decisions made at the conclusion of the council, but primarily because the council marked the first point in time when a significant attempt was made to gather the early church leaders from across the Mediterranean world to debate issues. Additionally, the council represents the point where the church emerged from the underground and began to function with an imperial endorsement. It is important to note, as Rodney Stark has shown, that "Constantine was not responsible for the triumph of Christianity. By the time he gained the throne, Christian growth already had become a tidal wave of exponential increase."[62] Nevertheless, the empowerment of the faith with Constantine's support provided an impetus that propelled Christianity to even higher levels of popularity throughout the Mediterranean world.

[62]Rodney Stark, *Cities of God: The Real Story of How Christianity Became an Urban Movement and Conquered Rome* (New York: Harper Collins, 2006), 189.

There are more thorough descriptions of the First Ecumenical Council at Nicaea than what can be added to this chapter.[63] But here we will attempt to outline what happened at that time.

At the beginning of the fourth century, the Roman Empire was ruled by a tetrarchy. The tetrarchy was a system instituted by Diocletian whereby the empire was governed by two senior emperors (*Augusti*) and two associate emperors (*Caesares*). Maximian ruled as emperor in the west, while Diocletian ruled the eastern empire. Constantius I and Galerius were appointed Caesars. Diocletian and Maximian both abdicated the throne in 305 and Constantius I (west) and Galerius (east) were elevated to *Augusti*. When Constantius I died of natural causes in 306, Constantius's army elevated Constantine I (son of Constantius I) to Caesar (begrudgingly supported by Galerius, who favored others). Constantine thus bypassed other throne claimants. A year later (307) Maximian was forced to promote Constantine to *Augustus*, in spite of Maximian's support for his son Maxentius. Constantine later defeated Maxentius's rebellion on October 28, 312 at the battle of the Milvian Bridge. The defeat and death of Maxentius solidified Constantine's control of the western empire. This was also the moment of Constantine's conversion to Christianity.

The factors leading to Constantine's conversion are debated. It is possible that Constantine may have seen the growth of the Christian faith within the empire and made a tactical move to embrace the faith. It is also possible that Constantine's mother, Helena, preceded him in converting to the faith. Perhaps she influenced her son. However much those factors may have played into Constantine's conversion, Constantine's testimony, as relayed to Eusebius[64] and Lactantius,[65] pointed to a vision or dream that Constantine had on the night before the battle of the Milvian Bridge.

---

[63]Khaled Anatolios, *Retrieving Nicaea: The Development and Meaning of Trinitarian Doctrine* (Grand Rapids, MI: Baker, 2011); Lewis Ayers, *Nicaea and Its Legacy: An Approach to Fourth-Century Trinitarian Theology* (New York: Oxford University Press, 2006); Y. R. Kim, ed., *The Cambridge Companion to the Council of Nicaea* (Cambridge: Cambridge University Press, 2021).

[64]Eusebius, *Life of Constantine* 1.27-32. Eusebius claims that Constantine personally reported this to him and confirmed it with an oath.

[65]Lactantius, *On the Deaths of the Persecutors* 44. Lactantius was appointed as a teacher of rhetoric by Diocletian and moved to Nicomedia. There, Lactantius converted to Christianity and fled from the city. After Constantine became emperor, he brought Lactantius back to Nicomedia to tutor his son and to act as one of his advisers.

Figure 1.5. Emperor Constantine, Museo Capitoline, Rome

According to Eusebius, Constantine looked up in the sky around noon and saw a cross above the sun with the words ἐν τούτῳ νίκα ("by this conquer"). Constantine's troops also saw the sign. Unsure of what the vision meant, Constantine had a dream that night in which Christ appeared to him commanding him to make a representation of the sign as they entered the battle. The next day Constantine had the chi-rho symbol affixed to the shields of his troops. Constantine routed Maxentius's troops, Maxentius perished in the Tiber, and the victory was attributed to Christ's miraculous intervention.

Meanwhile in 308, Licinius was appointed *Augustus* by Galerius. In 310 Licinius defeated Maximinus II (also known as Daza), who was functioning as Caesar in the eastern empire. Licinius thus controlled Rome's dominions in the eastern Mediterranean. When Galerius died in 311, the tetrarchy was effectively dissolved. Constantine and Licinius divided the empire into the east, controlled by Licinius, and the west, controlled by Constantine.

Shortly before his death in 311 Galerius issued the Edict of Serdica (Edict of Toleration) ending the persecution of Christians in the Eastern Roman Empire and granting Christians the right to worship freely. The edict was posted at Nicomedia but was not strictly observed throughout the empire. In 313 Constantine and Licinius jointly issued the Edict of Milan, reaffirming and broadening the Edict of Toleration. This edict not only granted religious freedom to the Christians but also required that property that had been seized be returned to the Christians.

Relations between Licinius and Constantine deteriorated and wars between Licinius and Constantine were intermittently fought over the next decade until 324, when Licinius was ultimately defeated. Licinius was banished to Thessalonica and killed a year later. Constantine thus consolidated his power as the sole ruler of the empire.

Following the Edict of Milan theological disputes that had been festering prior to the edict threatened to divide the church. Eusebius opined,

> The trouble was this. The people of God were in a splendid state, flourishing by imperial benefactions. There was no external terror to disturb, so newly did serene and deepest peace by God's grace protect the Church on every side. Envy therefore laid its snare against our prosperity, creeping inside and openly flaunting itself in the very assemblies of the saints. Indeed, it set even the bishops against each other, imparting divisive quarrels with divine doctrines as the excuse. Then it broke out like a great fire from a little spark. It began

> from the summit of the Alexandrian church and spread through all Egypt and Libya and the further Thebaid [southern Egypt].[66]

Arius, a prominent theologian from Alexandria, Egypt, promoted the belief that Christ was divine, yet a created being—the highest created being. Arius's point was that the Son was subordinate to the Father. Arius was a student of Lucian, a distinguished teacher and martyr from Antioch. Arius's beliefs may have been a reflection of some of Lucian's teachings. Alexander, the bishop of Alexandria, opposed Arius's views, believing that Christ was not created, but eternally generated and equal in divinity to the Father. Arius's teachings spread and were supported by many presbyters and bishops, not only in Egypt but elsewhere in the Mediterranean world.[67] Alexander exiled him in spite of the many Christians that supported Arius.

In an attempt to unify the empire as well as the church, in 324 Constantine sent a letter with Hosios (Osios), a bishop of Cordoba and personal adviser, to Egypt to try to resolve the dispute between Alexander and Arius. The letter highlighted Constantine's concerns: "My first concern was that the attitude towards the Divinity of all the provinces should be united in one consistent view, and my second that I might restore and heal the body of the republic which lay severely wounded."[68] Constantine's letter and Hosios's visit failed to produce a resolution to the issue.

Later in 324, a synod was held in Antioch, at which time bishops who supported Arius were suspended. Constantine determined that the issue had to be resolved before matters got out of hand. He decided to convene a council to address the issue and to bring about reconciliation and unity within the church. The council was first planned to meet in Ancyra

---

[66]Eusebius, *Life of Constantine*, 2.61.3-5. All translations of Eusebius's *Life of Constantine* are from Averil Cameron and Stuart G. Hall, *Life of Constantine: Introduction, Translation and Commentary*, Clarendon Ancient History Series (Oxford: Clarendon, 1999).

[67]Thompson notes, "Patristic scholars today warn against lumping together as 'Arians' all the early theologians who had reservations about granting the Son full equality with the Father. They argue that it was the opponents of Arius who created this persona of Arius as the leader and arch-heretic of this theological tendency. . . . Arius and those with similar ideas are seen as continuing an already existent theological trajectory which emphasized the Son as 'substantially different' than the Father." Glen L. Thompson, "Documents of the Early Arian Controversy," Fourth-Century Christianity www.fourthcentury.com/documents-of-the-early-arian-controversy/.

[68]Eusebius, *Life of Constantine* 2.65.1.

(modern Ankara) but it was later changed to Nicaea. Constantine's explanation for the change in venue was due to easier access to Nicaea for the travelers, better weather, and the convenience for Constantine to attend in person. The choice of Nicaea for the First Ecumenical Council may also be due to the logistics of hosting the event. Accommodations for the attending bishops and their retinue would be a challenge without a large Christian community to house the guests. This suggests that the Nicaean church was strong and vibrant during the early fourth century.[69]

Invitations were issued to around one thousand bishops in the eastern empire and another eight hundred in the west. In order to encourage attendance, Constantine made arrangements that all the attendees' expenses would be covered by the state. Eusebius explained that the bishops were permitted to travel with two priests and three deacons. Only a little over three hundred bishops showed up, most of them from the east. Eusebius described the assembled group: "In the present band the number of bishops exceeded 250 and the number of presbyters and deacons and of the many other attendants who accompanied them was beyond calculation."[70] Jacobs asserts that the total number of visitors to the city may have been between 1,200 and 1,900 people and that housing may have been provided in private homes across the city.[71]

Constantine presided over some of the proceedings, but the task of leading the council was chiefly delegated to Hosios. Arius and Alexander

---

[69]Contrary to Ine Jacobs, "Hosting the Council in Nicaea," in *The Cambridge Companion to the Council of Nicaea*, ed. Young Richard Kim (Cambridge: Cambridge University Press, 2021), 69, who doubts that Nicaea had a large Christian population at that time.

[70]Eusebius, *Life of Constantine* 3.8.1. Eusebius's guess was a minimal baseline exceeding 250 people. Eusebius did not count the bishops. Eusthathius of Antioch, who was also in attendance, estimated around 270, although he also did not count the number. A third attendee, Athanasius of Alexandria, actually counted 318 bishops. The 318 became the official number and is supported by Hilary of Poitiers, Rufinus, Jerome, Dionysius Exiguus, and Evagrius.

It is sometimes imagined that the number 318 was adopted from Genesis 14:14 as the number of Abraham's descendants. However, the 318 people mentioned in Genesis searched for Lot, meaning that Abraham's men (including Lot) numbered 319. It is not so easy to dismiss the number 318. Yet some scholars insist the number was lower. Gwynn follows Honigmann's reconstructed list and suggests 200–250 bishops attending the council. D. M. Gwynn, "Reconstructing the Council of Nicaea," in Kim, *Cambridge Companion to the Council of Nicaea*, 93. The appendix to this volume (368–75) contains the names of attendees that Honigmann considered authentic. Honigmann believed that number exceeded the 199 authentic bishops on his list, perhaps numbering as many as 250.

[71]Jacobs, "Hosting the Council in Nicaea," 77.

both attended the meeting along with other notables, including Eusebius of Caesarea, Eusebius of Nicomedia, Nicholas of Myra, and Athanasius. Arius argued for the superiority of God the Father and that the Son was the first creation, created before the world or anything else. The Son was nevertheless God but was subordinate to God the Father and not coequal to the Father. Arius was supported by Eusebius of Nicomedia and Theognis of Nicaea along with twenty-one other bishops. Eusebius of Caesarea as well had Arian leanings.[72] When Arius was expelled from Alexandria, Eusebius welcomed him at Caesarea. The opposition was led by Alexander and Athanasius, who argued that the Son was of the same essence as the Father (ὁμοούσιος—*homoousios*) and was eternal with the Father.

The debates raged for over two months and were contentious. At one point it was reported that Saint Nicholas of Myra struck Arius in the chops. Not content with just checking who's naughty or nice, jolly ol' Saint Nick took matters into his own hands. Perhaps someone spiked the eggnog.[73] In the end, Alexander, Athanasius, and their supporters won out. A vote was taken and Arius was supported only by Theonas of Marmarica and Secundus of Ptomemais.[74] The three were exiled to Illyricum and others who previously supported Arius succumbed to the pressure and signed the decree, including Eusebius. According to Philostorgius, Secundus remarked to Eusebius upon his departure, "You submitted, Eusebius, in order to escape being sent into exile; but I place my confidence in a revelation made to me by God, that within a year you too will be sent into exile."[75]

In 327 Alexander died and Athanasius became the bishop of Alexandria. Constantine, influenced by Eusebius of Nicomedia, had Arian sympathies, but had gone along with the decision of the Nicaean Council. Eventually, the emperor allowed Arius and those who were exiled to return to their homes. In 335 Athanasius was summoned to the Synod at

---

[72]Robert M. Grant, "Religion and Politics at the Council of Nicaea," *Journal of Religion* 53, no. 1 (1975): 2.

[73]Most assume this story to be fictitious. Cf. Gustav Anrich, *Hagios Nikolaos: Der Heilige Nikolaos in der Griechischen Kirche. Texte und Untersuchungen*, 2 vols. (Berlin: B.G. Teubner, 1913).

[74]Philostorgius, *Ecclesastical History* 1.9.

[75]Philostorgius, *Ecclesastical History* 1.10.

Tyre to answer charges brought against him. As a result, Athanasius was exiled, and Arius was restored to the ministry. Arius died in Constantinople in 336, followed by Constantine's death in 337. On his deathbed, Constantine was baptized by Eusebius of Nicomedia.

Arian theology sprang back to life during the reigns of Contantius II, Julian, and Valens. Some within the Arian movement adopted the term ὁμοιούσιος (*homoiousios*), that is, the Son was "similar in essence" to the Father, as opposed to ὁμοούσιος (*homoousios*), that the Son was the "same essence" as the Father. Finally, the issue was laid to rest by a council called by Theodosius I, who convened the Second Ecumenical Council in 381. The council met in the church of Hagia Irene in Constantinople. It reaffirmed the decisions made by the Council of Nicaea and once again condemned the teachings of Arius. The council also denounced the teachings of the Pneumatomachians, who denied the divinity of the Holy Spirit.

SUMMARY

Nicaea has had a rich history as one of the two most important cities in Bithynia, along with Nicomedia to the north. Located on the eastern shore of Lake Ascania, the site was ideally located with access to the freshwater lake and trade routes to locations in all directions. Not surprisingly, the site was populated early with unknown origins. However, by the fourth century BC, Nicaea was large enough to be described as a city and by the early third century BC it was named the capital of Bithynia. Shortly thereafter, the capital was moved to Nicomedia which possessed an outlet to the sea. In the centuries thereafter, both Nicaea and Nicomedia contended for prominence in the province.

It is not known when Christianity first arrived in Nicaea, but evidence indicates that by the end of the first century the new faith was firmly established in the city. Some of Paul's disciples may have first evangelized the area. Based on the reference to Bithynia in 1 Peter, some have suggested that Peter engaged in ministry in Nicaea, and early patristic references support this theory.

In the early second century the newly appointed governor of Bithynia, Pliny, wrote to the Emperor Trajan asking advice on how to deal with the numerous Christians in the province. Pliny acknowledged the policy of his predecessors and tried those accused of being Christians. He offered Christians the opportunity to deny their faith under the threat of death. Those who refused, he had executed. Yet he recognized that many in the province, the young and old, the peasants and nobility, as well as those in the cities and countryside, had embraced the faith.

For the next two centuries the persecutions and executions of Christians were sporadic as various emperors and governors took it on themselves to eradicate the faith. Many funerary inscriptions from this area bear testimony of martyrs and others who proclaimed their faith on tombstones despite the dangers to family and friends who survived. Among the notable martyrs from Nicaea, Neophytos was particularly honored for his faith and testimony. The traditions of Neophytos are preserved in late Byzantine menologia currently in Baltimore and the Vatican. Neophytos is presumed to have been buried on the shore of Lake Ascania, and the submerged basilica was later built as a memorial church.

The Edict of Milan in 313 effectively brought the persecutions of Christians to an end. This edict was a crucial point in Christian history. A decade later, Constantine, who himself converted to the faith, called a council to settle theological disputes that had been broiling for several years. The First Council of Nicaea brought together for the first time Christian bishops, theologians, and leaders, who spent roughly two months on the shores of Lake Ascania fellowshipping and debating important theological issues that have become the foundational beliefs of Protestants, Catholics, and Orthodox believers today.

CHAPTER TWO

THE EARLIEST CHRISTIAN PLACES OF WORSHIP

CHRISTIANITY PRIOR TO CONSTANTINE—AN UNDERGROUND MOVEMENT

With rare exception, dedicated structures for worship, similar to the churches and basilicas of today, were not constructed until after the Edict of Milan in the early fourth century. In the beginning, Christianity was an offshoot of Judaism, and the faithful initially worshiped in synagogues. The apostles and earliest Christians were Jews who believed Jesus was the Messiah and that the kingdom of God would soon arrive. They also believed that the kingdom would be rooted within God's covenant community—the Jewish nation. The Christians believed and hoped that the Jews would recognize their Messiah and adopt the new faith. But that did not happen. A decisive split took place during the Council of Jamnia near the end of the first century.[1] Meeting in Yavneh sometime after the destruction of the temple, influential Jewish rabbis adopted a benediction (known as the *birkat ha-Minim*), commonly read in the synagogues, anathematizing slanderers. The slanderers are widely thought to be Jewish-Christians who continued to fellowship in the synagogues. The introduction of this benediction into the synagogue liturgy brought about the final division between Jews and Christians. Once the Christians departed from the synagogues, the earliest places of worship for the Christians were the homes of the believers.

When the Christians were forced out of the synagogue, they congregated in their homes and began to appoint leaders to guide them in the

[1]David Instone-Brewer, "The Eighteen Benedictions and the Minim Before 70 C.E.," *Journal of Theological Studies* 54 (2003): 25-55.

faith. These early Christian leaders were not well trained. Lacking any or having only a few writings of the Christian canon, the new churches and their leaders were dependent on the scattered visits from the second or third generation disciples of the apostles. The Christian Scriptures were not quickly copied and dispersed throughout the Mediterranean world. Outspoken and assertive leaders themselves were cobbling together an understanding of the faith based on what they had previously heard from other Christians. They commonly merged their beliefs with the philosophies and beliefs circulating in the broader society. This process, known as syncretism, resulted in diverse and commonly heretical manifestations of Christianity. The early church struggled with many cults that developed from these practices, particularly with Gnosticism.

The apostle Paul recognized the problem early in his ministry. All of his letters to the churches were attempts to correct misguided theological issues and disputes within the congregations. The apostle made it a practice to take representative disciples from the various churches with him on the road, whom he would teach and train on his travels (Acts 20:4). These disciples would be the key foundational leaders of their home churches once they returned home. Moreover, Paul established the School of Tyrannus during his three-year ministry in Ephesus (Acts 19:9). These helpers were then sent out into the surrounding regions to evangelize with the result that "all the Jews and Greeks who lived in the province of Asia heard the word of the Lord" (Acts 19:10).

The practice of itinerant ministry continued throughout the first century and probably into the early second century.[2] Both 2 and 3 John describe the problems of such ministry. John cautions his readers: "If anyone comes to you and does not bring this teaching, do not take them into your house [church], or welcome them [give them an opportunity to address the congregation]" (2 John 10). Third John is more specific. An assertive Diotrephes had assumed control of the church, and he would not allow John's disciples to speak to the congregation: "He even refuses

---

[2]James D. G. Dunn lists more than forty-five persons who were associates or coworkers of Paul who circulated among the churches or were stationed at locations to anchor the churches. *Beginning from Jerusalem*, vol. 2 of *Christianity in the Making* (Grand Rapids, MI: Eerdmans, 2009), 566-72. The anonymous disciples and coworkers of other early Christian leaders must have been expansive to bring about the exponential growth of Christianity in the first century.

to welcome other believers. He also stops those who want to do so and puts them out of the church" (3 John 10). The late first-century *Didache* likewise instructed congregants to be leery of those claiming to be prophets. The false prophet can be detected by their behavior. Those who act contrary to the teachings of the Lord are false prophets (*Didache* 11:8). Those who ask for money and those who act contrary to their own teaching are also false prophets (*Didache* 11:6, 10). Still, the letters of John and the *Didache* testify that itinerant ministry was the norm for most of the early churches. The lack of control over prophecy is best illustrated by the Montanism that took root in Phrygia, not far from Nicaea.

Montanus, the leader of the group, lived in the middle of the second century and held beliefs similar to the basic orthodox tenets of Christians elsewhere. He claimed to receive new revelations. Montanus and his followers believed that the Holy Spirit was working through them. They advocated a rigid lifestyle and settled in the "New Jerusalem"—Pepuza, in the rugged interior of Phrygia. While some fellow Christians embraced them, the movement was ultimately condemned as a heresy.

Numerous congregations lacked the needed theological grounding during this early formative period. Some remained within the confines of orthodox Christianity, others flirted on the fringe of the faith and still others departed from the faith while still clinging to elements of Jesus' teachings. There were no seminaries or monasteries until much later in time. However, as time progressed, as the Scriptures were reproduced in larger numbers, and as the writings were circulated broadly across the Mediterranean world, a broader theological consensus emerged regarding the central tenets of the faith. This consensus was promoted by Christian scholars, some of whom were converted from the philosophies, who articulated the faith through their teaching, preaching, and writings. Nevertheless, the Christian faith struggled throughout the first three centuries, theologically as well as socially within secular society.

The home churches where the earliest Christians gathered together had limited capacities.[3] Depending on the home of the host, seating

[3]Wayne A. Meeks, "The Formation of the Ekklesia," in *The First Urban Christians: The Social World of the Apostle Paul* (New Haven, CT: Yale University Press, 1983), chap. 3; James S. Jeffers, *The Greco-Roman World of the New Testament Era: Exploring the Background of Early Christianity*

around twenty-five people would typically be the maximum capacity. As the number of Christians grew in a particular locale, additional meetings were established in other homes elsewhere in the villages and towns. Wealthier Christians who adopted the faith had larger homes or villas that could accommodate more people, but even those early assemblies held no more than sixty people in any one location. We know a few of these churches from Paul's writings. Aquila and Priscilla opened their home to a congregation in Ephesus (1 Cor 16:19). Philemon and his wife Apphia had the Colossian Christians assemble in their home (Philem 1-2). Gaius likewise welcomed Corinthian Christians in his home (Rom 16:23). So, we can imagine that the congregations addressed in Paul's letters to the Romans, Corinthians, Ephesians, Philippians, Thessalonians, and Colossians met in several locations and his letters circulated among the house churches in these cities. Similarly, the warning against receiving false teachers in your "house" in 2 John 10 does not refer to a home per se, but rather was an instruction to not allow false teachers to promote their doctrines in the house churches.

Beginning in the latter half of the first century and continuing for roughly the next 250 years, the Christians were persecuted for their faith. These persecutions ebbed and flowed in their intensity. There were times of relative peace interspersed with times of brutal suppression of the faith. Unknown thousands of Christians were martyred for no other reason than their belief in Christ. It is impossible to know the full extent of these persecutions. Moreover, the treatment of Christians varied from one location to another, depending on the provincial governors and local rulers. Some rulers did little to harass their Christian populations, while others were harsh. At the beginning of the second century, Pliny the Younger's letter to Trajan indicates that some Christians apostatized under the threat of death. For those who persisted in the faith, "I ordered to be executed." Others "stated that they were Christians and then denied it. They said that in fact they had

(Downers Grove, IL: InterVarsity Press, 1999), 83-86; Jonathan L. Reed, *The HarperCollins Visual Guide to the New Testament: What Archaeology Reveals About the First Christians* (New York: HarperCollins, 2007), 109-15, 146-48; Dunn, *Beginning from Jerusalem*, 601-8.

been, but had abandoned their allegiance, some three years previously, some more years earlier, and one or two as many as twenty years before. All these as well worshipped your statue and images of the gods, and blasphemed Christ."[4]

Several early Christian apologists described the unjust persecution of Christians and pled for tolerance. Tertullian, writing at the end of the second century, noted "You hang Christians on crosses and stakes . . . with hooks you tear the flanks of Christians. . . . We lay down our necks [to lose our heads] . . . we are driven to the beasts . . . we are condemned to the mines . . . we are banished to the islands."[5] Written around the same time in the second century, the *Epistle to Diognetus* summarized the Christian faithful:

> They live on earth, but their citizenship is in heaven. They obey the established laws; indeed in their private lives they transcend the laws. They love everyone, and by everyone they are persecuted. They are unknown, yet they are condemned, they are put to death, yet they are brought to life. They are poor, yet they make many rich; they are in need of everything, yet they abound in everything. They are dishonored, yet they are glorified in their dishonor; they are slandered, yet they are vindicated. They are cursed, yet they bless; they are insulted, yet they offer respect. When they do good, they are punished as evildoers, when they are punished, they rejoice as though brought to life. By the Jews they are assaulted as foreigners, and by the Greeks they are persecuted, yet those who hate them are unable to give a reason for their hostility."[6]

The consequence of these persecutions was that the church became an underground movement. The dangers of physical abuse, ostracism from the community, property seizure, and martyrdom had an impact on the presence of Christians and Christian symbols in the public sphere. Christian symbols such as the cross or fish (ichthus) are rare prior to the time of Constantine. The Christians were careful with respect to

---

[4]Pliny the Younger, *Letter* 96. Translation by P. G. Walsh, *Pliny the Younger Complete Letters: Translated with an Introduction and Notes by P.G. Walsh* (Oxford: Oxford University Press, 2006), 278.

[5]Tertullian, *Apologeticus* 12.3-5. Translation by T. R. Glover, *Tertullian: Apology, De Spectaculis*, LCL 250 (Cambridge: Harvard University Press, 1931), 85.

[6]*Epistle to Diognetus* 5, 9-17. Michael W. Holmes, ed., *The Apostolic Fathers: Greek Texts and English Translations* (Grand Rapids: Baker, 1999), 541.

sharing the faith with unknown people. The betrayal of trust by revealing the identities of Christians to civic authorities often led to dire consequences for the Christian community.[7] The gathering places of the Christians were not marked with crosses or Christian symbols. The exterior of the house churches looked no different from the homes of their neighbors. Thus, it is difficult for archaeologists today to identify the early house churches.

Nevertheless, the evangelistic efforts of faithful Christians continued, although these efforts were circumspect and discreet. "Being excluded from the normal social gatherings, their points of contact with non-Christians lay quite inevitably at street-corners or at places of employment, or in the working quarters of dwellings."[8] MacMullen adds that if the topic of religion was broached, the conversation most likely involved Christians describing the wonderful cures and miracles as a manifestation of the truth of the gospel.

The relative silence of Christian voices, however, was broken by the testimony of their lives. There was a sense that Christians could be identified by their behavior. Tertullian notes the comments of the unbelievers: "'Look,' they say, 'How they love one another . . . and how they are ready to die for each other.'"[9] The moral conduct of the Christians stood in stark contrast to the depravity of others that went unpunished by Roman authorities. Yet, it was the law-abiding and morally upright Christians that were being punished.

The silence of the Christian voices in the streets, baths, and agoras was shattered by the sound of public martyrdoms in the amphitheaters, stadiums, and theaters. Untold thousands of Christians were mocked, humiliated, tortured, and killed in the arenas. Yet, those who affirmed their faith in the face of death spoke loudly to the spectating crowds filling the seats. In one of Tertullian's more familiar statements, he

---

[7]"Relations between the clusters of Christians and their neighbors determined how much 'presence' the former might have, how much 'noise' they might make—in short, how openly they might indulge their evangelical impulse. . . . Their neighbors looked on them with suspicion. They were ready to believe the worst of them, indeed freely to invent it." Ramsay MacMullen, *Christianizing the Roman Empire, A.D. 100–400* (New Haven, CT: Yale University Press, 1984), 103.

[8]MacMullen, *Christianizing the Roman Empire*, 40.

[9]Tertullian, *Apologeticus* 39. Translation by Glover, *Tertullian: Apology*, 177.

asserts, "But go to it, my good magistrates; the populace will count you a deal better, if you sacrifice the Christians to them. Torture us, rack us, condemn us, crush us; your cruelty only proves our innocence. . . . We multiply whenever we are mown down by you; the blood of Christians is seed."[10]

The Christians could furtively convey their faith through symbols that could be drawn in the sand or elsewhere. The Greek tau (*t*) could represent the cross. Likewise the chi (*x*) written in an inscription could be turned upright to represent the cross (see plate 10). A fish drawn on the ground could represent the acrostic ΙΧΘΥΣ, the Greek word for fish. As noted earlier, the individual Greek letters served as initials for the profession *Jesus Christ, God's Son, Savior*. Examples of the fish acrostic were found on the funerary epitaph of Licinia Amias, currently in the Vatican, and also on a broken alabaster piece from Villa Quintiliorum just outside Rome.

Since the early house churches were not distinguished from the homes of the other residents, it is not easy to identify homes that doubled as churches (see plate 11). Exterior identification was uncommon, so archaeologists have had to rely on the interiors of these house churches. Some of these house churches were modified for the addition of a baptistry. In other cases an apse facing Jerusalem or Christian frescoes or graffiti suggest that the home was used for Christian worship. It is generally considered that Dura-Europos contains the earliest known house church.[11] Located on the banks of the Euphrates River in Syria, not far from the Iraqi border, Dura-Europos was established as a fortress around 300 BC. In addition to the house church, Dura-Europos had a well-preserved synagogue, dating to the second century AD. The house church was located around three hundred meters to the south of the synagogue. It was converted into a church around 240. The size and construction of the home suggests that the residents were wealthy. The conversion involved the removal of a wall to combine two rooms for worship and the construction of a baptistry, and another room was used for the celebration of the Eucharist.

---

[10]Tertullian, *Apologeticus* 50. Translation by Glover, *Tertullian: Apology*, 227.

[11]Reed, *HarperCollins Visual Guide to the New Testament*, 154-55.

The home of another wealthy Christian in Laodicea (Phrygia) was converted into a house church. This recent discovery, led by Celal Şimşek and his team of excavators from the University of Pammukkale, is now open to the public. Excavations of the house revealed a twenty-room peristyle home that occupied around 21,000 square feet. The home can be dated to the first century, but the conversion took place sometime later. A large room on the eastern side of the peristyle was originally a dining hall. It was overlaid with marble facing on the walls, with an opus sectile floor, and an apse was constructed on the north. Objects used for worship were found in the room.

Figure 2.1. House church, Laodicea

THE EARLIEST CHURCHES FOLLOWING THE EDICT OF MILAN—AD 313

The Edict of Milan allowed Christians the freedom to practice their faith without the fear of persecutions. The Christians now enjoyed full legal protection. Property confiscated in the years prior to the edict was returned to the Christians or they were compensated. The edict brought about sweeping changes for the Christian community.[12] Not only could they share their faith with their neighbors openly, but they could now worship publicly. In short order, the church emerged from the underground to operate in full view of those who previously sought their destruction. Paul McKechnie points to an imperial letter addressed to Eusebius of Caesarea instructing him and other bishops to build, enlarge, and repair the churches:

> 'Be diligent about the sacred edifices, either by repairing those which remain standing, or enlarging them, or by erecting new ones wherever it may be requisite.' Bishops in every province received the same direction and were told to turn to governors of provinces and officers of the praetorian prefecture for supplies. . . . Complex as fourth-century change was to prove to be throughout Phrygia, it moved decisively during that century beneath a Christian and Byzantine sacred canopy.[13]

The most visible manifestation of this change was the construction of dedicated places for worship. Not having an architectural plan of their own, the Christians adopted the plans of Roman structures that were already used for public gatherings. The basilica was a large, rectangular, covered hall used for political gatherings, the administration of justice, commercial purposes, and various public functions. The earliest known basilica was the Basilica Porcia, built in the Roman Forum in 184 BC. The oldest surviving basilica was discovered in the forum at Pompeii. This was built sometime between 120 and 78 BC.

The Christians constructed basilicas for worship. The Christians modified the Roman basilica plans by adding an apse at the end, generally facing Jerusalem. The apse was the place for an altar and for the priest to speak and administer the sacraments. Further modifications might include pastoria, consisting of a room to the north of the apse (prothesis) and another room to the south of the apse (diaconicon). These rooms functioned as places for relics and sacred objects. In other instances, one of the rooms of the pastoria was used for a baptistry. Additional

---

[12]"Nothing counts for more than the years 312, which brought Constantine's conversion, or 313, with the Edict of Milan." MacMullen, *Christianizing the Roman Empire*, 102.

[13]Paul McKechnie, *Christianizing Asia Minor: Conversion, Communities, and Social Change in the Pre-Constantinian Era* (Cambridge: Cambridge University Press, 2019), 262.

modifications in large basilicas might include an elevated ambo in the center of the basilica for preaching. Large basilicas also divided their central length into a nave with flanking aisles, typically separated with columns. The columns helped to support the superstructure and roof. Occasionally, the area above the aisles contained a balcony for additional seating. The entrance of the basilica churches was generally at the western end of the structure, far opposite the apse. Here, a small enclosed courtyard, known as the narthex, greeted the worshipers. Occasionally an open-air atrium preceded the narthex.

Many of the earliest basilica churches were built as martyrions. A martyrion was a basilica church that was constructed to remember and commemorate the life of a martyr or saint. These were generally constructed at the place of the martyrdom or the burial of the saint. Consequently, these martyrion basilicas were often located in or near a necropolis. Prior to the Edict of Milan, the early Christians remembered and celebrated the lives of the martyrs by marking the sites as small shrines. As time passed, Christians wished to be buried near the saint. Over the years, a Christian necropolis would grow up around the tomb of the saint. Even after a larger basilica martyrion was constructed around the tomb of the saint, additional tombs were sometimes placed within the structure as well as outside the basilica. An interesting feature of these necropolises is that they are not always located at the main city necropolises.

Several fourth-century martyrions are located in southwestern Cilicia, in an area known as Rough Cilicia. These martyrions bear several features similar to the one at Nicaea. It is important to note that all of these martyrions were built in the fourth century, within a century of when the faith became legal and persecutions ceased. These churches constitute some of the earliest basilica churches in Christendom. These martyrions were generally located in necropolises. In some instances, the martyr was buried in the civic necropolis. In these cases, the martyrion church was built in the necropolis among the tombs of believers and nonbelievers. In other cases when the site of martyrdom or burial was elsewhere in or around the city, the martyrion was built at the site of the execution or burial and a new Christian necropolis developed around it. Another feature of these Cilician martyrions, common with the Nicaean one, is the presence of the martyr's tomb prominently featured in the church, generally in the pastoria. There is evidence of the gathering of the relics of the martyr at many of these sites.

Figure 2.2. Yanikhan martyrion basilica

Cilician fourth- or early fifth-century martyrions have been identified at Corasion, Corycos, Diocaesarea, Elaiussa Sebaste, Kanytelis, Öküzlü, Seleucia ad Calycadnum, and Yanıkhan. More specific details regarding these martyrions will be shared in a later chapter.

Research by Ayşe Aydın has determined that eleven objects in the Museums at Adana, Tarsus, Silifke, and Taşucu contained relics of martyrs from Cilicia and Isauria.[14] Most of these objects were created as miniature limestone or marble sarcophagi that were placed under the altars of the basilicas. Aydın notes there was an unusually large number of martyrdoms in Cilicia and Isauria during the reign of Diocletian (284–305). Later, in the early Byzantine period, Cilicia and Isauria became a region rich with the relics and traditions of the martyrs.[15]

[14]Ayşe Aydın, "Hıristiyan Dinindeki Martir-Aziz ve Rölik Kültünün Kilikya-Isaurya Bölgesi Hıristiyanlığına Yansımaları (Märtyrer, Heilige und Reliquienkult im Kilikisch-Isaurischen Raum)," *Olba* 17 (2009): 63-82.

[15]Aydın, "Hıristiyan Dinindeki Martir-Aziz," 75.

IMPERIAL EDICTS REGARDING CHRISTIANITY AND THE PAGAN TEMPLES

It will be helpful to briefly review some of the more important imperial edicts that were issued regarding the rights of Christians to practice their faith. Also, we will need to describe imperial edicts that curtailed the rights of pagans to practice their religion.

During the first two centuries, no official decrees were issued banning the practice of the Christian faith. There are several reasons for this. The Christian faith was new, a small movement, and it was not well understood by the emperors. Moreover, the founder of the faith and the earliest Christians were Jews. Due to Judaism's antiquity and staunch monotheism, the Jews were granted an exemption from the worship of the Roman gods and participation in the imperial cult. However, beginning in the latter half of the first century, it became evident that the bulk of those embracing the Christian faith were not Jews, but rather Gentiles. As Christianity grew and expanded beyond the borders of Palestine, governing officials took aim at the new faith. Even then, decrees against the Christians were not issued. Unauthorized organizations or associations were already forbidden in the empire.

As early as the Republican Period, the Romans had concerns about new associations, guilds, or societies (known as *collegia*). The state feared that such organizations could be subversive to Roman interests and could cause trouble. Thus, in 64 BC all *collegia* were banned by the Senate. The ban was later removed, but as part of Julius Caesar's reforms (*lex iulia*), any new *collegium* had to be approved by the Senate or emperor. When Christians gathered together (*collegia*) and refused to participate in the imperial cult, the rulers assumed that the Christians were disloyal and seditious. Thus, the Christians were prohibited from gathering together for fear that the Christian gatherings might be cover for illegal or rebellious activity.

The first persecutions of the Christians are reported in the Bible. The persecutions of the seven churches in Revelation are variously interpreted. Those who follow Leonard Thompson[16] believe there was no per-

[16]Leonard L. Thompson, *The Book of Revelation: Apocalypse and Empire* (New York: Oxford University Press, 1990).

secution of Christians during the time of Domitian. Thompson's analysis elevates the positive portrayals of Domitian by Statius and Quintilian (both of whose works were commissioned by Domitian) along with Martial (a contemporary of Domitian's) over the works of numerous writers such as Tacitus, Pliny the Younger, Dio Chrysostom, Juvenal, Suetonius, Dio Cassius, and Philostratus, who portray Domitian as evil, corrupt, and tyrannical. In Thompson's estimation, all of these later writers were supposedly biased and untrustworthy. Perhaps a better question would be to ask if Statius and Quintilian were biased, having received the patronage of Domitian. Even so, Thompson fails to address the reason why the Roman Senate declared *damnatio memoriae* upon the emperor's death. According to Thompson, the author of Revelation created the persecution scenario in order to polarize the Christian community against the Roman pagan society.

More likely, the persecutions mentioned in the text of Revelation were real, but not directly administered by Domitian himself. The local governors and civic leaders knew that the withdrawal of a significant Christian population from the imperial cult would have a damaging effect on the benefactions from the emperor. Additionally, the governing administrative officials in Asia knew that their neglect of maintaining the emperor cult would have a detrimental impact on their careers. Consequently, the persecutions reflected in Revelation were primarily carried out by the provincial governors, local officials, and the spiteful population.

Rather than offering a lengthy and detailed account of the first three hundred years of interaction between the Christians and the Roman government, it would be best here to offer a short timeline with brief descriptions of key moments in the developments. Those interested in a more detailed discussion of this period can consult works on this period.[17]

[17]P. R. Coleman-Norton, *Roman State and Christian Church: A Collection of Legal Documents to A.D. 535*, 3 vols. (London: SPCK, 1966); Bernard Green, *Christianity in Ancient Rome: The First Three Centuries* (London: T&T Clark, 2010); MacMullen, *Christianizing the Roman Empire*; Clyde Pharr, *The Theodosian Code and Novels and the Sirmondian Constitutions* (Princeton, NJ: Princeton University Press, 1952). For much of the timeline that follows, I am indebted to Glen L. Thompson's website Fourth Century Christianity, which offers a timeline with more details than what I include above: www.fourthcentury.com/imperial-laws-chart/.

Table 2. Brief timeline of Christian and Roman government interactions

Late first and second centuries AD—The persecution of Christians during this time was sporadic and localized, although these persecutions generally met with the emperor's approval.
AD 249—The Edict of Decius required all inhabitants of the Roman Empire to sacrifice to the gods. This was the first official decree demanding the worship of the Roman gods. The edict also had the effect of bringing about the persecution of Christians.
AD 257—The emperor Valerian issued an edict that banned Christian assemblies, ordered the priests to sacrifice to the gods and exiled the clergy who refused.
AD 258—Valerian issued a second edict ordering the execution of Christian deacons and clergy.
AD 303-304—During this time Diocletian issued four edicts ordering the arrest, imprisonment and execution of Christians.
AD 311—The Edict of Toleration[18] was issued by Galerius, Constantine and Licinius. This edict did away with Diocletian's persecutions of Christians.
AD 313—The Edict of Milan[19] was jointly issued by Constantine and Licinius. This edict legalized the practice of Christianity and ordered that property which was seized from Christians be returned to them.
AD 323—An edict of Constantine[20] proclaiming that Christians would not be forced to participate in pagan worship rites
AD 341—An edict of Constantius and Constans[21] whereby pagan sacrifices were banned in compliance with a law of Constantine
AD 346—An edict of Constantius[22] ordering the closure of pagan temples and stating that violators who attempt to worship in the temples were to be executed
AD 353—An edict of Constantius[23] prohibiting night-time pagan sacrifices
AD 361-362—Several edicts of Julian legalized all forms of Christianity, even those previously considered heretical, and legalized the practice of Judaism and Paganism.
AD 380—Edict of Thessalonica,[24] an Edict by Theodosius I, Gratian, and Valentinian II, making Christianity the official religion of the Roman Empire
AD 392—An edict of Theodosius[25] imposing a complete ban on sacrifices to pagan images

It should be noted that just as the persecution of Christians for the first three centuries was not consistent, neither were the bans on the practice of pagan worship consistent in the years after Constantine. The general unwritten policy of persecuting the Christians was implemented by some governors and local officials, but laxly employed by others. Once

[18]Eusebius, *Ecclesiastical History* 8.17.3-10.
[19]Eusebius, *Ecclesiastical History* 9.5.15-20.
[20]*Codex Theodosianus* 16.2.5.
[21]*Codex Theodosianus* 16.10.2.
[22]*Codex Theodosianus* 16.10.4.
[23]*Codex Theodosianus* 16.10.5.
[24]*Codex Theodosianus* 16.1.2.
[25]*Codex Theodosianus* 16.10.12.

it became an official edict with Decius and the emperors that followed, the persecutions intensified but were still not systematically executed.

Likewise, the edicts that banned the worship of pagan deities and closed the temples were not enforced consistently. The attitudes and beliefs of local populations and officials made it unlikely that the laws were applied strictly. Some governors and civic officials even benefited economically from the pagan rites. Others sided with popular support for the pagan practices by turning a blind eye to the temples. The edicts were repeated over the years to remind the people and civic officials of the imperial position. As Richard Bayliss states, "A date given for an individual law cannot be relied on to provide a ubiquitous *terminus post quem* for the archaeological evidence or as an accurate reflection of the prevailing religious climate in the empire as a whole at the time of enactment."[26]

It is important to remember that the Edict of Milan in AD 313 did not abolish the worship of the Greek and Roman gods. The temples continued to be used throughout most of the fourth and fifth centuries. Constantine did not favor paganism, but he was tolerant of those who continued to worship the Roman gods. It was not until the decree by Theodosius I in AD 380 (known as the Edict of Thessalonica) that Christianity became the state religion of the Roman Empire, and the pagan cults were banned. Even then, the worship of the ancient gods continued. Slowly, in the fifth and sixth centuries, the temples were abandoned, destroyed, or converted into churches or public buildings.

Earlier in his reign, Theodosius was tolerant of the pagan religions, and it was only in 391 that his legislation on paganism became more restrictive. These measures may have been taken as a token of Theodosius's penance after the massacre at Thessalonica in 390. After the massacre, Ambrose booted Theodosius from the church.[27] Less than a year later, Theodosius was reinstated. In 391 Theodosius issued a law banning pagan sacrifices in Rome. The following year, another law banned pagan worship in Alexandria and

---

[26]Richard Bayliss, "Provincial Cilicia and the Archaeology of Temple Conversion," 2 vols. (PhD diss., University of Newcastle upon Tyne, 2001), 243.

[27]Christopher S. Mackay, *Ancient Rome: A Military and Political History* (Cambridge: Cambridge University Press, 2004), 329.

later that year a more stringent third law was issued to ban pagan worship in the eastern empire. At the same time, however, Theodosius appointed several pagans to high offices in the western empire, perhaps in an attempt to placate the many pagans still under Roman rule.[28] As Mary Beard, John North, and Simon Price note, "Some traditional cults of Rome continued into the fifth century, but repeated imperial enactments continued to clamp down on the practices of paganism. We cannot tell how far the repetition of these bans on traditional religion was a consequence of widespread disobedience; how far the series of different laws addressed subtly different aspects of traditional cult; or how far the point of the legislation was the public declaration of the emperor's support for Christianity."[29]

WHEN WERE TEMPLES CONVERTED INTO CHURCHES?

There is a consensus among scholars that pagan temples in Anatolia were not directly converted into churches until the middle of the fifth century.[30] Peter Talloen and Lies Vercauteren follow Bayliss's classification of temple conversions into two categories: indirect conversions and direct conversions.[31] Indirect temple conversions did not use the remaining standing structure of the earlier temple. Instead, they were new and independent constructions built on the *temenos* (the sacred precinct) of the destroyed temple, or they used some of the materials of the old temple for a new basilica built elsewhere. Indirect temple conversions can be subdivided into two categories: (1) examples of churches built upon the temenos of the earlier temple, but not incorporating the church into the standing ruins of the temple. The new construction might not have, but whenever possible did utilize *spolia* (reused architectural pieces) from one or more earlier temple(s). Bayliss refers to these as Temenos-Churches. In other instances, (2) an indirect conversion might reuse many of the architectural pieces from the earlier temple (spolia) even though the new structure was not located on the *temenos* of the earlier temple. Bayliss refers to these as Temple-Spolia-Churches.

[28]Alan Cameron, *The Last Pagans of Rome* (New York: Oxford, 2010), 60-61, 63-65.

[29]Mary Beard, John North, and Simon Price, *Religions of Rome*, vol. 1 (Cambridge: Cambridge University Press, 1996), 375. "Emperors through the fifth into the sixth century elaborated Theodosius' ban on sacrifices—presumably in the face of the continuing practice of traditional sacrifice," 387.

[30]Peter Talloen and Lies Vercauteren, "The Fate of Temples in Late Antique Anatolia," in *The Archaeology of Late Antique "Paganism"* (Leiden: Brill, 2011), 347-87.

[31]Bayliss, "Provincial Cilicia and the Archaeology," 79.

Bayliss lists twenty-four Temenos-Churches in the Mediterranean realm. Examples of Temenos-Churches in Anatolia include the small church at the Artemis temple in Sardis (late fourth century),[32] a basilica church at the Apollo and Athena temples in Side (fifth century), the basilica of Mary at the Olympieion in Ephesus (fifth century), and the basilica church constructed in the temenos of the Letoon temples (sixth century). Bayliss lists another forty-three Temple-Spolia-Churches in the Roman world. Examples in Anatolia include the Basilica E1 at Sagalassos (late fifth or early sixth century), Basilica A at Kyaneai in Lycia (around 500), and the Basilica of Saint John in Ephesus (sixth century). In his broad study of conversions throughout the Mediterranean world, Bayliss concludes, "Temple conversions of the 4th and early 5th centuries are almost entirely of the indirect variety."[33]

Figure 2.3. Sardis, indirect temple-church conversion

[32]Talloen and Vercauteren ("Fate of Temples") assert that the attribution of a fourth-century date is "an exceptionally early date" and note Bayliss's reservations on this date. Bayliss questions the excavations techniques used in 1912 and also claims the design of the church argues for a later date. Bayliss, "Provincial Cilicia and the Archaeology," 114n36.

[33]Bayliss, "Provincial Cilicia and the Archaeology," 119. Talloen and Vercauteren concur: "The indirect conversion of temples and their material remains into churches took place throughout Late Antiquity, from the 4th to the 7th c." "Fate of Temples," 373. Later, they comment that "the indirect conversion of temple remains into churches likewise dates from the first half of the 5th c. onwards (or perhaps even earlier)," after which they cite three possible exceptions.

Figure 2.4. St. John Basilica, utilizing spolia from Artemission, Ephesus

Direct temple conversions, what Bayliss calls Temple-Churches, were built directly on the site of the earlier temple, utilizing its in situ remains. The remains of the walls and columns of the earlier temple were refurbished and transformed into a basilica. Bayliss counts ninety-one examples of Temple-Churches in the Mediterranean region. Examples in Anatolia include the temple of Aphrodite in Aphrodisias (converted in the late fifth or early sixth century), the temple of Apollo in Sagalassos (converted in the second half of the fifth century), the temple of Serapis (a.k.a. the Red Hall) in Pergamon (converted in the second half of the fifth century), the temple of Apollo in Didyma (converted in the late fifth or early sixth century), the temple of Zeus in Aizanoi (unknown conversion date), the temple of Zeus Olbios in Diocaesarea (converted in the second half of the fifth century), and the temple of Zeus at Selge (converted in the late fifth or early sixth century) (see plate 12).

Such direct temple conversions do not appear until the middle of the fifth century. After examining the archaeological and literary evidence, Bayliss argues, "Direct temple conversions are not attested with certainty before the middle of the 5th century, either archaeologically or historically."[34] Hanson had earlier drawn the same conclusion. Hanson

[34]Bayliss, "Provincial Cilicia and the Archaeology," 120. Bayliss clarifies this: "it is not my intention here to propose that no temples were used as churches before the middle of the 5th century; in the next chapter I will discuss evidence which suggests that some might have been occupied by

believed that a law of Theodosius II in 435 provided the impetus for temple conversions.[35] The law banned pagan sacrifices and commanded that the pagan temples and shrines should be torn down and replaced by the sign of the cross.[36] Talloen and Vercauteren claim that this decree did not have far-reaching effects and that the temple conversions must have occurred even later.[37] Nevertheless, they agree that direct conversions "appear to have occurred only from the middle of the 5th c. onwards, half a century after the indirect conversions began."[38]

SUMMARY

The earliest churches were located in the homes of the Christian believers. Paul's letter to the Romans greeted the church in the house of Prisca and Aquila (Rom 16:5). Before returning to Rome, they also used their home in Ephesus as a house church (1 Cor 16:9). At Laodicea, Nympha's house also functioned as a church (Col 4:15-16). In nearby Colossae, Philemon opened his home as a place of worship (Philem 2). Likewise, the congregation addressed in 2 John met in a believer's home (2 Jn 10). Acts 2:46 notes that the early Christians in Jerusalem met in the homes of Christians. This practice continued in large part up until the Edict of Milan in 313, when Christianity became a legal religion in the Roman Empire.

The leaders of these early churches were not well trained. Consequently, the apostles and disciples of the apostles circulated from church to church to share the faith and to assist the new believers to get a better grip on the faith. In time, the Scriptures were written to address theological misunderstandings and to resolve problems in the congregations. But even after the Scriptures were written, the individual books were circulated independently, and nobody had a complete Bible as we have it today.

Christians before this time. However, it seems clear that these early occupations were not accompanied by the kind of structural transformation that we see from the mid-5th century onwards," 112.

[35]R. P. C. Hanson, "The Transformation of Pagan Temples into Churches in the Early Christian Centuries," *Journal of Semitic Studies* 23 (1978): 257-67.

[36]*Codex Theodosianus* 16.10.25.

[37]"Moreover, the evidence does not show a sudden spate of direct conversion activity after A.D. 435." Talloen and Vercauteren, "Fate of Temples in Late Antique Anatolia," 374.

[38]Talloen and Vercauteren, "Fate of Temples in Late Antique Anatolia," 373.

Due in part to the immaturity of these early congregations, many of the churches fell prey to false teachings, causing some of the early Christian communities to splinter into Christian sects and heresies. Compounding the problem, from the latter part of the first century up until the early fourth century, Christians came under the scrutiny of Roman governing authorities who misunderstood and mistrusted them. This resulted in sporadic persecutions.

The lack of financial resources as well as the fear of persecution were factors contributing to the lack of dedicated structures for Christian worship. That all changed with the Edict of Milan. The edict, jointly issued by Constantine and Licinius, returned to the Christians property that had been seized from them. Additionally, the governors were encouraged to assist the Christian communities to build places of worship. The edict had far-reaching consequences beyond making Christianity legal and eliminating persecutions.

The Christians generally adopted the Roman basilica as the template for their places of worship. Modifications were made to the basilicas to better suit the purposes of Christian worship. Many of the earliest basilica churches were martyrions. These were churches that remembered and celebrated the lives of the local martyrs and saints and were often located in places where the martyrs died.

In the years after the Edict of Milan, the emperors issued a number of additional edicts that restricted or banned the practice of paganism and established Christianity as the official religion of the Roman Empire. The edicts banning worship at the pagan temples were not consistently enforced, and paganism continued alongside Christianity in Roman cities for at least another three hundred years.

Eventually, however, the temples were abandoned, and several of them were converted into Christian churches. The manner in which these temples were converted varied between direct conversions and indirect conversions, depending on the state of the ruins and the preferences of the local Christian communities. For our purposes, it is important to note that archaeological evidence indicates that direct temple conversions did not begin until the middle of the fifth century.

CHAPTER THREE

THE DISCOVERY, EXCAVATION, AND RESEARCH OF THE UNDERWATER BASILICA

DISCOVERY AND RESEARCH

Archaeology is a detailed process of marking out the parameters of a site, carefully excavating it, and cleaning, examining, and cataloging artifacts from the dig. Aside from the excavators, experts such as epigraphists, metallurgists, pottery analysts, chemists, paleobotanists, sociologists, and historians may be employed for a particular site.[1] As Currid notes, "Archaeology can speak to every aspect of ancient society."[2] Much like a modern crime scene, the examination of ancient remains is a puzzle to be pieced together. Naturally, working underwater complicates the process of excavation and requires special expertise and equipment. Working with scuba gear, the excavators suction the lake floor with a tube that transports the debris and small artifacts to the shore where the mud, gravel, and artifacts are separated and set aside for examination.

As early as 1838 the ruins of a structure were observed beneath the surface of Lake Iznik (ancient Ascania), when the waters of the lake receded. But in the years thereafter, the ruins were forgotten. The remains were rediscovered in 2014 when aerial photography revealed the structure submerged about one hundred feet offshore. Mustafa Şahin, head of the

[1]Good introductory texts on biblical archaeology include John D. Currid, *Doing Archaeology in the Land of the Bible: A Basic Guide* (Grand Rapids, MI: Baker, 1999) and Ellen White, *Layer by Layer: A Primer on Biblical Archaeology* (Winona, MN: Anselm, 2019). A broader and more rigorous text on the methods and theories of archaeology is Guy Gibbon, *Critically Reading the Theory and Methods of Archaeology: An Introductory Guide* (New York: Altamira, 2014). A glossary of terms is provided in the appendix below.

[2]Currid, *Doing Archaeology in the Land of the Bible*, 16.

Figure 3.1. Submerged basilica suction tube tray, Nicaea

Department of Archaeology at Uludağ University in Bursa, began exploratory excavations late in 2015 in collaboration with authorities from the Iznik Museum. I first became aware of the discovery in the summer of 2017 and visited the site in August of 2017. Following the visit, Professor Şahin and I wrote a preliminary report, which was published in the November 2018 issue of the *Biblical Archaeology Review*.[3]

The first season of work at the lake was in 2015, when Şahin and his staff conducted an underwater field survey.[4] The boundaries of the excavation were marked with mooring buoys and floats. A grid consisting of ten-meter squares was superimposed over the basilica and surrounding area. The squares were designated with letters denoting the north/south positions and numbers indicating the east/west positions. The basilica lies underwater in a roughly east/west direction. The cardinal reference line was set at the center of the basilica running the length of the nave and bisecting the basilica into a northern half and a southern half. Squares

[3]"Nicaea's Underwater Basilica," *Biblical Archaeology Review* 44, no. 6 (November–December 2018): 30-37, 61.

[4]Mustafa Şahin and Ahmet Bilir, "Underwater Survey in Lake Iznik—2015," in *North Meets East 3: Aktuelle Forschungen zu antiken Häfen*, ed. M. Seifert and L. Ziemer (Aachen: Shaker, 2016), 75-84.

to the north were designated with the letter *K*, the first letter of the Turkish word for north—*kuzey*. South of the reference line, the squares were designated with the letter *G*—*güney*, the Turkish word for south.

An illustration was made of the in situ remains (the ruins as they were originally found) in alignment with the grid lines, and photographs were taken of the site. Among the finds during this season were thirty-six tombs. Eighteen of these were located outside of the basilica and another eighteen were located inside the basilica. Five of these were in the narthex, six were located in the western end of the central nave, another six were found in the eastern end of the central nave, and one was found in the northern aisle. The graves were terracotta *cappuccina*[5] tombs constructed from roofing tiles. South of the central apse in the diaconicon,[6] the remains of a sarcophagus were observed. Additionally, a partially buried pithos, a broken amphora, potshards, a large number of clay roofing tiles, and human skeletal remains were found on the bed of the lake.

A curved wall measuring 49 feet in length was found west of the basilica, farther from shore. It has been suggested that a portion of the wall could have been a temenos wall for an earlier temple. This seems unlikely, however. The wall is not square with the basilica, and it turns in an arch toward the south. More likely, the wall may have been a seawall to keep the waters of the lake away from the basilica. This was probably built later as the waters rose and began to threaten it. Another hundred feet west-northwest of this wall there is another structure measuring roughly 37 by 20 feet. Very little of this structure has survived aside from its foundation, and its function is unknown.

The basilica itself measures 136 by 61 feet with a nave measuring 66 feet in length and 26 feet in width. The nave was flanked by aisles on the north and south. Based on similar-sized basilicas, the aisles were separated from the nave by five columns on both the north and south. It is possible

---

[5]*Cappuccina* tombs were generally used by peasant families who could not afford a stone tomb (sarcophagus). Large roofing tiles entombed the deceased within an *A*-shaped enclosure, which was sealed airtight.

[6]The two rooms flanking the central apse of a Byzantine basilica were collectively known as the pastophoria. These served priestly functions. The northern room, known as the prothesis, sometimes contained a baptistry. The southern room, the diaconicon, could serve a variety of functions.

that the columns supported balconies, as was common in many basilicas of this size. But so many of the remains have been taken for secondary use, it is difficult to say. The basilica probably had a wooden roof. Several of the column fragments have been reused to surround a well in the atrium. A semicircular apse stood at the eastern end of the nave. The diaconicon was located south of the apse and contained a sarcophagus measuring 6.48 by 2.30 feet. The sarcophagus was not constructed of one piece, suggesting that it was placed inside the basilica after its construction. To the north of the apse there was another room for the priests, known as the prothesis. On the west side of the structure, a narthex measured 13 feet in width, and an atrium lay further to the west, measuring 26 by 54 feet. Attached to the eastern wall of the atrium, a water source, perhaps a well, is surrounded by damaged, reused architectural pieces.

Excavations resumed in 2016, focusing on the eastern side of the nave, bordering the bema.[7] The work concentrated on a small area in the northeast, reaching a depth of two meters, whereupon workers reached the foundation of the structure. This area contained five terra cotta graves, designated KM-01 through KM-05. The skeletal remains of the tombs were scattered around but the remains in KM-04 were intact and well-preserved. KM-01 contained the remains of a middle-aged adult and the bones of a five-year old child. KM-02 contained the bones of a child around eighteen months old and KM-03 held the remains of two children ages three and one. A golden earring and a coin dated to the time of Valens (AD 364–378) were found in KM-03. The remains of KM-04 were the best preserved and contained the bones of an adult man. A coin found in this tomb was dated to the time of Valentinian II (AD 378–383). A portion of tombs KM-02, KM-03, KM-04, KM-05, and KM-08 all lay underneath the apse-bema wall and are 50 centimeters (1.64 feet) lower than the wall. The floor of the foundation was neither stone, ceramic, nor mosaic, suggesting that the floor of the original structure was either earthen or wood.

The 2017 season saw work in the apse of the basilica. Here a wall of a later date was found that suggested that the basilica may have been used for different purposes. Coins were found here along with a second-century

[7]Mustafa Şahin, "İznik Gölü Bazilika Kazıları—2016," *TINA Denizcilik Arkeolojisi Dergisi* 6 (2016): 64-79.

oil lamp. Work in the prothesis, north of the apse, revealed a continuation of the later wall extending into the prothesis. Most importantly however, a second floor was located 64 cm (2.10 feet) below the later walled room. The floor was covered with terra cotta tiles, suggesting that additional tombs may exist in the area. A deeper probe beneath the foundation floor resulted in the discovery of a first-century erotic oil lamp. This suggests that the lamp was deposited at the site before any structure existed.

Further work in 2017 was carried out south of the apse in the diaconicon, where a sarcophagus once existed.[8] In the northeast of this room, opposite of the sarcophagus, a floor consisting of square terra cotta tiles measured 185 by 70 cm (6.07 by 2.30 feet). Like the tiled floor in the prothesis, tombs may lie beneath this floor. Excavations in this area resulted in the discovery of nineteen coins, with the earliest being a bronze of Theodosius I (AD 392–395), and several fragments of tableware. The diaconicon has a small apse pointing east, and the perimeter construction of the diaconicon is larger and different from the parallel prothesis on the north, thus disturbing the symmetry of the basilica. This asymmetrical construction indicates that the diaconicon was originally an independent shrine (probably a small chapel enclosing the burial site of a saint). Later, this chapel was incorporated within an early basilica. The differential in the floors (mentioned above) suggests that the current masonry structure was a third stage in the development of the basilica. I suggest that the diaconicon originated as a small martyrion chapel. Later, a small basilica church was built that incorporated the chapel. Still later, a larger and more durable masonry basilica replaced the smaller basilica.

The focus of the 2018 season was on the narthex of the basilica.[9] Nothing of the northern wall of the narthex exists, but the archaeologists surmise that the main entrance to the basilica was on that side. Seventeen nails and fragments of charcoal were found in this area, suggesting that a wooden door opened into the narthex. Five terra cotta tombs were

---

[8]Mustafa Şahin, "Neue Forschungen und Ausgrabungen in Der Basilica des İznik Sees," in *Asia Minor Studien*, Band 96 Imperial Residence and Site of Councils (Bonn: Rudolf Habelt, 2020), 93-106.

[9]Mustafa Şahin, "İznik Gölü Bazilika Kazıları 2017–2018," *TINA Denizcilik Arkeolojisi Dergisi* 10 (2018): 116-26.

found in the narthex along with several intact oil lamps of the fifth and sixth centuries and a coin dating to the time of Gordion III (AD 238–244). Overall, 871 coins have been found in the basilica. The largest number of them come from the period AD 370–390.[10] This was likely the period of the basilica's masonry construction and early use.

In 2019 the excavations concentrated on a u-shaped stone formation in the atrium.[11] Şahin notes that the British pilgrim and monk Willibald visited Nicaea between the years AD 727 and 729. According to Willibald, the church where the council took place had images of the bishops who attended the First Council of Nicaea. Willibald also mentioned that there was a well or pool (a colymbion or stoup) in which sacred water or oil was dispensed. To explore the possibility of the u-shaped structure as a well, the formation was excavated to a depth of 150 cm (4.92 feet). Inside, the formation was filled with rubble stones, tile fragments, and pieces of wood. The southwest wall of the formation had levels of wooden girders, evidently for support. The 2019 season was shortened after work on the u-shaped structure. Work at the site was suspended during the Covid years and began again in 2023.

HOW WAS THE BASILICA SUBMERGED?

Earthquakes have plagued Anatolia for millennia. Turkey is located in an area of significant seismic activity with major faults on the north, east, south and west. The bulk of modern Turkey sits on the Anatolian Plate, which some claim is the most active in the world. This is a large tectonic plate located between even larger tectonic plates. The Anatolian Plate is being squeezed by the Arabian Plate on the southeast and the Eurasian Plate on the north. The Arabian Plate is pushing north. The Anatolian Plate is confined by the massive Eurasian Plate on the north, so the Anatolian Plate is forced to move to the west and the southwest.

The movement of the plate occurs along several fault lines. The East Anatolian Fault runs roughly from Van southwest to Antakya. In May 2011, I spent several days in Van researching ancient Urartian sites in the

[10]Şahin, "Neue Forschungen," 103.

[11]Mustafa Şahin, "Underwater Excavation at the Basilica Church in İznik Lake—2019," *International Journal of Environment and Geoinformatics (IJEGEO)* 9 (2022): 71-80.

area. Five months later, in October, a 7.2-magnitude earthquake struck Van, killing over six hundred people and destroying much of the city, including the hotel where I stayed. In February 2023, a 7.8-magnitude earthquake hit the area near Gaziantep. This was followed nine hours later by another 7.7-magnitude earthquake in the area. The most severe damage occurred ninety miles southwest along the fault at Antakya, a city of two hundred thousand people. Almost all the city's high-rise buildings were leveled or severely damaged. Over fifty-nine thousand people were killed, almost fifty-one thousand in Turkey and over eight thousand in Syria.

I visited Antakya three and a half months later, in May 2023, and the devastation was hard to believe. By that time, most of the buildings that pancaked were removed, and cranes were tearing down the newer, recently constructed high-rises that were structurally unsound. Very few structures survived, and the city was almost bare. There were few people in the city; most of the residents had relocated, and there was a large military presence. A resettlement camp was located a short distance to the north of the city center, with many tents lettered with the names of countries that contributed to the relief of the displaced residents.

Figure 3.2. February 2023 earthquake remains at Antakya

The North Anatolian Fault runs along the northern mountains of Turkey bordering the Black Sea, extending from near Van through Istanbul and into the Sea of Marmara. Some of the most recent and destructive earthquakes along this fault include a 7.8 magnitude earthquake in 1939 that hit the area of Erzincan, killing over thirty-two thousand people. The western end of the North Anatolian Fault branches into three sections. The northern branch runs through Izmit. In 1999 a 7.6 earthquake struck Izmit, killing eighteen thousand people. The southern branch runs directly through Iznik.

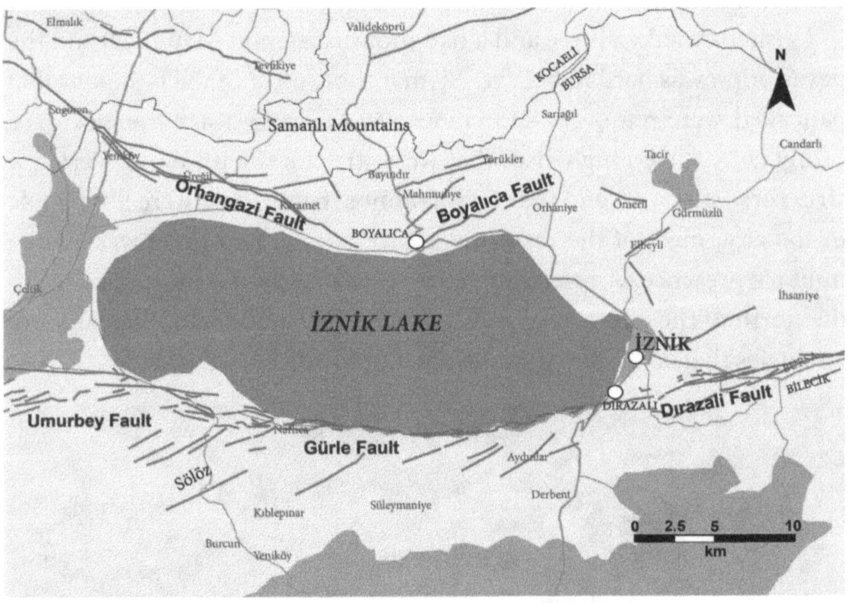

Figure 3.3. Fault lines at Lake Iznik

The East Anatolian Fault and the North Anatolian Fault are strike-slip faults, meaning that the plates are sliding past the adjoining plates in horizontal directions. In contrast, the southern border of the Anatolian Plate is being pushed by the African Plate. The collision of the Anatolian Plate and the African Plate has resulted in a subduction zone. The African Plate is moving north, sliding below the Anatolian Plate, resulting in the rise of the Taurus Mountains, which define the southern boundary of modern Turkey. This activity is likely the cause of the submergence of ancient cities and structures on the southern Mediterranean coast of

Turkey. Portions of Aperlai, Kekova, Simena, and Theimussa now lie below the Mediterranean Sea. With a boat ride along the coast in these areas, one can see ancient, submerged tombs, harbors, and structures.

Completing the picture, on the west, the Anatolian Plate is colliding with the Aegean Plate. This is a relatively smaller plate that is subducting below the Anatolian Plate. The process has resulted in the wrinkles on the Aegean Sea floor that appear as the Greek islands between Turkey and Greece. Submerged structures in the ancient towns of Cenchrea and Archampoli may have been a consequence of the Aegean subduction (see plate 13).

The active seismic activity of ancient Anatolia is only one theory to describe why the basilica at Nicaea currently lies underwater. Did the waters of Lake Ascania rise, or did the land surrounding the basilica sink? The issue is complicated by an incomplete understanding of environmental factors in the past and the seismic history of the last seventeen hundred years. Long before the discovery of the underwater basilica in Iznik, there have been a number of geologists, environmentalists, and seismologists that have studied the North Anatolian Fault (NAF). The NAF runs the length of Turkey south of the Black Sea for more than 930 miles. East of Iznik the NAF fragments into three branches, one running through Izmit (ancient Nicomedia), the other running through Iznik (Nicaea), and the other running further south. The fault is a strike-slip fault with the Anatolian Plate (southern plate) moving in a western direction.

Since the discovery of the basilica, several scientists have zeroed in on Iznik to study the lake's climate changes and geophysics, as well as the fault lines that surround Lake Iznik. But more specifically, several faults encircle Lake Iznik. In recent years, French seismologists Yacine Benjelloun, Renaldo Gastineau, Julia de Sigoyer, and others began an examination of the geologic changes that have taken place around the lake over the past two thousand years.[12] Their working hypothesis is that

[12]R. Gastineau et al., "Active Subaquatic Fault Segments in Lake Iznik Along the Middle Strand of the North Anatolian Fault, NW Turkey," *Tectonics, American Geophysical Union (AGU)*, 40 (2021): 1-38; Y. Benjelloun et al., "Historical Earthquake Scenarios for the Middle Strand of the North Anatolian Fault Deduced from Archeo-Damage Inventory and Building Deformation Modeling," *Seismological Society of America* 92 (2021): 583-98; Y. Benjelloun et al., "Segmentation and Holocene Behavior of the Middle Strand of the North Anatolian Fault (NW Turkey)," *Tectonics* 40 (2021): 1-32.

earthquakes over the hundreds of years have slowly resulted in the submersion of the eastern portion of Lake Iznik and have lowered the basilica beneath the waters. Sedimentary cores taken from Lake Iznik revealed fourteen earthquake-induced turbidite deposits that correspond to known earthquakes in the past two thousand years. Two subaquatic fault lines pass through the lake in an east–west direction: the Boyalıca Fault to the north and the Iznik Fault in the south. These form part of the middle strand of the North Anatolian Fault (MNAF). The research observed a continuous strike-slip fault along the southern shore of Iznik Lake with movement in an east–west direction.

> The fault displays morphological features typical of strike-slip deformation, associated locally with a smaller vertical component. We collected 114 measurements of horizontally offset markers, providing evidence for large, repeated earthquakes along the MNAF. Through a statistical analysis of the offsets, we particularly documented at least two major surface-rupturing earthquakes whose deformation was preserved in the landscape. They are characterized by coseismic horizontal displacement ranging from 3.2 to 6.2 m, which indicates moment magnitudes ranging between 7.2 +/- 0.2 and 7.4 +/- 0.2.[13]

One of these, the AD 1065 earthquake, "may have induced ground-level variation that led to the destruction and submersion of the basilica of Nicaea, explaining why this basilica has never been rebuilt."[14]

Michael Attaleiates, who lived in Constantinople at the time, documented a series of cataclysmic earthquakes for two years, from 1063–1065. The last one, an earthquake in Nicaea, destroyed the church of the Nicaean Council.

> In the Hellespont, Kyzikos was especially struck, where the ancient Greek temple was also shaken and most of it collapsed. This had been quite a sight to behold on account of the solidity of its construction. . . . From that time on and for two years earthquakes continued to occur sporadically at various times, leaving mortal men speechless in wonder. . . . That the earth would shake for two years is something altogether unheard-of and found in no book of history. . . . After the two-year period, an earthquake occurred that was larger

[13]Benjelloun, "Segmentation," 27.

[14]Gastineau, "Active Subaquatic Fault Segments," 19.

> than the frequent aftershocks, but smaller than the initial one. It happened in Nikaia in Bithynia and brought almost total devastation and ruin to the place. Its most important and large churches—the one founded in honor of the Wisdom of the Word of God, which was also the cathedral, and the one of the Holy Fathers, where the Council of the most Holy and Orthodox Fathers against Areios confirmed its decisions and where Orthodoxy was proclaimed openly to shine brighter than the sun—those churches, then, were shaken and collapsed as did the walls of the city along with many private dwellings.[15]

Kyzikos, less than one hundred miles due west, shared fault lines with Nicaea. The devastating earthquakes over these two years were not the first earthquakes to shake the area. A great deal of seismic activity is known to have occurred in the preceding centuries. However, the earthquakes of 1063–1065 may have been the last straw to submerge the church of the Council of Nicaea.

A number of scientists, however, disagree with the theory that earthquakes caused the submersion of the basilica. A study by six researchers at Çanakkale Onsekiz Mart University has argued that the water level of Lake Iznik has risen over the last sixteen hundred years with the result that the basilica is now underwater.[16] Using electrical resistivity technology (ERT), electrodes were driven into the ground around the basilica, and current was applied to determine the geologic structure of the surrounding ground. Measurements of the resistivity of the current enable the scientists to determine the underground geological materials. The research contends that the basilica was built on bedrock consisting of beachrock, a naturally occurring cementation of gravel, sand, and other materials. The lakebed is located two meters below the surface of the lake and the beachrock lies another two meters below the floor of the lake. Most importantly, there is no evidence for tectonic deformation in the beachrock, which raises doubts about the theory of earthquakes as the cause of submersion. "It was concluded that the Basilica of St. Neophytos was built entirely on the surrounding beachrock formation.

---

[15]Michael Attaleiates, *The History*, trans. by Anthony Kaldellis and Dimitris Krallis (Cambridge, MA: Harvard University Press, 2012), 165-67.

[16]H.E. Çınar et al., "Is Submergence of the Saint Neophytos Basilica (Lake İznik, NW Turkey) Caused by AD 740 Earthquake or Climate Change? Discussion of Geoelectrical Data," *International Conference on Science and Technology (ICONST)* (2019): 1-9.

Therefore, the main reason why the basilica is submerged today is that the lake water [rose] significantly over time."[17] This view was reinforced with a later study by eight Turkish seismologists. The research concluded that there is nothing underneath the basilica except for the beachrock. "This implies that the base structure beneath the basilica is probably the most lakeward extension of this buried beachrock, rather than the remains of an earlier archaeological structure."[18] Moreover, the submersion of the basilica was due to "climate-related processes." "We propose that submergence of the 1.5 m-thick beachrock and remains of the basilica structure should be related to a rise in the lake's water level during the last 1500 years instead of earthquake-related subsidence in AD 740 or on another date."[19]

In 2020 a French film company led by director Pascal Guerin began work on a documentary film to tell the story of the discovery. Guerin and his associates interviewed the French seismologists, but sometime later, as they prepared an interview with the Turkish experts, permission for the interview with the Turkish experts was inexplicably revoked. Professor Şahin and I have been interviewed over the past two years for the film. Interviews were conducted both in Iznik and in Rome at the Vatican Libraries, where we were granted permission to examine the Menologion of Basil II (mentioned above). The film was released in 2023 and aired on PBS stations across the country in October.[20]

OTHER ANCIENT REMAINS AND BYZANTINE CHURCHES IN NICAEA

Nicaea was laid out as a grid on the eastern shore of Lake Ascania, following the Hippodamian plan with city streets intersecting at right angles. Walls were first constructed during the Hellenistic period, but they were degraded over the centuries. They were of little help when the Goths sacked and burned the city in the middle of the third century. The people of Nicaea

[17]Çınar et al., "Is Submergence of the Saint Neophytos Basilica," 7.

[18]A.E. Erginal et al., "Co-sesmic Beachrock Deformation of 8th Century AD Earthquake in Middle Strand of North Anatolian Fault, Lake İznik, NW Turkey," *Tectonophysics* 799 (2021): 1-8.

[19]A.E. Erginal et al., "Co-seismic Beachrock Deformation," 7.

[20]"The Sunken Basilica," Les Batelieres and Scope Pictures, *Secrets of the Dead*, PBS, season 20, episode 5.

reoccupied the city when the Goths moved on, and they promptly built sturdy walls for the city's protection. Today, these massive walls are the most prominent and impressive feature of the city. These walls still stand at a height of thirty-three to forty-three feet, encircling the city for more than three miles. There were 114 defensive towers and four gates, one each in the north, south, east, and west. They have been repaired frequently over the years. The earlier Hellenistic walls have largely disappeared. The third-century walls reused some of the Hellenistic materials and encompassed a larger city than the one that existed during the Hellenistic period.

Figure 3.4. Map of Byzantine Nicaea

Strabo, the Roman geographer, claimed that at the intersection of the main north–south street (Cardo Maximus) and the main east–west street

(Decumanus Maximus) there was a gymnasium. From that point it was possible to see all four of the city gates. Today, the Hagia Sophia basilica occupies that spot, and there is no evidence of the gymnasium. The Hagia Sophia is currently around ten feet below the level of the modern city İznik, and this was probably the ground level of Nicaea fifteen hundred years ago (see plate 14).

The gates of the old city are older than the third-century walls and they contain several interesting features. They were originally constructed as triumphal arches by Vespasian and Titus in the late first century AD. The enlarged third-century walls used these triumphal arches for the entrances into the city. The reconstruction of the walls and their incorporation into the gates has resulted in an interesting mixture of masonry.

In the north, the Istanbul Gate was a triple gate with one entrance inside of the other (see plate 15). These gates are currently being excavated. The excavations began in 2018 with the objective of uncovering the Roman road that remained buried below. The present road leading into Iznik is around eight feet above the first century road. In the process of the excavation, a church was discovered between the second and third gates. The church had a nave and two aisles, and it contained *cappuccina* tombs (tombs constructed with terracotta roof tiles). The church has been dated to the thirteenth century.[21] Of the three gates, the middle gate was the earliest one and is a Roman structure. The gate has three arches. The central arch was for wagons, carts, and animals. The arch was flanked by smaller arches for pedestrian traffic. A bronze dedication was inset above the middle arch, but it has not survived. In the past only the upper two-thirds of the gate was visible, but recent excavations have unearthed much more of it below. Above the pedestrian entrances, there were two niches on the sides of the gate for statues. The innermost gate is crowned with two massive theatrical mask reliefs, which probably came from the Roman theater in the south of the city. The masks face north, welcoming visitors to the city. A relief of cavalry and another of three individuals can be seen in secondary use (spolia) on the outermost gate. These were probably the remains of an ornately decorated sarcophagus. The secondary use of an

[21]Halük Çetinkaya, "Byzantine Churches of Nicaea," Collection of Scientific Works, *Nis and Byzantium* 19 (2020): 68.

ornate sarcophagus can also be seen at the outermost gate at the Lefke Gate. The outer Istanbul Gate is flanked by two towers.

Similar to the Istanbul Gate, the eastern city gate, known as the Lefke Gate, has a series of three gates inside one another. Like the Istanbul Gate, these gates were constructed at different times. The outermost gate is a composite construction with spolia, including two statue bases built into the wall on either side of the opening. Two marble relief pieces are on the right wall, one of a sacrificial scene and the other of Roman infantry. Like the pieces in the outer gate of the Istanbul Gate, these were probably parts of a sarcophagus with high relief panels. This outer gate is flanked by two circular towers. Also like the Istanbul Gate, the middle gate of the three successive gates is the oldest and dates to the Roman period. Its construction was similar to the middle Istanbul Gate, and it must have been constructed at the same time. Like the Istanbul Gate, this gate has been excavated down to its original ground level, so one can see not only the statue niches but also the pedestrian entrances flanking the center entrance. Both of the pedestrian entrances have inscriptions crediting Marcus Plancius Varus for the construction of the arch (see plate 16). During the reign of Vespasian (AD 69–79) Varus lived in Nicaea and served as the proconsul of Bithynia.

During excavations in 2008 to uncover the street passing under the Lefke Gate, a small church was discovered within the gates. Outside of two apses, very little has survived, so it is not possible to date the church. However, since a similar church was found inside the Istanbul Gate, a date in the thirteenth century has been suggested. Further outside of the triple gate an aqueduct still stands. The aqueduct was built during the reign of Hadrian and was renovated at the time of Justinian in the sixth century.[22]

On the south side of the city, the Yenişehir Gate is a double gate. The innermost gate is Roman, but its construction differs from the Istanbul and Lefke Gates. Here there are no statue niches or pedestrian entrances. An inscription indicates that it was constructed (probably reconstructed) in AD 268 by Claudius II Gothicus. The outer gate is of later construction and is flanked by two circular towers. The gate that originally stood on

---

[22]Yacine Benjelloun, et al. "Construction History of the Aqueduct of Nicaea (Iznik, NW Turkey) and Its On-fault Deformation Viewed from Archaeological and Geophysical Investigations," *Journal of Archaeological Science* 21 (2018): 391.

the west side of the city facing the lake (Göl Kapı) has been destroyed, and only a pile of rubble marks the spot of the piers that supported the arches.

Figure 3.5. Yenisehir Gate, Nicaea

In the southwest quadrant of the city, a Roman theater has been uncovered and is in fairly good shape (see plate 17). The theater was constructed during Pliny the Younger's term as governor of Bithynia in the early second century AD. It has been suggested that the theater could hold fifteen thousand people, but the estimate seems too large compared with the capacity estimates of other theaters. The theater is currently being excavated.

There are several important Byzantine churches in the city. Çetinkaya lists fifteen in Iznik and claimed that there may have been as many as twenty-six.[23] The churches within the Lefke and Istanbul gates of the city have already been mentioned, but several others that played important roles in the city should be noted.

In the sixth century Justinian built a church in the center of the city at the site of the gymnasium mentioned by Strabo. This church measures

[23]Çetinkaya, "Byzantine Churches," 75.

ninety-eight by seventy-two feet and is known as the Hagia Sophia. Two sixth-century dedicatory inscriptions were found in the church.[24] Justinian's church was destroyed by an earthquake in the eleventh century and the current basilica was constructed afterward. Archaeologists have noted two more phases of construction since then. The basilica has a nave with two side aisles and an apse at the front. Two pastophoria (rooms for sacred objects) flank the apse. Both have the remnants of frescoed walls from the early church. The apse contains a *synthronon*, a semicircular seating area for the clergy, and an altar. The seventh and last ecumenical council met at this church in 787. In 2011, the church was converted into a mosque.

Figure 3.6. Nave of Hagia Sophia, Nicaea

In the north of the city, the church of Saint Tryphon was discovered in 1946. The church was built to commemorate the life of the martyr, who was executed during the persecutions of Decius. The church has since been neglected, and not much remains today. The church had a nave with flanking aisles, each with its own apse. It measured sixty-four by seventy-four feet and was cruciform in shape. It had an opus sectile floor with

[24] Çetinkaya, "Byzantine Churches," 59.

Figure 3.7. Synthronon of Hagia Sophia, Nicaea

Figure 3.8. Diaconicon of Hagia Sophia, Nicaea

Plate 1. Submerged basilica at Nicaea

Plate 2. The ancient walls and one of 114 towers encircling Nicaea

Plate 3. Underground pool and menorah, east of the Koimesis church, Nicaea

Plate 4. Flavia Prisca, Christians for Christians funerary inscription, Kutahya Museum

Plate 5. Boteris funerary inscription, Nicaea Museum

Plate 6. Christians for Christians, Bursa Museum

Plate 7. Alexandros Martyr funerary inscription, Kutahya Museum

Plate 8. Christians for Christians funerary inscription, Kutahya Museum

Plate 9. Menologion of Neophytos, Vatican Library

Plate 10. Laodicea pavement chi-rho, alpha-omega graffiti

Plate 11. Laodicea step graffiti—a church with eight crosses

Plate 12. Zeus temple—direct conversion to a basilica, Diocaesarea, Cilicia

Plate 13. Submerged Byzantine basilica at Cenchreae, Greece

Plate 14. Hagia Sophia, Nicaea

Plate 15. Istanbul Gate, Nicaea

Plate 16. Marcus Plancius Varus, Lefke Gate, Nicaea

Plate 17. Roman theater, Nicaea

Plate 18. Lake Iznik ruins, Nicaea

Plate 19. Atrium well and column pieces

Plate 20. Valens and Valentinian coins

Plate 21. Joint of narthex wall and southern nave wall

Plate 22. Submerged *cappuccina* tombs

Plate 23. Skeletal remains

Plate 24. Atrium well

Plate 25. Diaconicon sarcophagus remains

Plate 26. Yanikhan martyrion, Cilicia

Plate 27. Neophytos sacrophagus panel, Nicaea Museum

Plate 28. Inside Neophytos sarcophagus panel, Nicaea Museum

Plate 29. Remains of submerged sarcophagus

rooms on the sides of the aisles. The rooms are thought to be part of a school that functioned in the church. The church was built by Theodore Laskarsis in 1255 or 1256 after the saint appeared to Laskarsis in a dream.[25] Çetinkaya believes the church was built on the ruins of an earlier church that was destroyed in the 1065 earthquake.[26] He also suggests that a reliquary found among the northern city walls may have contained the remains of the saint.

In the southeast quadrant of the city rests the largely destroyed Koimesis church, also known as the Dormition church. The original structure has been variously dated from the sixth to the ninth century. This ciborium-style Byzantine basilica was still standing largely intact in 1922, but was intentionally destroyed by the people of Iznik as retaliation for the destruction of mosques by Greeks during a tumultuous period of Turkish history.[27] Today, very little is left. Inscriptions indicate that the church was founded by a monk named Hyakinthos.[28] Old photographs reveal opus sectile flooring and mosaics of angels, the Virgin Mary, and Jesus Christ.[29] The Koimesis basilica also had a monastery associated with it. Several sarcophagi were located in the basilica, including the sarcophagus of Neophytos, located in the narthex.[30] Neophytos's sarcophagus was rescued from the rising waters of Lake Ascania and relocated to the Koimesis basilica at an unknown date. Fragments of the sarcophagus are in the new Iznik Museum containing artifacts from the underwater excavation.

One hundred and fifty feet to the east of the Koimesis church are the remains of a Byzantine structure, perhaps a fountain house, known as Böcek Ayazma. It is not clear how the structure functioned. Several steps lead down to a locked gate and an underground room with a small square pool, which may have functioned as a baptistry or perhaps a

---

[25]Clive Foss, *Nicaea: A Byzantine Capital and Its Praises* (Brookline, MA: Hellenic College, 1996), 104.

[26]Çetinkaya, "Byzantine Churches," 67.

[27]Cyril Mango, "The Date of the Narthex Mosaics of the Church of the Dormition at Nicaea," *Dumbarton Oaks Papers* 13 (1959): 245.

[28]Çetinkaya, "Byzantine Churches," 63.

[29]These are dated to the eleventh century. Mango, "Date of Narthex Mosaics," 245.

[30]Çetinkaya, "Byzantine Churches," 63.

Figure 3.9. Remains from the Koimesis basilica, Nicaea

mikvah. The pool is framed with stones in secondary use. One of the stones, dating anywhere from the fourth to the sixth century AD, is inscribed with a menorah and the Greek text of Psalm 136:25.[31] The inscription is enough to indicate a Jewish presence in the city, but how the piece ended up at this pool is unknown.

Three churches have been found around the theater.[32] One of them lies about 160 feet away from the theater and has been dated to the thirteenth century. It was probably a basilica with a nave and two side aisles. Another church was located in the cavea of the theater. This was a small church, only about twenty-six by thirty-nine feet, with tombs inside and outside the church. After the theater was damaged and no longer used, the site became a small necropolis, and this church may have been a funerary chapel. A more recent discovery in 2005 was a chapel or prayer niche in the orchestra of the theater. Frescoes of Mary with the baby Jesus on the walls were dated to the sixth century. A graffiti was inscribed on the wall with the words ΚΥΡΙΕ ΒΟΗΘΙ

[31]Çetinkaya, "Byzantine Churches," 63-65, dates the inscription to the fourth century. He does not believe the pool was a baptistry.

[32]Çetinkaya, "Byzantine Churches," 70.

Figure 3.10. Excavations at the Roman theater, Nicaea

ΩΥΔΕ . . . ONONIA.[33] A possible translation is "O Lord, help. There is no other name."[34]

Near the Yenişehir Gate another church was discovered in 1964. The church measures sixty-six by seventy-five feet and is shaped like the Koimesis church. The church has been dated between the eleventh and thirteenth centuries, but Çetinkaya argues for a date in the fifth or sixth century.[35] He suggests that the church might be the Hagia Antonios.

According to Çetinkaya another three churches have been found in the northeastern part of Iznik. These probably date to the later Byzantine period. Another church of uncertain date was found near the old Iznik Museum in the northeast corner of Iznik. Foss mentions other churches that were described in literary sources, but their whereabouts are unknown. In particular, Foss notes a church dedicated to the martyr Diomedes located outside of the city walls and close to the city.[36]

---

[33]Çetinkaya, "Byzantine Churches," 71.

[34]My translation, assuming that the damaged word ΩΥΔΕ . . . is ΟΥΔΕΙΣ and ONONIA is ONOMA.

[35]Çetinkaya, "Byzantine Churches," 65-66.

[36]Foss, *Nicaea*, 114-15.

Figure 3.11. C. Cassius Philiscus obelisk, Nicaea

The Iznik archaeological museum has a splendid collection of artifacts, inscriptions, and sarcophagi from Nicaea. A new museum was opened in 2023, and many of the archaeological artifacts from the earlier museum have been moved to the new structure, including many pieces from the submerged basilica. The older museum has been renovated and now functions as the area's ethnographic museum.

Three miles north of Iznik there is a thirty-nine-foot-tall obelisk constructed as a burial monument to C. Cassius Philiscus. The obelisk, known as the Beştaş (or Dikilitaş), probably dates to the first century AD. This probably stood near the Roman road that led to Nicomedia and Constantinople. Four and a half miles north of town in Elbeyli, there is a fifth century underground tomb known as the Yeralti Mezar. The tomb is a family tomb with well-preserved frescoes of peacocks and flowers. A short distance outside of the Lefke Gate on the east of the city there are the fragmentary pieces of what is called Berber Rock. This was a monumental tomb that probably dates to the Hellenistic period. It has been suggested that the tomb may be the tomb of Prusias II, king of Bithynia, who was killed in 149 BC. However, Prusias II was killed in Nicomedia.[37]

The location of the palace of Constantine is unknown. Several years ago a marker was placed near ruins in the İnciraltı area of Iznik, about three hundred yards north of where the underwater basilica was discovered. There, the remains of a structure can be seen jutting out from

[37] Appian, *Mithridatic Wars* 2.7.

Figure 3.12. Berber Kaya tomb, Nicaea

the shore into the lake (see plate 18). More recently, scholars have become convinced that these ruins are not associated with the palace and the sign has been removed. By comparing the city plans of similar sites in the empire, Ibrahim Mert contends that the location of the palace must have been in the center of the city where the Cardo Maximus and Decumanus Maximus met.[38] He opts for a location opposite the gymnasium mentioned by Strabo, on the west side of the Cardo. Melda Ermiş argues for a location in the northwestern part of Nicaea, near the lake.[39] Ermiş believes that the concentration of churches, tombs, and structures on Şeyh Bedrettin Street and Arabacı Street, between the Istanbul Gate and the lake, strongly suggest that the palace was located there.

The ancient city wall west of the Istanbul Gate contains solid Roman ashlar construction that remains relatively undamaged. This is the best-preserved section of Nicaea's wall circuit. Given the strength of the wall, it would not be surprising that the palace would be located in this area.

[38]İbrahim Hakan Mert, "Nikaia (İznik) Kent Plani Tipolojisi," in *The Proceeding of the International Workshop: Localisation of the 1st Council Palace in Nicaea*, ed. Mustafa Şahin and İbrahim Mert (Bursa: Uludağ Universitesi, 2011), 171-82.

[39]Ü. Melda Ermiş, "İznik Sarayı Çevresindeki Kiliseler," in Şahin and Mert, *Proceeding of the International Workshop*, 79-103.

Figure 3.13. Nicaea north walls, near the Istanbul Gate

SUMMARY

After the discovery of the submerged structure in 2014, Mustafa Şahin, head of the Archaeology Department at Uludağ University, assembled a team of archaeologists and researchers to determine the function of the building and to ascertain the date of the structure. Another question had to do with the issue of how the structure was submerged beneath the waters of Lake Iznik.

The initial observations of the structure revealed the presence of a central nave flanked by aisles and an apse pointing toward the east. These observations made it clear that the structure was a Byzantine basilica. But was the basilica originally built as such, or was the basilica converted into a basilica at a later date? The excavations over the following years uncovered thirty-six terracotta *cappuccina* tombs, sixteen inside of the basilica and another sixteen outside of the structure. Some of these tombs still contained the skeletal remains of the deceased. Noteworthy is the fact that a few of the tombs were partially buried underneath the masonry walls near the central apse. Broken pottery, coins, and a few column fragments were uncovered in the excavations. Based on the coins, Şahin dates the basilica to the late fourth century.

In the diaconicon, a room to the right of the central apse, the scant remains of a sarcophagus were found. The asymmetrical construction of the prothesis (located to the left of the central apse) compared with the diaconicon (on the right) suggest that the diaconicon was originally a shrine or chapel for the burial of a saint. The presence of these tombs indicates that the larger basilica functioned as an early Christian martyrion. A curved wall west of the basilica measuring almost fifty feet in length apparently was built as a retaining wall to keep the waters of the lake away from the basilica.

To deal with the question of the submersion of the basilica, several Turkish and French seismologists have studied the tectonics of the area. Turkey has suffered from many catastrophic earthquakes over the years. South of the Black Sea, along Turkey's northern shoreline lies the North Anatolian Fault line. This fault runs through Iznik and Lake Iznik. This is a very active fault that has produced several significant earthquakes since the first century. Several seismologists believe that these earthquakes have slowly lowered the eastern shores of Lake Iznik, thus submerging the basilica. A massive earthquake in AD 1065 demolished the city of Nicaea and was probably the last straw for the basilica.

Elsewhere in Iznik, there are many remains from the past. Most impressive are the ancient city walls that surround the city that are more than three miles long. These massive walls date to the third century AD and are punctuated with 114 defensive towers. Entrance to the city was gained through gates on the north, east, and south, all of which are still standing. Two of these were originally first-century triumphal arches and are beautifully decorated. The ruins of an early second-century theater still remain. Research in Iznik has revealed fifteen Byzantine churches scattered throughout the city. Of these the underwater basilica is the only one located outside of the city and is the only one dated as early as the fourth century.

CHAPTER FOUR

WAS THE UNDERWATER BASILICA ORIGINALLY A CONVERTED PAGAN TEMPLE?

THE TEMPLE THEORY

The discovery of the underwater basilica in Nicaea created a media storm. The mystique of a previously unknown submerged basilica lying in relatively shallow water in ancient Nicaea piqued the interest of historians and the media. The discovery was proclaimed one of the top ten most important archaeological discoveries of 2015.[1]

Once assigned as the director of the excavation, Mustafa Şahin began investigating ancient sources to see if anything was mentioned in the early literature that could offer clues about the structure. The Roman and early Byzantine literature makes no reference to a structure to the south of Nicaea. However, a later Byzantine document, originally written in the seventh century, known as the *Chronicon Paschale*, claimed that a temple of Apollo was built outside of the walls of Nicaea during the reign of Commodus.[2] Commodus ruled from AD 180 to 192.

The *Chronicon Paschale* offered no specifics of where this temple may have been, other than that it was outside the walls (ἔξω τειχῶν). Neither the distance from the city, nor the cardinal directions, nor any surrounding structures were mentioned. This Apollo temple has never been found anywhere in the vicinity of Nicaea. However, Professor Şahin thinks that this

---

[1] *Archaeology*, January–February 2015. Archaeological Institute of America, www.archaeology.org /issues/161-1501/features/2789-turkey-submerged-byzantine-basilica.

[2] The *Chronicon Paschale* was compiled by an anonymous priest and consisted of a chronological list of people and events from creation up to the year 627. The earliest copy of the *Chronicon* comes from the Vatican and dates to the tenth century. See Ludwig August Dindorf, ed., *Chronicon Paschale*, vol. 1, *Corpus Scriptorum Historiae Byzantinae* (Bonn: Weberi, 1832).

building may have been the temple mentioned in the *Chronicon*. Şahin suggests that a colonnaded peripteral temple of six by eleven columns was laid out at the site, extending in a direction from east to west. Two columns were set in antis at both the front and back. Knowing that pagan temples were sometimes converted into Christian basilicas, Şahin proposed that the temple, originally dedicated to Apollo, was later converted into a basilica church, two hundred years later in the late fourth century.[3]

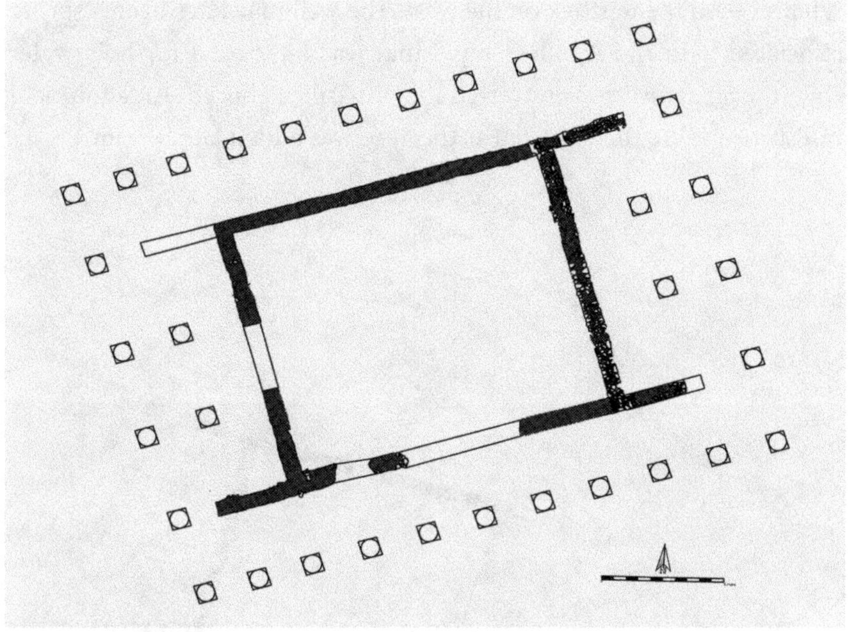

Figure 4.1. Apollo temple, phase 1

As we mentioned earlier, perhaps a decade before the Edict of Milan, in AD 303, Neophytos, a native of Nicaea, was martyred during the Diocletian persecutions. Sometime after the martyr's execution, the saint's remains were buried in the southeast of the temple. This happened while

[3]M. Şahin, "Neue Forschungen und Ausgrabungen in Der Basilica des İznik Sees," in *Imperial Residence and Site of Councils: The Metropolitan Region of Nicaea / Nicomedia*, vol. 96, *Asia Minor Studien*, Imperial Residence and Site of Councils. (Bonn: Rudolf Habelt, 2020), 98, 103; M. Şahin, "Underwater Excavation at the Basilica Church in İznik Lake—2019," *IJEGEO* 9 no. 2 (2022): 71; Mustafa Şahin and Ahmet Bilir, "Underwater Survey in Lake Iznik—2015," in *North Meets East 3: Aktuelle Forschungen zu antiken Häfen*, ed. M. Seifert and L. Ziemer (Aachen: Shaker, 2016), 83.

the temple was still operating as a functioning pagan temple. Around seventy years after the Edict of Milan, in the late fourth century, the temple was converted into a basilica church by adding two short parallel walls running the length of the temple in an east–west direction. This cut the temple into a central nave flanked by two aisles. At that time an apse was added on the east side of the basilica and the west entrance was converted into a narthex. An additional antechamber (atrium) with a well preceded the narthex on the west. The well may have been a spring associated with the Apollo temple that was later used for holy water when the structure was converted into a basilica church. An additional wall surrounding the tombs near the apse was added later in time.

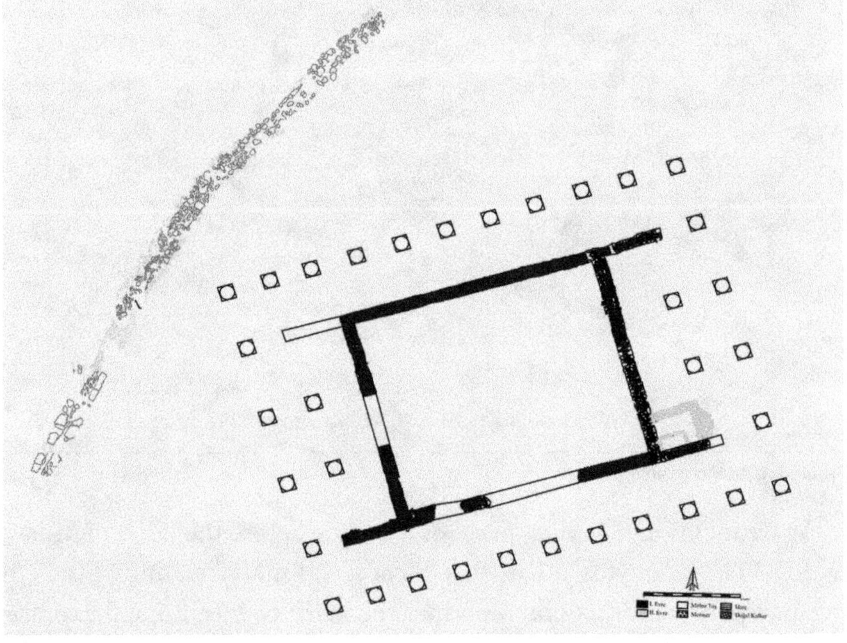

Figure 4.2. Apollo temple, phase 2

SUPPORT FOR THE THEORY

In his volume on ancient inscriptions from the museums in Iznik, Sencer Şahin cited the *Chronicon Paschale*, which stated, "During Emperor Commodus' fourth year, while Victorinus was consul, the Apollonion was built

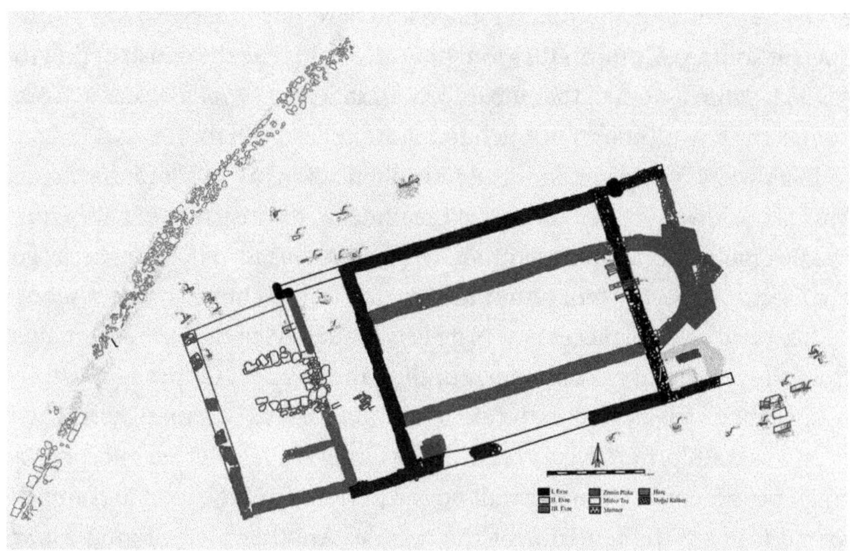

Figure 4.3. Temple-basilica conversion, phase 3

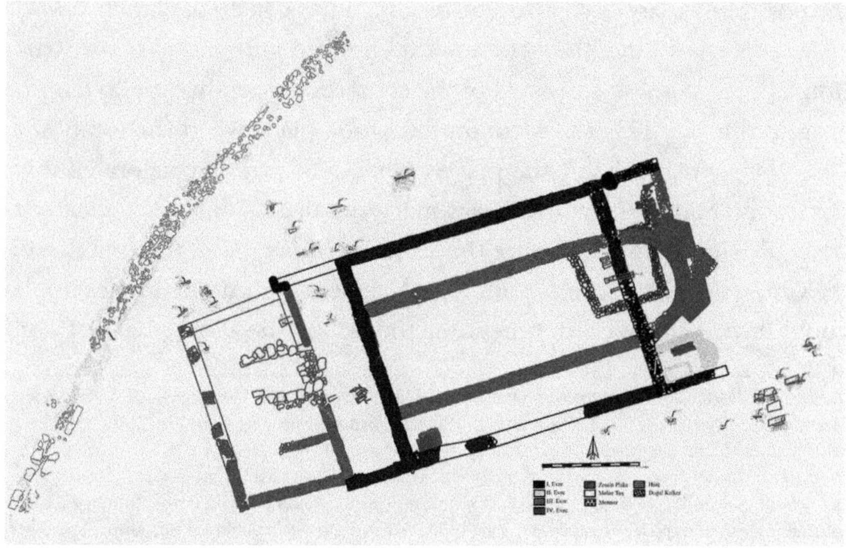

Figure 4.4. Converted basilica, phase 4

outside the walls of Nicaea in Bithynia. The work was supervised by Bactyanus, while Severus was governor of Bithynia."[4] The Bithynian governor Severus and the builder Bactyanus are not otherwise known in ancient sources. Commodus's fourth year would date the construction to AD 183. Şahin assumed that the information in the *Chronicon* came from an inscription, although no such inscription has been found.

In a variety of popular and academic publications as well as in the media, Mustafa Şahin has conjectured that the underwater structure in Lake Iznik was originally this temple mentioned in the *Chronicon*.[5] For instance, large architectural pieces were found in the area of the church narthex along with several column pieces (see plate 19). Şahin interprets these as remains from the peripteral columns surrounding the temple. Additionally, Şahin posits that a well located in the atrium of the basilica was thought to have been a sacred spring associated with the temple of Apollo. He interprets a small portion of a perimeter wall on the periphery of the temple complex as the wall for the temenos of the temple. Another piece, found a few meters away, is construed to be a part of the pediment. Finally, the discovery an erotic terracotta oil lamp among the ruins is thought to rule out the possibility that the structure was originally a Christian church.[6]

Şahin suggests that the structure experienced four phases of construction.[7] The first phase consisted of the construction of the Apollo temple around the year 183. The second phase took place when the tomb of a Christian saint, probably the martyr Neophytos, was incorporated into the Apollo temple. Neophytos was martyred in 303, during the persecutions of Diocletian. Following the Edict of Milan (313), the practice of the Christian faith became legal. The placement of the tomb in the temple could have followed any time after the edict. The third phase of con-

[4]Sencer Şahin, *Katalog der antiken Inschriften des Museums von Iznik (Nikaia) / İznik Müzesi Antik Yazıtlar Kataloğu*, Band 10, 3. *(Testimonia)* Teil II,3 (Bonn: Rudolf Habelt, 1987), 15. Text from Dindorf, trans., *Chronicon Paschale*, 491. Translation mine.

[5]M. Şahin, "Underwater Excavation at the Basilica Church," 71-80; M. Şahin, "Neue Forschungen," 93-106; M. Şahin, "Hava Fotoğrafları ve Arkeoloji Biliminde Yeni Bir Keşif: İznik Gölü Bazilikası," *Yüksek Öğretim Dergisi* (Nov. 2018): 79-81; M. Şahin, "Nikaia'nın Kayıp Apollon Tapınağı," *Bursa'da Zaman* (July 2017): 52-53; M. Şahin, "İznik Gölü Bazilika KalıntısıSualtı Yüzey Araştırması—2015," *TINA Denizcilik Arkeoloji Dergisi* 4 (2015): 32-51.

[6]M. Şahin, "Neue Forschungen," 98-99; M. Şahin, "Hava Fotoğrafları ve Arkeoloji Biliminde," 80; M. Şahin, "Nikaia'nın Kayıp Apollon Tapınağı," 52-53.

[7]M. Şahin, "Neue Forschungen," 103.

struction was marked by the conversion of the temple into a basilica church. In 392 Theodosius issued an edict that banned the sacrifice to idols and pagan deities.[8] This ban reinforced earlier bans by Constantine, Constantius, and Constans,[9] but it is not believed that any of these bans were strictly enforced.[10] Coins found in one of the terracotta tombs (KM-04) under the foundation walls date to the time of Valens (364–378) and Valentinian II (375–392) (see plate 20). Since four of these tombs were located under the walls, the coins suggest that the walls were not built until after 390.[11] The conversion of the temple to a church involved dividing the temple into a central nave with aisles and adding a narthex. An additional antechamber (or atrium) with a well preceded the narthex on the west. The final phase of construction consisted in the addition of the apse, prothesis, and a wall that ran around the tombs at the front of the church, extending into the apse.

EVALUATION OF THE THEORY

Would a Christian martyr be buried in an active pagan temple? Şahin's theory triggers a number of questions that need to be addressed. Foremost among these questions is the issue of why the priests of a functioning pagan temple would allow the remains of a Christian martyr who vehemently opposed pagan worship to be deposited in the temple of Apollo. Even after the Edict of Milan, the pagan temples continued to function for almost two hundred years before they were abandoned.[12] It seems unlikely that the priests and worshipers of Apollo would have permitted Neophytos's remains to be deposited in the temple.

An associated question is how would the Christian community accept the prospect of having the bones of their patron saint deposited in a functioning pagan temple. Christian aversion to paganism was one of

---

[8]*Codex Theodosianus* 16.10.12.

[9]*Codex Theodosianus* 16.10.2.

[10]Bayliss states, "The repetition of laws against sacrifice is usually interpreted as indicative of the general failure of the enforcement system, but it also reflects the tenacity especially of officials to find loopholes in the legislation." Richard Bayliss, "Provincial Cilicia and the Archaeology of Temple Conversion," 2 vols. (PhD diss., University of Newcastle upon Tyne, 2001), 242.

[11]Mustafa Şahin, "Neue Forschungen," 99; M. Şahin, "Nikaia'nın Kayıp Apollon Tapınağı," 53.

[12]Feyo L. Schuddeboom, "The Conversion of Temples in Rome," *Journal of Late Antiquity* 10 (2017): 166-86.

the chief characteristics of the Christian faith from the time of Paul throughout the Byzantine period. Thus, from both a Christian and pagan perspective, it seems unlikely that Neophytos would have been buried in a temple of Apollo. This is a significant obstacle to embracing the theory that the structure was originally a temple.

In response, Şahin asserts that Babylas, a martyred saint from Antioch on the Orantes, provides a precedent for such a burial.[13] Babylas was the bishop of Antioch. According to tradition, Babylas was imprisoned during the Decian persecution and died around 253. He was buried outside Antioch. During the reign of Constantius Gallus, in 354 Babylas's remains were dug up and transferred to the nearby temple of Apollo in Daphne in order to counteract the paganism of the oracle. It was believed that the power of the holy relics of the saint would cancel any of the powers of the cult of Apollo. At that time, a church was built over the temple. Şahin assumes this is what happened at Nicaea as well. Neophytos's remains were buried in a temple of Apollo in Nicaea to invalidate the cult and later the temple was converted into a church.

Bayliss and others, however, do not believe that Babylas's remains were ever placed in the Apollo temple.[14] As Bayliss notes, the church historian Sozomen continued to refer to the structure as a temple even after the supposed conversion.[15] Moreover, contemporary historians Socrates and Theodoret described the Babylas structure as a neighbor to the Apollo temple.[16] "It seems therefore that the shrine and tomb of the martyr was built not in the temple itself, but nearby."[17] Later, Julian ordered the relics of Babylas removed from the martyrion in Daphne in 362. The remains subsequently were placed in the church of Qausiyeh at Antioch.[18]

---

[13]Şahin, "Neue Forschungen," 103.

[14]Bayliss, "Provincial Cilicia and the Archaeology," 111. Likewise, Jennifer Barry, *Bishops in Flight: Exile and Displacement in Late Antiquity* (Oakland: University of California Press, 2019), 157-60 and Christine Shepardson, "Rewriting Julian's Legacy: John Chrysostom's On Babylas and Libanius's Oration 24," *Journal of Late Antiquity* 2, no. 1 (2009): 99-115.

[15]Sozomen, *Ecclesiastical History* 5.19-20.

[16]Socrates, *Ecclesiastical History* 3.18; Theodoret, *Ecclesiastical History* 3.6.

[17]Bayliss, "Provincial Cilicia and the Archaeology," 111.

[18]The church at Qausiyeh was a cruciform martyrion church with seventeen graves in the structure. Downey dates the church to around 360. G. Downey, "The Shrines of St. Babylas at Antioch and Daphne," in *Antioch On-the-Orontes II*, ed. R. Stillwell (Princeton, NJ: Princeton University Press, 1938), 45-48. See also Wendy Mayer, "The Late Antique Church at Qausiyeh Reconsidered:

If this is the case, then the placement of Babylas's tomb in Daphne cannot be used as a precedent for the placement of Neophytos's tomb in what is thought to be a temple of Apollo in Nicaea. The case of Babylas in Daphne was neither an indirect temple conversion, nor a direct temple conversion. Julian later came to the temple of Apollo in Daphne and tried to extract a response from the oracle. Failing to receive a response from Apollo, Julian was told that the proximity of Babylas's remains prevented the oracle from speaking. For this reason, Julian ordered the removal of the remains. Julian's actions demonstrate that the temple of Apollo was still considered to be a functioning temple and that a conversion of the temple had never taken place. Thus, it seems, we have two conclusions: (1) that Babylas's tomb was not in the Apollo temple at Daphne but rather was placed in a martyrion near the Apollo temple, and (2) that the temple of Apollo in Daphne was still considered a pagan temple after Babylas's remains were brought nearby.

Temple conversions. If we apply the research of Hanson, Bayliss, Talloen, and Vercauteren, mentioned in the second chapter, to the underwater basilica at Nicaea, it seems highly unlikely that the basilica was built over a pagan temple.[19] Archaeological and literary evidence indicates that direct temple conversions into basilica churches did not take place before the middle of the fifth century. The dating of coins found under the walls and the carbon dating of skeletal remains in the tombs of the Iznik underwater basilica point to a date in the late fourth century. The proposal that the Iznik underwater basilica was a direct conversion of a pagan temple is untenable. Such direct conversions did not take place until almost a century later.

An examination of the walls. According to Şahin's theory, when the temple was converted into a church two hundred years later, interior walls were constructed in the Apollo temple to divide the interior into a nave with aisles on the sides. Secondary construction is clearly visible from the construction methods, from the materials used, and from the seams

Memory and Martyr Burial in Syrian Antioch," in *Martyrdom and Persecution in Late Antique Christianity*, ed. J. Leemans (Leuven: Uitgeverij Peeters, 2010), 161-78.

[19]R. P. C. Hanson, "The Transformation of Pagan Temples into Churches in the Early Christian Centuries," *Journal of Semitic Studies* 23 (1978): 257-67; Peter Talloen and Lies Vercauteren, "The Fate of Temples in Late Antique Anatolia," in *The Archaeology of Late Antique "Paganism"* (Leiden: Brill, 2011), 347-87, and Bayliss, "Provincial Cilicia and the Archaeology," 120.

where the later construction was attached to the earlier structure. People did not build structures the same way they were constructed two hundred years earlier and later additions are evident by examining the remains.

When it comes to a close examination of the submerged basilica, we find no difference in the materials or the construction methods, and there is no seam suggesting that the interior walls were added later (see also plate 21). With more than two hundred years separating the time of the temple's construction until the time of the conversion to a basilica, one would expect the construction to exhibit secondary construction. However, the walls of the so-called secondary construction in the submerged basilica demonstrate no difference from the walls thought to be of an earlier temple. The interior parallel walls separating the nave from the aisles have the same masonry as the exterior walls of the basilica. The same can be said of the remains of the back western wall that separates the narthex from the atrium. The antae wall of the supposed temple appears to be of the same masonry as the western narthex-atrium wall. If so, instead of being a later addition that enclosed the antae of the temple and thus created a narthex, the western wall must have been constructed at the same time as the southern antae wall. Particularly telling are the joints where these interior walls connect with the exterior walls. The interior walls, running east and west, are interconnected or interlaced with the walls running north and south. Thus, the walls were constructed at the same time and not at some later period. One would expect that a wall added later would have a straight seam where it connects with a wall that was constructed earlier. Instead, the masonry of the inside walls and the western narthex wall overlap with the intersecting outer walls.

What do the tombs suggest? As mentioned earlier, the Edict of Milan did not ban the worship of pagan deities. Even the many fourth-century edicts banning the practices at the temples did not shut down the pagan temples. The fact that these edicts were reissued in later years indicates that pagans continued to visit and sacrifice at the temples and that the edicts were not strictly enforced. The temples and sacrifices continued into the fifth and even the sixth centuries, in spite of legislation and pressure to abandon the cults.

Figure 4.5. Joint of narthex wall and southern nave wall

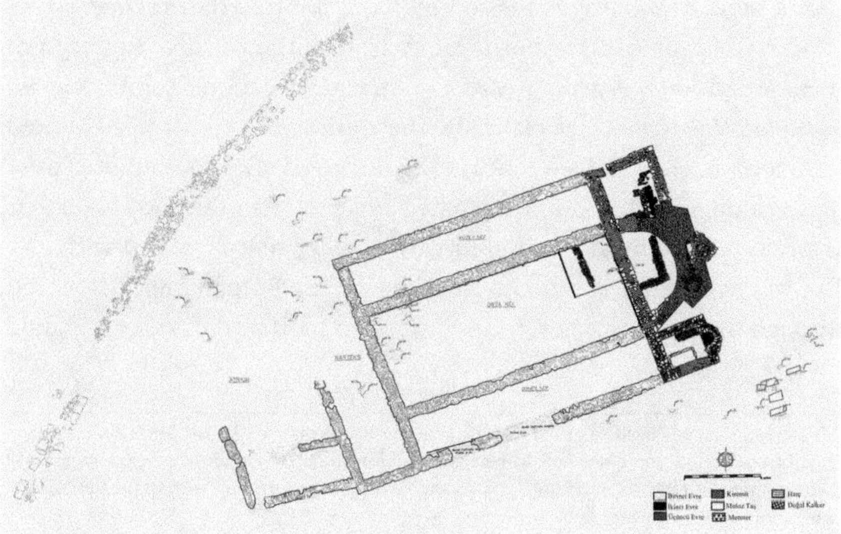

Figure 4.6. Diagram of tombs in submerged basilica

The continued use of the temples is difficult to reconcile with the presence of tombs in the underwater structure. Temples were sacred spaces that were kept separate from the necropolises of ancient cities. Tombs were rarely, if ever, located in pagan temples. The main necropolises of Nicaea were located to the north and east of the city. The underwater structure is located to the south of the city and the tombs in and around the structure were not an early necropolis for the city.

On the other hand, it was common for Christians to build churches over the burial sites of their saints. The tombs of martyrs, in particular, were frequently remembered and celebrated as shrines and places of worship in the years following their martyrdom. Other Christians wished to be buried near the martyrs and additional tombs often encircled the tomb of the saint. After the Edict of Milan, many of these shrines were incorporated into new basilicas, known as martyrions. Thereafter, additional tombs were added within and outside of the martyrions.[20] This practice was motivated not only by a desire to honor the saint, but also by the belief that somehow the spiritual power of the saint could be transferred to those nearby.[21] Augustine was aware of these practices, and he rejected the idea that the dead received any benefit from being buried near a saint.[22] Still, Augustine's opinion did not stop the practice.

Thirty-six tombs have been found around the basilica. Eighteen of them are inside the structure. Most of these are ceramic tombs, known as *cappuccina* tombs (see plate 22). These are tombs constructed of fired terracotta roofing slabs to encase the deceased. The roofing tiles were placed alongside the body at a pitched angle to cover the body like a tent. The seam at the top was covered with smaller tiles or sealed with clay. This method of burial was common during the Roman imperial period through the Byzantine period and was often used by the poor who could

[20]The fourth-century basilica of Pope Mark, south of Rome on the Via Ardeatina near the catacombs of Balbina, contained almost two hundred burial chambers containing the remains of almost three hundred people. One hundred and thirteen of these tombs were inside the basilica, covering almost the entire floor of the structure.

[21]Robert Wisniewski, *The Beginnings of the Cult of Relics* (New York: Oxford, 2018). Cf. Peter R. L. Brown, *The Cult of the Saints: Its Rise and Function in Latin Christianity* (Chicago: University Chicago, 1982), 55.

[22]Augustine, *De Cura Pro Mortuis Gerenda* 22.

not afford a sarcophagus.[23] Examples of these kinds of burials are found throughout the Mediterranean world and elsewhere in Anatolia (Çatalhöyük, Gordion, and Hierapolis).[24] A few of these *cappuccina* tombs were also recently unearthed near the Yenişehir Gate.

Figure 4.7. *Cappuccina* tombs near the Yenişehir Gate, Nicaea

Radiocarbon dating of the skeletal remains in the tomb KM6 place the death of the individual between the years AD 335 and 418 (see plate 23). Similar dates are established by several coins found in the graves that come from the time of Emperor Valens (364–378) and Emperor Valentinian (378–383). These dates confirm the time of the burials and provide clues regarding the construction of the basilica.

[23]Liana Brent, "Disturbed, Damaged and Disarticulated: Grave Reuse in Roman Italy," in *TRAC 2016 Proceedings of the Twenty-Sixth Theoretical Roman Archaeology Conference* (Rome: Edizioni Quasar, 2017), 37-50; Andrew L. Goldman, "New Evidence for Non-elite Burial Patterns in Central Turkey," in *Life and Death in Asia Minor in Hellenistic, Roman and Byzantine Times*, ed. J. Rasmus Brandt et al. (Oxford: Oxbow, 2017), 149-75.

[24]Mauro Puddu, "Connecting the Dots: Between Sulci, Masullas and Karales," in *Funerary Archaeology and Changing Identities: Community Practices in Roman-Period Sardinia* (Oxford: Archaeopress, 2018), 113-22; Donatell Ronchetta, "The South-East Necropolis in Hierapolis in Phrygia: Planning, Typologies, and Construction Techniques," in Brandt et al., *Life and Death in Asia Minor*, 39-68.

At least four of the ceramic tombs (KM-2, KM-3, KM-4, and KM-6) are underneath the eastern wall that separates the apse from the nave. Coins dating to the late fourth century were found in one of these tombs. According to the temple theory, this wall was one of the exterior walls of the Apollo temple. The dates of the coins demonstrate that this wall could not have been a wall of the second-century Apollo temple. Instead, the wall was constructed sometime in the fourth century.

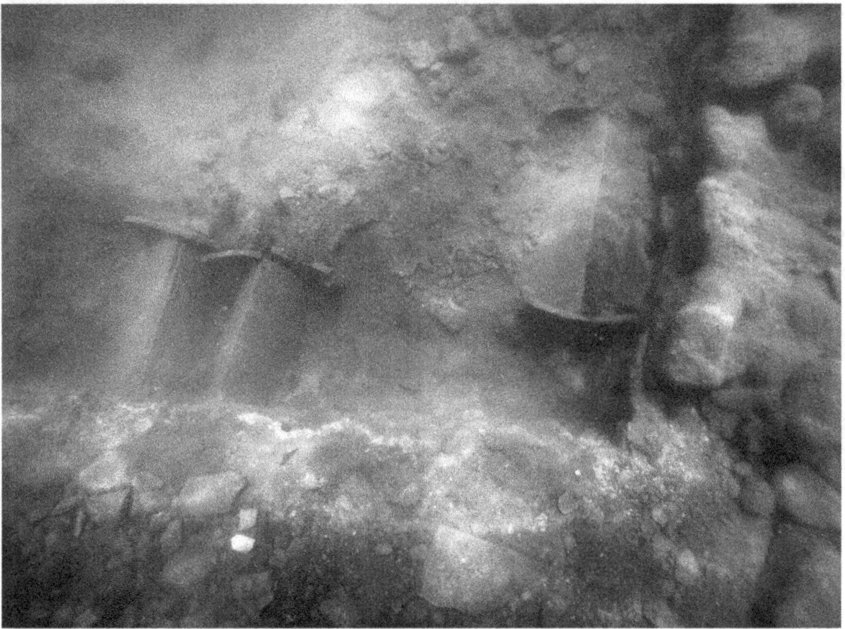

Figure 4.8. *Cappuccina* tombs partially buried under wall

The issue of sacred space is also pertinent to this discussion. Public worship at the pagan temples took place outside of the temple. The interior room (*cella*) was considered the home of the deity. The *cella* was sacred space, reserved for the priests and the cult statue. In front of the temple, altars were constructed for the worshipers to perform their votive duties. The doors of the temple would generally be opened when sacrifices were being performed so that the deity could observe the proceedings. The sights and smells of the sacrifice would arouse the god and compelled the god to act or speak. The common people did not generally enter the inner precincts except at certain times or under special circumstances.

By contrast, worshipers in the churches were taken inside of the structure. This transformation of space reflected changed perspectives of the deity. Whereas the pagan gods were considered transcendent and aloof, the Christians considered their God to be immanent and personal. "The pagan temple as *domus dei* or house of god—a building for the cult-effigy of the deity—was replaced by the church as *domus ecclesiae* or house of the community—a structure primarily intended to host a congregation of worshippers that came together in the name of an omnipresent God who could be worshipped in any location."[25]

So, the question is, If the structure in Lake Iznik was a temple to Apollo, why was the tomb of Neophytos placed inside the temple and why were a number of additional tombs placed in the structure? The only way of avoiding this question is to assume that the temple was converted into a basilica church in the late fourth century. However, as we noted earlier in chapter 3, such conversions did not occur until the middle of the fifth century.

The erotic oil lamp. During the 2017 excavations, an erotic terracotta oil lamp was discovered. In some publications it had been suggested that the lamp was evidence that the site was originally a temple. Şahin cites the lamp as a clear sign of this.[26] The argument follows the assumption that an erotic lamp of this sort would have been inappropriate for a basilica following Christianity's moral code.

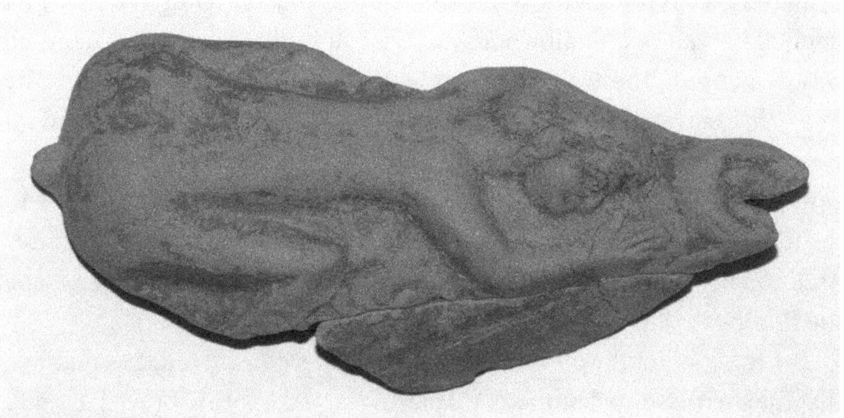

Figure 4.9. Erotic oil lamp, Nicaea

[25]Talloen and Vercauteren, "Fate of Temples," 376.
[26]Şahin, "Hava Fotoğrafları ve Arkeoloji Biliminde," 81.

The erotic oil lamp was found on a deep probe of the prothesis. The lamp was found under the foundation of the structure. Turkish seismologists, using electrical resistivity technology (ERT), have determined that nothing lies further beneath the foundation of the basilica except the beachrock of the lake. By comparing the erotic oil lamp with similar items found at Pompeii, Şahin dates the artifact to the first century.

The date of the lamp in the first century and the discovery of the lamp beneath the foundation both lead to the conclusion that the lamp was deposited on the shore of the lake before any structure was built. In any case, the erotic oil lamp is not proof of an Apollo temple at the site. Eroticism was not associated with the worship of Apollo any more than the worship of Christ. Based on this evidence, it seems unlikely that the lamp has anything to do with either a temple or the basilica.

The well or spring. The presence of a well at the western end of the structure has been introduced as supporting evidence for an Apollo temple (see plate 24). This well was surrounded by secondary-use architectural pieces, and it extended from the back (western) wall of the narthex and stretched out west into the atrium. It is suggested that this could have originally been a sacred well or spring associated with Apollo temples.

Evidence of a well at the site is supported by the eighth-century British traveler Willibald. Willibald claimed that the church of the first council had an open hall where there was a well from which sacred oil was dispensed. The well was excavated during the 2019 season.[27] The well was excavated to a depth of 4.6 feet. Whatever the structure might have been, it was filled with rubble including stones, pieces of tile, and wood. Levels of wooden girders were also found in the area, along with eighty-two coins dating from the early fourth to the thirteenth centuries. Additionally, nails, ceramics, glass pieces, and marble pieces were among the findings.

The function of the construction needs to be considered. It is possible that the surrounding architectural pieces framed a spring or well to serve an Apollo temple. However, it is also possible that the structure was used

[27] Şahin, "Underwater Excavation at the Basilica Church," 73-79.

as a baptistry for the church. Or if Willibald was describing the same structure, the item may have been a colymbion serving holy water (or oil) at the entrance to the church.

The structure was set in the atrium and attached to the back wall of the narthex. The northern and southern sides had architectural pieces placed on the perimeter, but the western side was open. A well would typically be entirely encircled by a wall. But this structure had an open end on the west. On the other hand, a colymbion or baptistry would be open for the worshiper to receive water or oil from the colymbion or for the initiate to enter the pool for baptism.

Whatever the structure may have been, in the years after the waters of Lake Ascania began to encroach on the basilica from the west, the structure was abandoned and filled with debris. Perhaps the baptistry was fouled by the waters of the lake or the holy waters of the colymbion were soiled by the impurities of the lake water. In either case, the structure was no longer functional and was plugged with discarded materials.

Current remains of the temple of Apollo. Compounding the matter, we must note that there is the problem of the lack of architectural remains for the temple. Only a few column fragments have been found in Lake Iznik to date, and the columns do not appear to be the columns of a temple. Columns from Apollo temples at the Smintheion, Claros, Delos, and Corinth (all similar in size to the underwater structure at Nicaea) are much larger in circumference and are fluted. The column pieces at Nicaea are smaller and unfluted. They were more likely the columns of a church basilica that separated the nave from the aisles. This was the standard architectural plan of basilicas.

We might also ask, Where is the crepidoma, the entablature, and the pediment? The entablature and pediment are the horizonal architectural pieces that rest on the columns of ancient temples. This would commonly include a frieze with figures in relief. The crepidoma is the level foundational platform of the temple on which the entire structure rests. It could be argued that the entablature and pediment were repurposed in later generations, but the crepidoma would have been impossible to move. In fact, Şahin acknowledged in a 2018 publication that "we have not observed any foundation remains of a possible temple yet."[28] In 2020, after two more seasons of excavations Professor Şahin again confirmed, "No architectural remains of this temple have yet been identified."[29] The lack of a crepidoma is particularly significant. Tombs located next to the walls of the basilica indicate there was no crepidoma, and excavations in the narthex (sounding #10) revealed five more graves, but no crepidoma.[30]

Once it became evident that the basilica would be lost to the lake, it is likely that much of the structure was reused as building material for other structures and churches in the city. The architectural remains of older buildings that were no longer used or had been irreparably damaged were commonly foraged for secondary use. Building materials were not easily obtained, so why not reuse pieces (spolia) that can be utilized for new construction? This was a major source of building materials, particularly in the Byzantine period. Thus, it could be argued that the artifacts from the Apollo temple (and the later basilica) were taken and used in other buildings in Nicaea.

This is a plausible explanation for the lack of remains, but this explanation fails to go far enough. The foundation platform of a temple, the crepidoma, cannot be found. Typically, the crepidoma consists of three steps. The top step, known as the stylobate, is where the walls and columns of the temple rest. On uneven ground, the crepidoma provides a level area for the superstructure of the temple. Thus, the three steps are not always visible above ground, but may be partially buried. If the steps of the crepidoma were too large, smaller steps often accompanied the entrance. In the case of the underwater basilica at Nicaea, the crepidoma has never been found. The lack of a stone floor (stylobate) suggests that the structure originally had an earthen or wooden floor. This would be unusual in Roman architecture for a temple.

Looking at the largest and most well-known Apollo temples, a common element is inscriptions inscribed on the temple walls and on other structures nearby. So, for instance, the Apollo temple in Delphi is

[28]Mustafa Şahin, "İznik Gölü Bazilika Kazıları 2017-2018," *TINA Denizcilik Arkeoloji Dergisi* 10 (2018): 125.
[29]M. Şahin, "Neue Forschungen," 103.
[30]M. Şahin, "İznik Gölü Bazilika Kazıları," 121.

loaded with inscriptions by worshipers who have come to the temple to inquire of the god. Likewise, the important Apollo temples in Claros, Didyma, Miletos, and Delos are surrounded by inscriptions. Yet, no Apollo inscriptions have been found near the underwater basilica or elsewhere in secondary use in the later structures of Nicaea.

Sources for the existence of an Apollo temple in Nicaea. Finally, it can be noted that documentation for the existence of an Apollo temple in Nicaea is scant. There is the previously mentioned seventh-century *Chronicon Paschale* that briefly mentioned the temple. Elsewhere, there are no literary sources, inscriptions, or archaeological finds to suggest there was an Apollo temple near Nicaea. Temples were the focal point of pagan urban culture—not just the religious rites, but these temples also constituted the social urban fabric of a city's culture, and they played pivotal political roles as well. Yet, there are no clues of an Apollo temple in the literature or inscriptions of the city. What are we to make of this? The author of the *Chronicon* may have received erroneous information or may have received information and incorrectly assumed that the temple was associated with Nicaea. Given that the *Chronicon* was written five hundred years later, what was the source of the *Chronicon*'s information?

Even if the *Chronicon*'s data is correct, the location of the Apollo temple is ambiguous. Was the temple north or east or south of the city? Was the temple a rural temple located at a sacred site some distance from Nicaea? The temple may have been marginally related to the life of Nicaea, and the *Chronicon*'s author may have connected it with the closest nearby city. For example, the Apollo temple at Didyma was located at the end of the sacred way twenty kilometers from the nearest city, Miletus. Likewise, the temple of Apollo Smintheus was connected to Alexandrian Troas via the sacred way at a distance of thirty-five kilometers, and the temple of Apollo Claros was located twelve kilometers to the south of Colophon. If there was an Apollo temple in the area of Nicaea, the site may have been some distance away from the city.

If the structure was originally a temple to Apollo, why was it constructed just a few meters outside of the city walls, rather than inside of the city? A temple outside of the walls would suggest that the deity was excluded from the civic life of the city. Elsewhere in Anatolia, there are temples outside of cities.[31] However, the temples located outside of cities were typically built at remote locations because there were ancient sacred traditions associated with springs, mountains, or geographic features. Likewise, it is unlikely that a temple would be built on the beach of Lake Ascania. Altogether, the *Chronicon*'s statement alone is not specific enough to identify the submerged structure in Lake Iznik as an Apollo temple, and the lack of corroboration by any other data calls into question the identification as such.

SUMMARY

For a host of reasons, it appears unlikely that the underwater basilica originated as an Apollo temple that was later converted into a Christian basilica. First, from both a Christian and a pagan perspective, a Christian martyr, who opposed the pagan cults, would not have been buried in a pagan temple. Neophytos was martyred in AD 303, and the Edict of Milan was not issued until ten years later, in AD 313. The Edict of Milan did not ban pagan worship, and the worship of the pagan deities continued for another two, or in some instances, another three centuries. If the structure was originally an Apollo temple, it would have been an active pagan temple when the remains of Neophytos were placed in the temple. The burial of the saint in the temple would not have been acceptable for either Christians or pagans.

Second, an examination of temples that were later converted into basilica churches demonstrates that such conversions did not happen until the middle of the fifth century at the earliest. The underwater basilica has been securely dated to the fourth century, before any direct temple conversions took place. Pagan temples continued to be used for many years after the Edict of Milan. It was only after the pagan temples were abandoned that they were repurposed and reconstructed.

Third, an examination of the walls of the underwater structure show that the construction of the interior walls (supposedly added later to

[31]In Acts 14:13 the temple of Zeus was located outside of the city of Lystra. Likewise, the temple of Zeus at Diocaesarea was located around three miles away from Olba. The temple of Zeus was constructed at the ancient sacred site before people later settled around it. Afterward the place was given the name Diocaesarea.

divide the temple into a nave and aisles) were constructed at the same time as the exterior walls. The interior and exterior walls utilized the same building materials and made use of the same building techniques, and the interior walls were interwoven into the exterior walls, demonstrating that they were constructed at the same time as the exterior walls.

Fourth, the presence of thirty-six tombs in and around the basilica contributes to our understanding that the structure was a Christian martyrion, rather than a pagan temple. Pagan temples were not constructed in burial grounds and people were not buried in or near the temples. On the other hand, it is well attested that Christians were commonly buried near the tombs of the saints and martyrs. Even after the construction of the basilicas, Christians continued the practice of burying the faithful on the grounds.

Fifth, nothing has currently been excavated at the site that can be clearly identified as part of an earlier pagan temple. Perhaps most telling is that a crepidoma (the temple platform) is not present at the site. Additionally, there is only one source that supports the existence of an Apollo temple in the vicinity of Nicaea. This source, the *Chronicon Paschale*, was written five hundred years after the structure was supposedly built. The information provided by the *Chronicon* is not supported by any other literary, inscriptional, or archaeological data, and the brief description in the *Chronicon* is not specific enough to identify the submerged basilica as a temple.

For these reasons, it is hard to imagine that the underwater basilica at Nicaea was originally a second-century Apollo temple that was later converted into a basilica church during the late fourth century. Rather, the structure was a church from the beginning. In particular, the presence of the tombs in and around the church suggests to us that the church was a structure built to remember the life and death of a martyr, a structure known as a martyrion.

CHAPTER FIVE

WAS THE UNDERWATER BASILICA A MARTYRION?

WAS THE BASILICA A MARTYRION BUILT TO COMMEMORATE NEOPHYTOS?

As mentioned above, two late illuminated manuscripts tell the story of Neophytos, a young man who was martyred in Nicaea. According to these manuscripts Neophytos was born in Nicaea to Christian parents Theodore and Florentia. He displayed great piety early in life and left Nicaea at the age of ten. When he was fifteen, Neophytos returned to the area and confronted the governor Decius, who was engaged in the persecution of Christians in the city. Neophytos was seized, tortured, and executed. The Menologion of Basil II, currently in the Vatican Library, depicts the execution on the shores of Lake Ascania.

From the first century onward, a tradition developed within the early Christian communities of remembering and commemorating the deaths of important figures of faith. The tombs of the saints and martyrs became places of prayer, worship, and veneration. As time passed, these tombs became shrines that were decorated or enlarged. Some of these shrines became sanctuaries and, in some instances, basilicas were built over the tombs of the saints. In the years thereafter, members of the Christian community were buried near the saint. It was believed that those buried near the saints would obtain benefits from them.[1] The practice became so popular that, at times, there was competition for the burial sites nearest

[1]Augustine addressed the issue (*De Cura pro Mortuis Gerenda*, sec 6) and claimed that those buried near the saints would only indirectly receive benefits, such as the prayers of those who visited the saint's tomb. Others, however, believed that the spiritual powers of the saint consecrated the burial ground and those interred nearby. See Augustine, "On the Care of the Dead," Fourth-Century Christianity, www.fourthcentury.com/on-the-care-of-the-dead/.

the saint.[2] At the beginning of the fourth century, following the legalization of Christianity with the Edict of Milan, basilica churches, known as martyrions, were built over the tombs of the saints, and these became the leading churches of Christian communities. Even after the construction of these basilica martyrions, later Christian tombs were added in the area immediately surrounding the basilica. Notable examples of these are the burial sites of Peter and Paul in Rome[3] and several martyrions in Cilicia.

The thirty-six graves in and around the basilica are important. The location of these graves south of the city is unusual. The main necropolis was located north of Nicaea, near Elbeyli. A second necropolis was east of the city, outside of the Lefke Gate.[4] The tombs here on the lakeshore, within and surrounding the church, can be best explained by the martyrdom and burial of Neophytos and the desire for fellow Christians to be buried nearby. In the following years, the burial site grew and expanded around the martyr's tomb. Shortly after the Edict of Milan, a memorial church was constructed to celebrate the life of the martyr.

In the diaconicon of the Nicaea martyrion, in the southeast of the basilica, Şahin has identified a small apse within which were two tombs, one a terracotta tomb and the other a sarcophagus (see plate 25). Şahin believes the apsed structure was a small sanctuary martyrion that was later enclosed within the larger basilica. The fact that several terracotta tombs were located under the walls of the basilica tells us that the current underwater walls were built after necropolis had been established and that the basilica was intentionally built over a necropolis. Skeletal remains were found in several of the tombs.

The location of the basilica outside of the city walls of Nicaea also contributes to the conclusion that the basilica was a martyrion. Following the legalization of Christianity with the Edict of Milan, one would

---

[2]Yvette Duval, *Aupres des Saints Corps et Ame: L'inhumation "ad Sanctos" dans la Chretiente d'Orient et d'Occident du IIIe au VIIe siècle* (Paris: Etudes Augustiniennes, 1988).

[3]Margherita Guarducci, *The Tomb of St. Peter: The New Discoveries in the Sacred Grottoes of the Vatican* (New York: Hawthorn, 1960). Peter Lampe, "Traces of Peter Veneration in Roman Archaeology," in *Peter in Early Christianity*, ed. H. K. Bond and L. W. Hurtado (Grand Rapids, MI: Eerdmans, 2015), 273-317. Nicola Camerlenghi, *St. Paul's Outside the Walls: A Roman Basilica, from Antiquity to the Modern Era* (Cambridge: Cambridge University Press, 2018), 24-30.

[4]Urs Peschlow, "Nicaea," in *The Archaeology of Byzantine Anatolia: From the End of Late Antiquity Until the Coming of the Turks*, ed. Philipp Niewönhner (Oxford: Oxford University, 2017), 207-8.

assume that a church would have been constructed within the walls of the city. However, it is known that burials were outside ancient cities. The choice of constructing a church outside of the city atop a necropolis can best be accounted for by reckoning the church to be a martyrion.

As we have mentioned above, the tradition regarding Neophytos is weak. The two earliest accounts of Neophytos date to the tenth and eleventh centuries. Both accounts of the life and martyrdom of Neophytos are heavily mythologized. According to these traditions, Neophytos, as a youth, struck a rock and produced water for his thirsty companions. He raised his mother from the dead, and during his martyrdom he survived several tortures, emerged unscathed from a fiery furnace, and tamed lions and bears unleased to devour him. These stories seem to echo stories of Moses, Daniel, Jesus, and some of the earlier martyrs. This calls into question the historicity of the narratives.

It is important at this point to describe the process that supported the tradition. This would have been similar to the process that undergirded the Synoptic tradition. John's Gospel states that "Jesus performed many other signs in the presence of his disciples, which are not recorded in this book" (Jn 20:30). And "Jesus did many other things as well. If every one of them were written down, I suppose that even the whole world would not have room for the books that would be written" (Jn 21:25). What John wrote was also true of the other Gospels and was also true for the traditions of the early church. It was impossible to record all of the stories regarding Jesus and the later church. This was particularly relevant regarding the oral culture of the first several centuries. Not all the incidents, events, and teachings of the early Christian leaders could be remembered, recollected, and accurately passed on in the oral tradition.

There is ample testimony to conclude that tens of thousands of Christians were executed for their faith over the first three centuries. Since most people could neither read nor write, most of these stories were never written down. The lives and martyrdoms of these individuals were recounted to later generations by word of mouth, primarily by the families and Christian communities who knew the individuals and the details. But as generations passed, many of the details were lost and forgotten. I suspect that most of the stories of those martyrs never survived for more than two hundred years. However, even in cases where the stories of the saints faded away, the names often survived much longer.

As with the Jesus traditions, only the more remarkable traditions persisted. Some of these entered the written tradition. One could ask, If Jesus performed other miracles, why were they not recorded? Why were other teachings of the Lord not recorded? Many of these circulated orally within Christian circles for at least a century. The Gospel writers selected the stories of Jesus that they thought were most pertinent to their audiences and that highlighted the theological issues the authors thought most important. Likewise, the purveyors of the later church tradition realized that as more stories were told, only a portion of them could be included in the written traditions.

During the early Byzantine period, the guardians of the traditions were the Christian monks, and the places where the Scriptures and church traditions were recorded were the monasteries. Contrary to the bulk of the population, most of the monks were literate, and one of their primary tasks was to preserve the sacred tradition of the Christian faith. The monks remained celibate in order to keep their focus on the tradition without the distraction of a wife and children. These were the people who preserved the Scriptures by copying the sacred texts while also maintaining the legacy of the saints and martyrs.

As with the production of newer copies of Scripture, once produced, the older copies were neglected and relegated to the pile of obsolete documents. Over time most of these documents perished. The monks trusted the accuracy of the newer documents and felt no need to keep the older ones. As the volumes in the libraries of the monasteries grew, space became a problem, and many of these sources were discarded or burned.

Thus, we see a gap that often exists between late traditions and the earlier events they recorded. The gap does not necessitate the assumption that the late tradition was concocted from nothing. Rather, it is more likely that the earlier sources were discarded once a newer copy was issued or when the contents of an earlier source were included in the later document. We need to realize that the monks seldom thought of preserving or documenting their sources as scholars and librarians do today. The textual tradition of the New Testament writings demonstrates that there was little difference between early copies of the biblical text compared with copies produced hundreds of years later. It is plausible to assume that some care was also given to the tradition of the saints.

A story from Constantin von Tischendorf's travels illustrates this point. Tischendorf, a German textual critic, traveled the Mediterranean in search of the earliest copies of the New Testament. In 1859, on one of his visits to Saint Catherine's monastery at the foot of Mount Sinai, Tischendorf was shown a fourth-century manuscript known today as Sinaiticus, one of our oldest and best copies of the New Testament. According to the monk who showed him the manuscript, the pages were being used as tinder to start fires. Tischendorf's exuberant response was enough to convince the monks of the manuscript's value. Although Tischendorf was not able to obtain the manuscript at that time, he later returned and was able to finagle the manuscript out of the hands of the monks. The story exemplifies monastic practices (even in the nineteenth century) for disposing of ancient manuscripts that were no longer used. If Scripture was discarded in this way, certainly other ancient documents of the Christian faith were discarded as well.

Figure 5.1. Codex Sinaiticus, St. Catherine's Monastery, Egypt

The veracity of the Gospel tradition has often been challenged due to the thirty- to forty-year gap between the crucifixion of Jesus and the writing of the Gospels. But textual criticism of the Gospels has shown that, once the stories were recorded, they have not essentially changed over the hundreds of years up to the present. Fortunately, we have thousands of early copies of books from the New Testament. These manuscripts help us to see the care put into preserving the scriptural tradition. Unfortunately, we do not have as many copies of the lives of the saints. We cannot trace the trail leading up to the later traditions. Why can we not assume a measure of the same care for preserving the traditions of the martyrs? These traditions were preserved by the same people—the monks.

With this in mind, I consider it plausible that the martyrdom of Neophytos was a historical event. The execution of Christians during these periods of persecution was a traumatic event deeply imprinted on the minds of the local Christian community. It is unlikely that the deaths of individuals would be quickly forgotten even if the details were lost. Oral and written traditions may be preserved for hundreds of years, even if the trail of sources is lost today. It was common for legends and miraculous stories to expand around the beloved saints. Yet that does not negate the reality of the martyrdom. If nothing else, we are at least able to establish the execution and burial of an individual, perhaps named Neophytos, at Nicaea.

It is also clear that the underwater basilica was a martyrion built to commemorate a martyr who was executed prior to the Edict of Toleration. The location of the basilica is telling. Fourteen other Byzantine churches were erected within the walls of Nicaea. It is unusual for a church to have been built outside of the walls of the city. The most likely explanation for the underwater basilica's location is that it marked the spot of a martyr's death or burial. The date of the structure is also important. As the oldest basilica in Nicaea, the structure followed the period when Christianity emerged from the time of its persecution and began to legally build places of worship.

In 2018 excavators at the basilica discovered a terracotta token. Şahin dates the token to the fifth or sixth century.[5] The obverse depicts Christ Pantocrator (Ruler of All), seated on a throne with a cross behind his head. His right hand is raised, offering a blessing, and his left hand holds a copy of

[5]This is consistent with Boero's observation: "Based on the limited evidence for dating tokens, it appears that tokens came into widespread use in the Near East in the first third of the sixth century." Dina Boero, "The Cultural Biography of a Pilgrimage Token: From Hagiographical to Archaeological Evidence," *Archiv für Religionsgeschichte* 21 (2020): 163n30.

the Scriptures laid on his lap. The reverse is blank. The token measures 1.5 inches in diameter and was made of terracotta, rather than bronze or silver, indicating that it had no monetary value. Instead, the token was a souvenir given or purchased by a pilgrim that visited the site. Boero notes, "Given a token's easy production and humble clay fabric, it is probable that pilgrims from various socio-economic backgrounds could purchase tokens."[6] The tokens had various uses. For some, the token was a souvenir that brought blessings, for others it facilitated prayer, and for yet others the token was thought to contain the power of the saints and thus to have apotropaic powers. The discovery of the token confirms that the site was a place of pilgrimage, either to celebrate the life of Neophytos or to remember the First Council of Nicaea. Perhaps the basilica was a place of pilgrimage for both.

Figure 5.2. Christ Pantocrator

[6]Boero, "Cultural Biography of a Pilgrimage Token," 167.

THE NICAEA BASILICA AND THE EARLY CHRISTIAN MARTYRIONS IN ROUGH CILICIA

The region of Cilicia has some of the earliest Christian basilicas constructed in the years following the Edict of Milan. The presence of several fourth-century churches stands out as a distinctive feature of this Roman province. There are few literary sources describing life in the area of Rough Cilicia, the southwestern half of Cilicia. However, the remains of several martyrions in this area bear witness to a turbulent period of persecution prior to the Edict of Milan. Here, there are eight fourth- or early fifth-century churches that have been identified as martyrions. Churches at Seleucia ad Calycadnum, Corycos, Yanıkhan, Corasion, Diocaesarea, Kanytelis, and two at Elaioussa Sebaste originated as martyrions to commemorate the deaths of local saints. This region has been sparsely explored, and it is reasonable to assume that more martyrions existed among the numerous church ruins in the area.

In Stephen Hill's examination of the early Byzantine churches of Cilicia, he maintains, "The regular provision of a passage behind the apse is easily the most remarkable characteristic of Cilician church planning. The feature was present in the earliest Cilician basilicas, and was, I believe, a major factor which influenced subsequent architectural developments."[7] By Hill's count at least thirty-seven of these early Byzantine churches in Cilicia had these eastern passages behind the central apse. Hill believes these passages were spaces for the celebration of martyrs. "I believe that the case for the eastern passages in Cilician basilicas being martyrial, or at least funerary, in basic purpose can therefore be supported from internal Cilician evidence, and by comparison with martyria in other parts of the late Roman world."[8]

The setting and plan of the underwater basilica at Nicaea is similar to these martyrions in Rough Cilicia. Nothing remains today of a martyrion at the site of ancient Corasion. The modern city of Susanoğlu has expanded toward the sea with shops and resort hotels that have destroyed the remains of the ancient town. Fortunately, the church was visited by

---

[7]Stephen Hill, *The Early Byzantine Churches of Cilicia and Isauria*, Birmingham Byzantine and Ottoman Monographs 1 (Aldershot, UK: Variorum Ashgate, 1996), 28.
[8]Hill, *Churches of Cilicia*, 37.

Josef Keil and Adolf Wilhelm in 1931 and later by Hill, who described and sketched the basilica.[9] Like the basilica in Nicaea, the church of Corasion was built near the harbor and near a necropolis. Facing east, the church measured 82 by 56 feet and had a nave with flanking aisles and a narthex. Keil and Wilhelm described a colymbion on the east wall of the narthex with a lion's head spout and a basin beneath it. An unusual feature of this basilica was an additional apse located midway along the north wall of the aisle. It is probable that this was the position of the martyr's tomb.

The coastal city of Corycos (Kizkalesi) possessed twelve churches. The largest, the so-called Tomb Church, was located in the necropolis of the ancient city and was particularly strange in its construction. It measured 262 by 98 feet with a large atrium and narthex on the west measuring 115 by 98 feet. An apse was located on the south wall of the narthex, and fragments of a marble water basin (probably a colymbion) were found there. Inside the basilica itself, the church was divided into three sections, each at roughly 49 by 98 feet. The western section, just inside the narthex, had a series of columns running in a north and south direction. Farther east, the central nave, if it can be described as such, had four piers that probably supported elevated wooden arches, running east and west and dividing the basilica into a nave and aisles. Strangely, this central nave had an apse facing west, jutting into the western section of the church. A sarcophagus was found here in the central nave in front of the apse. Farther east from the central section, there were three rooms, each with an apse facing east. The room in the southeast had terracotta water pipes, suggesting that a baptistry existed here. The unusual layout of the basilica is explained by Hill as "a successful attempt to combine the capacity of the basilica to hold crowds of people with the more specialized demands of commemorative churches in which there is a strong focus on a central shrine or sacred object. . . . This church was surely an important martyrium."[10] Hill dates the basilica to the late fifth century.

Another unusual martyrion church was found in the northern necropolis of Diocaesarea (Uzuncaburç). The eastern end of the basilica is

[9]Hill, *Churches of Cilicia*, 243, fig. 49.
[10]Hill, *Churches of Cilicia*, 135.

no longer visible. A road running north through the necropolis has buried this part of the structure. Fortunately, a drawing of the basilica's plan was made by Keil and Wilhelm before it was covered by the road.[11] The basilica was 46 by 85 feet with an apse on the east. At the western end of the structure, the basilica was cut into the hillside, and a rock-cut tomb was centered below an arch. At a later period, the tomb was faced with an ashlar arch, but this has disappeared. Above the tomb on the western wall there are sockets for wooden beams. The sockets continue along the north and south sides of the rock. This suggests that the tomb was covered with a roof. Further along the north and south sides of the basilica, there were piers that supported a superstructure. Hill supports a suggestion by Keil and Wilhelm that the basilica was built over the tomb of a local saint named Lukios.[12] Later in the fourth century the tomb was expanded into a martyrion church.

Figure 5.3. Diocaesarea martyrion, northern necropolis

[11]Josef Keil and Adolf Wilhelm, *Denkmäler aus dem Rauhen Kilikien*, MAMA 3 (Manchester: Manchester University Press, 1931), 61-62, fig. 92.

[12]Hill, *Churches of Cilicia*, 256.

Elaioussa Sebaste was an important port city and the residence of several Roman governors in Rough Cilicia. Two Byzantine churches were constructed in the Roman agora of the city. The agora was located at the southern foot of the theater. The agora itself was built over an earlier complex with a beautiful polychrome mosaic floor depicting fish. It is not known what kind of structure the earlier mosaic floor might have been a part of, although it has been suggested that it was part of a large residential building. Whatever, once existed there, the area was converted into the city's agora. In the center of the agora, there was a circular structure that may have been a tholos (a round structure sometimes functioning as a sacred site).

In the early Byzantine period, two martyrion churches were built in the center of the agora. Today, the two churches are bisected by a modern road. The church on the west is oriented in an east–west direction. It has a central nave with apses on both the eastern and western ends. The nave was flanked by aisles, and both the nave and aisles had opus sectile flooring. At least nine *cassa* tombs were found under the floor of the basilica. One of them was located inside the tholos. Some of the tombs contained more than one body. The western apse was constructed with spolia from the tholos. A tomb in this apse was probably that of a martyr. The two apses probably had different functions. The western one was used for commemorating the martyr, and the eastern apse was for the worship services. The eastern apse was slightly elevated and had an altar. It was located between a prothesis on the north, containing a baptistry, and a diaconicon on the south.

The basilica on the eastern side of the road is even more interesting. It is also oriented in an east–west direction. Like the western basilica, it has a nave flanked by aisles and has similar opus sectile flooring. It also has a baptistry north of the apse in the prothesis. It is slightly bigger than the church to the west and had a narthex on the western end. This basilica had at least six *cassa* tombs. The apse of the basilica faced east, and it surrounded a tomb centrally located within the apse. Like the basilica to the west, this was a martyrion.

A small church was later constructed inside of this apse, surrounding the tomb. This inner church has a small apse facing east and a small nave

Figure 5.4. Elaiussa Sebaste west martyrion, Cilicia

Figure 5.5. Elaiussa Sebaste east martyrion, Cilicia

with no aisles. The opus sectile flooring of the earlier church provided the floor for this new church. The walls of the inner church cover a portion of the benches on the larger outer apse. These walls were poorly constructed with a double thick wall from spolia, probably from the larger basilica surrounding it. One can surmise that the larger basilica was destroyed at some point and the smaller church was rebuilt as a chapel for the remembrance of the martyr that was buried at the site.

Eugenia Schneider dates the church in the west to the late fifth century.[13] Similarities between the two basilicas, particularly the patterns of the opus sectile flooring, indicate that both basilicas were constructed around the same time. The presence and location of the tombs in each church suggest that they were martyrions dedicated to different saints. The smaller church constructed inside the ruins of the eastern basilica insured that the residents would not forget what had happened here.

There were five churches built around the large sinkhole at Kanytelis (Kanlıdivane). The sinkhole measures 230 by 430 feet and is 200 feet deep. The sinkhole was considered a holy site dedicated to the Olban Zeus, the chief god of the Olban Kingdom. Local traditions hold that this was a place where people were thrown to their deaths. The name Kanlıdivane itself means "Bloody Lunatic." Just north of the sinkhole is a large necropolis. Squeezed into the small space between the necropolis and the sinkhole is Church Four.

Church Four is also known as the Papylos church. A barely legible inscription on the top of the lintel identified Papylos as the builder. A lower inscription states, "This is the door leading to God. People who enter are saved. God help me." The church measured 148 by 51 feet, had a nave flanked by aisles, and had second-story galleries over the aisles. The side of the basilica facing the sinkhole has collapsed into the chasm. The location of the basilica so close to the edge of the sinkhole and bounded by the necropolis on the north suggests that the church was a martyrion and that the location was determined by the place of the death of the martyr. It seems that the martyr was killed and thrown into the sinkhole.

---

[13]Eugenia Equini Schneider, *Elaiussa Sebaste: An Archaeological Guide* (Istanbul: Homer, 2008), 61.

Figure 5.6. Papylos martyrion basilica, Kanytelis, Cilicia

A mile south of Seleucia ad Calycadnum (Silifke) lie the ruins of the martyrion of Thecla. This was one of the most celebrated martyrions in the Mediterranean world and a major site for pilgrimages. As many as six basilicas were built or rebuilt at the site. Our primary interest is in the martyrion of Thecla and the basilica that was constructed over it.[14] According to Hill, this martyrion became the archetype of churches in Cilicia.[15]

A cave church at the site is thought to be the dwelling where Thecla spent her last days. The cave was converted into an underground church in the third century and measured 59 by 39 feet. The nave was paved with limestone and had an apse facing east. The nave was separated from flanking aisles by two rows of three Doric columns. These were brought to the cave as spolia from elsewhere.[16] The northern aisle was closed off to

[14]Hill, *Churches of Cilicia*, 208-25.

[15]"The overwhelming popularity of basilical plans for the Cilician churches is their single most remarkable feature: I am convinced that it arose out of the fact the most important Cilician martyrium and monastic church, St Thecla's at Meryemlik, was, from the fourth century, a basilica which included a martyrium within its plan." Hill, *Churches of Cilicia*, 55.

[16]Similar Doric columns were reused in a cistern 150 meters to the north, presumably from the same source.

Figure 5.7. Thecla basilica, Silifke, Cilicia

the nave with a solid wall that was probably added for support when another basilica was built on the ground above it. Tombs were later placed in this northern aisle. It is suggested that the cave area to the north and east of this aisle was the original cave where Thecla lived. This small, simple, underground basilica may have been the martyrion that the pilgrim Egeria saw in the fourth century.[17] Alternately, the basilica mentioned by Egeria may have been the basilica built above it earlier in the fourth century.

Above the cave church the remains demonstrate that there were two churches built during the fourth and fifth centuries. The earlier fourth century basilica measured 108 by 85 feet. The nave had an apse facing east and was flanked by aisles on the north and south. It is not possible to say if the aisles had chambers further to the east. To the west, a small narthex provided entrance into the nave. The apse was located directly over the area of the underground cave where it appears Thecla lived. In the center of the apse, there was a grave. This may have contained the relics of Thecla.

[17]Egeria, *Itinerarium Egeriae* 42.

Later, a fifth-century basilica was built over the fourth-century one. This basilica was the largest in Cilicia, measuring 266 by 141 feet. Very little of it remains. The southern side of the apse stands to a great height, but the rest has collapsed. Most of the remains have been taken by villagers and reused for other purposes. The apse of the fifth-century basilica almost doubled the size of the earlier basilica. The nave of the later structure incorporated the nave and northern aisle of the earlier basilica and extended the length of the nave considerably. Like the earlier basilica, the fifth-century basilica had a nave with flanking aisles. Its eastern-facing apse was flanked by a prothesis on the north and a diaconicon on the south, each of which had smaller apses facing east. Further to the west the basilica had a narthex. It is possible that the southeastern aisle provided access to the cave below, thus connecting both the fourth- and fifth- century basilicas to the cave church.

An unknown ancient village, known today as Yanıkhan, contains the ruins of two Byzantine basilica churches that Hill dates to the late fourth century.[18] The southern church was a martyrion (see plate 26). An inscription at the site identifies the basilica as a martyrion constructed to remember three unknown Christian martyrs: Georgios, Conon, and Christophoros.[19] The basilica was constructed in the late fourth century by an Isaurian official named Matronianus.

The church had a central nave flanked by aisles on the north and south. This church measured 49 feet wide and 98 feet long from the west to the east (from the narthex to the eastern apses). The basilica was expanded with an atrium further to the west, beyond the narthex. This atrium was wider than the width of the basilica and measured 66 by 33 feet. The central nave's apse had a window looking further east into a room where the martyr's relics were kept. This room was flanked by pastophoria on the north (prothesis) and south (diaconicon). Each of these had small apses that extended beyond the nave's central apse further to the east. Between these apses and directly behind the central apse was the small square room where the tomb and relics were kept. On the north side of

[18]Hill, *Churches of Cilicia*, 257, 262.

[19]Stephen Hill, "Matronianus, 'Comes Isauriae:' An Inscription from an Early Byzantine Basilica at Yanıkhan, Rough Cilicia," *Anatolian Studies* 35 (1985): 93-97.

this room, there was a recessed area with an arcosolium (arched tomb). This was where the tomb or relics of the martyrs were kept. Hill claims to have seen a sarcophagus lid under the debris that currently resides in the niche. A thirteen-foot-wide walkway ran along the length of the southern wall, providing access to the pastophoria without entering the basilica proper.

Figure 5.8. Yanikhan martyrion arcosolium, Cilicia

A common feature in all of these martyrions is the presence of a tomb that occupies a prominent position in the basilica. For the martyrion at Corasion, this tomb was located in a secondary apse in the north wall. At Corycos, the unusually shaped church was constructed with three walled areas for worship east of the narthex. Here, the tomb was located in the central section. In the basilica at Diocaesarea, an arched niche cut into the bedrock at the western end of the basilica held the remains of the martyr. Elaioussa Sebaste had two martyrions built end to end, facing east. The western basilica had apses in both the western and the eastern ends. The apse in the west contained the tomb of the martyr. The eastern church had the martyr's tomb in the eastern apse. When the eastern church was destroyed, a smaller basilica was constructed with reused materials framing the tomb. It is unknown where the martyr's tomb was located in the Kanytelis basilica. It is possible that the body of the martyr was thrown into the abyss that borders the basilica and was never retrieved. This may account for why the church was built on the sinkhole's edge. At Thecla's martyrion in Seleucia, the underground cave basilica was preserved by the fourth- and fifth-century churches that were built above it, thus marking and preserving the tomb. Finally, the martyrion at Yanikhan had a room constructed directly behind the apse, between the prothesis and diaconicon. A window in the apse looked directly into this room and the tomb.

There was no consistent place for the location of the martyr's tomb in these basilicas. The location of the tomb varied according to the plan of the basilica and the surrounding geographic features, but the tomb occupied a place of prominence. The tomb in the martyrion at Nicaea was likewise located in a prominent position. This was located to the south of the apse in the diaconicon. There, a decorative sarcophagus probably contained the remains of Neophytos. Portions of a sarcophagus have been recovered during the excavation. These match a sarcophagus panel found years earlier at the Koimesis church in Nicaea.

IS THE SARCOPHAGUS OF NEOPHYTOS IN THE IZNIK MUSEUM?

The Koimesis church in Iznik has been dated somewhere between the sixth and eighth centuries.[20] The church was first mentioned in the proceedings of the Seventh Ecumenical Council in AD 787, where the head priest of the Hyacinth Monastery, Gregory, complained about the theft of icons from the monastery. Hyacinth was thought to be the founder of the basilica, which also functioned as a monastery. His name and monogram were found among the ruins. This dates the church to the early eighth century or earlier.

[20]Çetinkaya, "Byzantine Churches of Nicaea," 62. Janin claims that a sixth-century date for the original church is broadly accepted. The original church was restored after earthquakes in 727 and 1065. Raymond Janin, *Les Eglises et les Monasteres des Grands Centres Byzantins: Bithynie, Hellespont, Latros, Galesios, Trebizonde, Athenes, Thessalonique* (Paris: Institut Francais D'Etudes Byzantines, 1975), 122.

In 1898 Oskar Wulff visited and examined the Koimesis church and published drawings, a plan, and photographs of the church and its remains.[21] Wulff stated that there were two sarcophagi in the church, one for Neophytos and the other for a tenth-century clerk at the church named Patricus Nikephoros.[22] According to Wulff, an earlier visitor to the church, Murawiew, claimed that the tomb of Neophytos was located in the northern extension of the narthex.[23] A lamp constantly burned here and the niche was protected by wire mesh, suggesting that it still contained the bones of Neophytos. Wulff observed that renovations in the church make it impossible to determine whether the marble slab in the niche was a part of a complete sarcophagus or just a parapet slab used for the front of the tomb niche. Wulff's volume includes a photograph of the piece. The panel has a tall, narrow cross flanked by two identical frames (see plate 27). The frames have a two-inch bevel on all sides. Inside the frame, there is an eight-armed cross surrounded by a laurel wreath. Beneath the wreaths, there are small circles that Wulff believes once contained precious stones. From these, branches extended to the left and right, terminating with ivy leaves. On stylistic grounds, Sedat Güngördü dates this panel to the fourth century.[24] Wulff simply states the motif is of very old origin and claims there are fifth-century sarcophagus examples elsewhere.

Wulff also notes that Murawiew claimed to have seen a picture of the martyr in the church.[25] At that time the rebuilt Koimesis church was in good shape, but the basilica was destroyed by the people of Iznik in retaliation for the destruction of mosques by Greeks in 1922. Today, the ruins are in very poor condition.

At some point after the underwater basilica was lost to the lake, the sarcophagus and remains of Neophytos were transferred to the Koimesis basilica. Following the destruction of the Koimesis church, the marble

---

[21]Oskar Wulff, *Die Koimesiskirche in Nicäa und ihre Mozaiken nebst den verwandten kirchlichen Baudenkmälern* (Strassburg: Heitz and Mündel, 1903).

[22]Wulff, *Koimesiskirche in Nicäa*, 184.

[23]Murawiew, Pissjma, and Wostoka, "Letters from the East" [Russian] (St. Petersburg, 1851), 97, cited by Wulff, *Koimesiskirche in Nicäa*, 181.

[24]Sedat Güngördü, "İznik Koimesis Kilisesi ve Önemi" (master's thesis, Uludağ Universitesi, 2019), 33.

[25]Wulff, *Koimesiskirche in Nicäa*, 181n2.

panel was found during work at the site by the Iznik Museum in 1955. The panel is now in the garden of the new museum at Iznik. Evidently, Wulff never saw the back of the panel. No photo or description is given in his book. The reverse side of the panel was decorated with two large rectangular beveled frames, each surrounding a large double beveled cross (see plate 28). Between the frames there is a cross graffito centrally located. The top of the backside has a two-inch wide ridge running the length of the panel to support a lid. This confirms the suggestion that the panel was part of a sarcophagus.

Two large pieces of the ambo were also collected from the site. These pieces have a few features similar to the Neophytos sarcophagus panel. Both have ivy branches ending in a heart, and the beveled crosses from the inside of the Neophytos sarcophagus panel are similar to crosses on the flanks of the ambo.

Figure 5.9. Koimesis ambo, Nicaea Museum

The remaining in situ pieces of the sarcophagus from the diaconicon of the underwater basilica are a similar match to the marble panel in the Iznik Museum (see plate 29). It can be surmised that the relics of Neophytos were first deposited in the sarcophagus that once sat in the basilica under the waters of Lake Iznik. As the waters encroached on the martyrion, the Christians attempted to build a retaining wall further to the west, hoping to keep the waters at bay. These efforts, however, were unsuccessful, and the parishioners were forced to abandon the structure. The date for this departure cannot be determined. At that time, the salvageable artifacts, particularly the holy relics, were transferred to the Koimesis church and remained there until its destruction in 1922.[26] It was several years before the remains of the church were collected and examined. All the surviving artifacts now reside in the new Iznik Museum.

SUMMARY

The discovery of thirty-six tombs in and around the basilica immediately raises the question whether it was constructed as a martyrion. The main necropolises of Nicaea were located north and east of the city. There was no civic necropolis south of the city in the area of the lake. The discovery of a basilica church resting on a small necropolis is a strong clue.

Necropolises (ancient cemeteries) generally have no monumental structures within their confines, aside from mausoleum tombs. The existence of a basilica church within a necropolis is a strong indication of a martyrion. Martyrions were commonly constructed at the place of the saint's execution or burial. In the years that followed, other Christians wished to be buried near the saint. At sites with no preexisting necropolis, the execution of a martyr may be the beginning of a Christian necropolis that developed over the years. Such is the case with the underwater basilica at Nicaea.

Of the thirty-six tombs, eighteen of them were located inside the martyrion. A few of these tombs were located partially buried beneath the masonry of the basilica, indicating that the martyrion was constructed after a small necropolis already began at the site. All of these were *cappuccina* tombs, consisting of terracotta roofing tiles. These inexpensive tombs were typically used by peasants. One additional tomb, however, was a decorative sarcophagus that was located in a place of honor within

[26]Janin acknowledges that Neophytos was martyred and buried on the edge of Lake Iznik, and he claims that a church (martyrion) was built in his honor outside the city walls. However, he asserts that it is unlikely that the anonymous sarcophagus in the church of Koimesis is that of Neophytos. His reasoning is based upon the fact that the ancient tradition is completely unaware of Neophytos at Koimesis. However, if Murawiew's observance of a picture of Neophytos at Koimesis before the destruction is accurate, it seems there must have been some tradition of Neophytos at the church before the church's final destruction. Janin, *Les Eglises et les Monasteres*, 118, 124.

the basilica to the right of the central apse, in the diaconicon. This, we suppose, was the martyr for which the basilica was constructed.

The fact that this basilica was built outside of the city walls also contributes to the conclusion that the structure was originally a martyrion. Fourteen other Byzantine churches have been discovered in Nicaea, all of them inside the city's walls. The discovery of a fifth- or sixth-century terracotta token may also be an indication that the site was recognized as a martyrion. The token probably marked the site as a place of pilgrimage. It cannot be determined with certainty that Neophytos was the martyr for whom the basilica was constructed, but of all the candidates, Neophytos seems most plausible.

A comparison of the martyrion at Nicaea with similar fourth- or fifth-century martyrions in Cilicia is instructive. At least eight of these martyrions can be identified in the southwest of Cilicia, an area known as Rough Cilicia. Several of these, like the one at Nicaea, are located in necropolises. Likewise, the style of construction for these martyrions is similar to that at Nicaea. Another eleven objects from the area around Rough Cilicia have been identified as reliquaries, containing the remains of the martyrs and saints.

The Koimesis church, constructed sometime between the sixth and eighth centuries, was destroyed in 1922. Early visitors to the church claimed that the sarcophagus of Neophytos was deposited in the Koimesis church at an unknown time. We surmise that the sarcophagus and relics of the saint were moved there after the lakeside basilica was submerged. Remains that have been recovered from the Koimesis church include portions of the ambo (the speaker's platform) and a side panel presumed to be all that remains of Neophytos' sarcophagus. Those remains are now visible in the new Iznik Museum.

Taking all of the evidence together, it is clear that the submerged basilica was originally constructed as a martyrion. At some point, the saint's remains were exhumed and interred in a sarcophagus. Other Christians were buried nearby. In short order, the site became a shrine and may have been embellished. Following the Edict of Milan, a basilica church was constructed over the site, enclosing the tomb of Neophytos and several of the nearby tombs.

CHAPTER SIX

WAS THE UNDERWATER BASILICA THE PLACE OF THE FIRST COUNCIL OF NICAEA?

IS THE UNDERWATER BASILICA THE PLACE WHERE THE FIRST COUNCIL OF NICAEA MET?

In AD 324 the Emperor Constantine consolidated his power with victories over Licinius, thus establishing himself as sole ruler over the Roman Empire. Thereupon, he turned his attention to consolidating the Christians within the empire. The Edict of Milan in 313, jointly issued by Constantine and Licinius, granted religious toleration for the practice of Christianity within the empire, but theological debates regarding the nature of Christ threatened to split the church. Arius, a priest from Alexandria, Egypt promoted the belief that Christ was a created being. According to Arius, Jesus was divine, but limited in power and knowledge. Opponents of Arius argued that this associated Christianity with polytheism and undermined the significance of Christ's work. The dispute embroiled the church in such discord that Constantine called a council of church leaders and theologians to Nicaea to discuss the matter and to unite the church on the issue. In 325, more than three hundred bishops from across the Mediterranean world came to Nicaea (Athanasius claimed the number was 318) and assembled for discussions in the main hall of the imperial palace and the nearby church. These discussions and debates lasted more than two months, from May 20 to July 25.[1]

It is commonly assumed that the council met in Constantine's palace. As Robert Grant wrote, "On May 20, as the council opened, the bishops

[1]Robert M. Grant, "Religion and Politics at the Council of Nicaea," *Journal of Religion* 53, no. 1 (1975): 5.

met in a palace at Nicaea that had recently been taken from Licinius."[2] More recently, Ine Jacobs echoed the view: "We risk falling into the trap of projecting the end result back in time, assuming that important church events and gatherings must have taken place in churches. Yet, literary sources leave no doubt that the council gathered not in one of the Christian basilicas of Nicaea, which as described above probably did not yet exist in this time, but inside the palace itself."[3]

The literary sources that Jacobs cited were Eusebius's *Life of Constantine* and the early eighth-century *Laudation of the 318 Fathers*. Both of these sources mentioned the palace as the place where the final decision was rendered. However, a more detailed examination of these sources makes it clear that there was a Christian structure (perhaps a basilica church) in Nicaea at that time and that the council first met in that "place of worship" (as Eusebius described it) before moving to the palace for the later proceedings.

Eusebius of Caesarea, a participant at the council, recounted the inaugural event: "From all the churches which filled all Europe, Libya, and Asia the choicest of the servants of God were brought together; and *one place of worship*, as if extended by God, took them in all together."[4] Here it is clear that Eusebius was describing a church where the bishops first gathered together. Several weeks later, at the end of the debates and discussions, Constantine gathered all of the participants in the central hall of the palace in order to reach a resolution of the issue. Eusebius described the central hall as the largest in the palace: "On the day appointed for the Council, on which it was to reach a resolution of the issues in dispute, everyone was present to do this, in the very innermost hall of the palace, which appeared to exceed the rest in size. Many tiers of seating had been set along either side of the hall. Those invited arrived within, and all took their appointed seats."[5]

---

[2]Grant, "Religion and Politics," 5.

[3]Ine Jacobs, "Hosting the Council of Nicaea: Material Needs and Solutions," in *The Cambridge Companion to the Council of Nicaea*, ed. Y. R. Kim (Cambridge: Cambridge University Press, 2021), 78; see also 87.

[4]Eusebius, *Life of Constantine* 3.7.1, in *Eusebius Life of Constantine: Introduction, Translation and Commentary*, trans. Averil Cameron and Stuart G. Hall, Clarendon Ancient History Series (Oxford: Clarendon, 1999), 124.

[5]Eusebius, *Life of Constantine* 3.10.1, p. 125.

Eusebius's narrative needs to be examined closely. His account described two places where the meetings convened. The first one, described as a "place of worship," was too small to hold the participants, although they somehow managed to fit. The expression "as if expanded by God" suggests that the church was not ultimately large enough for the gathering. Nevertheless, the participants seemed to squeeze into the structure as the building "took them in all together." The second place, utilized weeks later during the final proceedings, was a part of Constantine's palace complex. This space was larger and seemed to have sufficient room for the people. Since Eusebius clearly stated that the council met in Constantine's palace when the deliberations came to an end and the participants voted on the matter, it is often assumed that the council met in the palace for the entire period of the council.

The council met for several weeks, roughly two months. When the council first convened Eusebius clearly described the meeting place as a "place of prayer" (οἶκος εὐκτήριος), literally "a house of prayer" (3.7.1). The expression used a few lines later in 3.10.1 was "the innermost hall of the palace" (μεσαιτάτω οἴκω τῶν βασιλείων), literally "the innermost house of the kings (or emperors)." The distinction between these two places is clear. Moreover, when describing the house of prayer in 3.7.1 Eusebius used an adverb, ὥσπερ, to describe the *manner* in which they assembled. They gathered together in the house of prayer "as if it was widened within by God." The participle πλατυνόμενος should be translated "being widened or broadened," implying that the structure was not large enough to comfortably accommodate the churchmen. On the other hand, the later description in 3.10.1 makes it clear that there was ample space in the palace.

Likewise, the *Laudation of the 318 Fathers* needs to be read in more detail. Written in the early eighth century by Gregory, a presbyter from Caesarea in Cappadocia, the *Laudation* was written for the church at Nicaea to celebrate, remember, and acclaim the council. The bishop of Nicaea asked Gregory to write this memoir probably because Gregory still had access to the notes and documents that Eusebius kept in Caesarea. Mango translates a portion of the *Laudation* that described the palace:

> Having detached from the palace that is there a huge hall—the fairest part, as it were, of the imperial apartments, whose decorous beauty has been pre-

served to our days by the protection of the holy Fathers, the mighty Emperor assigned this hall, like an offering of first-fruits, to the holy synod.[6]

The *Laudation* was read in Nicaea when the palace was still standing. The *Laudation* also referenced an earlier catalog of the persons that attended the council. The earlier source mentioned two bishops who died during the council: Chrysanthus "was buried in the church of Nicaea," and Musonius, "too, was buried in the church."[7] Thus, the *Laudation*, like Eusebius, clearly states that there was a church in addition to the palace. It is interesting that the *Laudation* does not claim Chrysanthus and Musonius were buried in the palace, but rather states they were buried in the church. We have already mentioned that there are eighteen tombs in the submerged basilica in Nicaea. Could two of them be the tombs of Chrysanthus and Musonius? Mango posits, "It is possible, therefore, that two such tombs actually existed and were inscribed with the names Chrysanthus and Musonius, thus giving rise to the legend about them."[8]

Later pilgrims and travelers confirm that the first council met in a church. The British traveler Willibald, who visited Nicaea between 727 and 729, claimed to have seen the church that still had depictions of the bishops who attended the council.[9] Likewise, Michael Attaleiates, a Byzantine historian from Constantinople, claimed that the church was still standing in 1065 when the earthquake brought about its final destruction: "Its most important and large churches . . . and the one of the Holy Fathers, where the Council of the most Holy and Orthodox Fathers against Areios confirmed its decisions . . . those churches, then were shaken and collapsed."[10]

A final objection could be that there would not have been enough time between the Edict of Milan and the Council of Nicaea to build a basilica church. However, we know of several large basilicas that were constructed within a span of three to five years. Below, we will advance evidence that

[6]Cyril Mango, "The Meeting-Place of the First Ecumenical Council and the Church of the Holy Fathers at Nicaea," *Δελτίον της Χριστιανικής Αρχαιολογικής Εταιρείας* 26 (2011): 30.

[7]Mango, "Meeting-Place," 32.

[8]Mango, "Meeting-Place," 32.

[9]Mustafa Şahin, "Underwater Excavation at the Basilica Church in İznik Lake—2019," *International Journal of Environment and Geoinformatics (IJEGEO)* 9 (2022): 73.

[10]Michael Attaleiates, *The History*, trans. by Anthony Kaldellis and Dimitris Krallis (Cambridge, MA: Harvard University Press, 2012), 165-67.

the earliest church at Nicaea may have been constructed in large part with lumber. The twelve years between the Edict of Milan and the Council of Nicaea was ample time for a church to be constructed.

Grant believes that the palace was originally built by Licinius and later taken over by Constantine.[11] Mango asserts:

> The existence of an imperial palace at Nicaea need not surprise us.[12] Roman emperors maintained palaces in many provincial centres where they had occasion to stop on their peregrinations. We do not know when the palace of Nicaea was built, but it was still standing, though 'collapsed in part,' in the reign of Justinian, who ordered its complete restoration. Its main hall must have been big enough to afford room for the 200–300 seated bishops plus the emperor's bodyguard as well as various notables and consultants—in all a gathering of at least 400.[13]

Today, the remains of Constantine's palace are unknown. A few years ago, it was believed that a collection of foundation stones jutting out into Lake Iznik (Askanios) three hundred feet north of the underwater basilica marked the spot. In the past a sign was posted there to indicate the location, but today the sign has disappeared, and today the site is disputed. Jacobs suggests that the so-called palace was actually a large structure (perhaps a villa) that was taken over by Constantine and expanded to meet the needs of the council.[14] She speculates that the converted palace was located in the northern part of the city near the Istanbul Gate.[15]

The underwater basilica was constructed over a small necropolis. Eighteen of the necropolis's thirty-six tombs have been discovered inside the underwater basilica. Some of these tombs were found underneath the masonry walls of the basilica. The archaeologists suggest that the graves surrounded

---

[11]Grant, "Religion and Politics," 5.

[12]Jacobs not only doubts the existence of a church at Nicaea, but also questions the existence of a palace: "There indeed is no evidence for or mention of an imperial residence before it became the location of the council according to Eusebius. There would also not have been time to build a palace once the decision to move the council to Nicaea was made." Jacobs, "Hosting the Council in Nicaea," 78. So also Urs Peschlow, "Nicaea," in *The Archaeology of Byzantine Anatolia: From the End of Late Antiquity Until the Coming of the Turks*, ed. Philipp Niewöhner (Oxford: Oxford University, 2017), chap. 15.

[13]Mango, "Meeting-Place," 27.

[14]Jacobs, "Hosting the Council in Nicaea," 87.

[15]Jacobs, "Hosting the Council in Nicaea," 79-80.

the tomb of Neophytos. Several coins found at the graves are from the time of Emperor Valens (364–378) and Emperor Valentinian (378–383). From the excavations, it appears that the existing masonry church was constructed during the late fourth century or the early fifth century. However, the question remains: Was this church built on the ruins of an earlier church?

Excavators have discovered a second floor in the prothesis that was sixty-four centimeters (25 inches) lower than the floor of the current stone basilica. The measurable area of the floor was calculated as 13 by 2.7 feet.[16] The lower floor was covered with terracotta slabs. Is this evidence of an earlier church below the current one? If so, could this be the "house of worship" mentioned by Eusebius? Underneath the stone masonry basilica, there may remain the ruins of an earlier wooden church that functioned as the church of the Council of Nicaea.

After the Edict of Milan (313), Christianity became a legal religion in the Roman Empire, and Christians began to emerge from a clandestine underground movement to freely express their faith. At that time churches began to be constructed throughout the empire. Formerly, the Christians met secretly in house churches. Now, larger public buildings were necessary. In the twelve years before the Council of Nicaea, was a wooden church built at this site? Was a place of worship (a martyrion) constructed at the place where Neophytos was buried?

WAS THE UNDERWATER BASILICA ORIGINALLY CONSTRUCTED OF WOOD?

This question first comes to mind when we consider the two floors discovered in the prothesis. Terracotta floor slabs, similar to the terracotta *cappuccina* tombs mentioned above, were found in the northeastern prothesis of the church. Şahin believes these slabs indicate that more terracotta tombs lie in this area of the basilica.[17] In the southeastern corner of the prothesis there is a portion of flooring that stands sixty-four centimeters (25 inches) above these terracotta slabs. This is all that re-

[16]Mustafa Şahin, "Neue Forschungen und Ausgrabungen in Der Basilica des İznik Sees," in *Imperial Residence and Site of Councils: The Metropolitan Region of Nicaea/Nicomedia*, vol. 96, *Asia Minor Studien*, Imperial Residence and Site of Councils. (Bonn: Rudolf Habelt, 2020), 100.

[17]Şahin, "Neue Forschungen," 100.

mains of the higher floor that once covered the prosthesis. There were two separate floors to the church separated by around two feet. This is also an area that was on the exterior of what was thought to be the temple, but an area that would have been enclosed in the church. This indicates that there was an earlier floor not far below the floor of the masonry church. Could this be the floor of an earlier church that was later replaced by the current submerged masonry church?

It might be asked, Would there have been enough time to build a church in the years between the Edict of Milan (313) and the start of the Council of Nicaea (325)? Large masonry structures involved a great deal of work and time. Around the same time as the council, the massive Basilica of Maxentius in Rome was built in just five or six years (AD 307–313).[18] The church in Nicaea was much smaller than the Basilica of Maxentius. Likewise, the Lateran Basilica in Rome was built in seven years, from 313 to 320,[19] and the basilica at Trier was completed between the years 305 and 312.[20] Based on these examples, there was ample time to build a church or even a basilica church constructed with masonry before the Council of Nicaea. Eusebius reported that this was a distinctive of Constantine's conversion. While comparing Constantine with the emperors that preceded him, Eusebius listed several differences: "They completely destroyed the places of worship, demolishing them from roof to floor; he decreed that the existing ones be augmented, and new ones erected on a grand scale at the expense of the imperial treasuries."[21]

Richard Krautheimer claims, "The predominant basilica type by 300–320 was a single-naved structure, timber roofed or with a flat ceiling, preceded by a narthex, and terminated by an apse; and it was strictly longitudinal."[22] If that is the case, we need not look for a structure with a nave and flanking aisles. The early church at Nicaea may have been much simpler.

---

[18]Leland M. Roth, *Understanding Architecture: Its Elements, History and Meaning* (Boulder, CO: Westview Press, 1993), 30; Verena Jaeschke, "The Roman Civic Center Under Maxentius (AD 306–312)—Buildings for a New Concept of Sovereignty," in *History Takes Place: Rome; Dynamics of Urban Change*, ed. Anna Hofmann and Martin Zimmermann (Berlin: Jovis Verlag, 2017), 179.

[19]Richard Krautheimer, "The Constantinian Basilica," *Dumbarton Oaks Papers* 21 (1967): 119.

[20]Krautheimer, "Constantinian Basilica," 117.

[21]Eusebius, *Life of Constantine* 3.1.4, p. 121.

[22]Krautheimer, "Constantinian Basilica," 124-25.

The construction of a wooden church would have taken even less time than a masonry church. Xavier Laumain has recently done important work on the use of timber in Roman construction.[23] As wood is a perishable building material, there are few wooden structures with remains that have survived. Consequently, scholarship has largely ignored the use of lumber in ancient structures. Laumain observes that several factors contribute to the lack of scholarly research on the use of wood.[24] First, wood is seldom described as a source for building materials in the ancient literature. Wood was cheap and thought to be inferior. Vitruvius notes that wood was commonly used for structures, but he greatly discouraged the use of lumber.[25] Additionally, there are very few wooden remains that have survived the hundreds of years of decay. Thus, there is little material for scholars to examine and compare. And finally, the prominence that stone masonry assumed in the eyes of the public overshadowed the use of other materials such as mud and lumber.

Laumain, however, points out that the construction of walls with *opus craticium* was widespread. The low costs, the speed of construction, and the light weight all contributed to many structures employing this construction technique. Stefania Stellacci and Vasco Rato go so far as to say, "Timber-framing is the most common mixed construction technique utilized by Romans and many other builders throughout history."[26] The fill used within the walls consisted of a variety of materials, including stones, mud, brick,

---

[23]Xavier Laumain, "The Roman Timber Framework: A Neglected Construction Method," in *Structures and Architecture: Concepts, Applications and Challenges*, ed. P. J. S. Cruz (London: CRC Press, 2013), 2240-47; X. Laumain and Angela Lopez Sabater, "Roman *Opus Craticuium*, A Rediscovered Construction Technology," in *International Conference on Structural Analysis of Historical Constructions*, ed. Jerzy Jasienko (Wroclaw, Poland: DWE, 2012), 1213-19; X. Laumain, "Nuevas Perspectivas sobre el *Opus Craticium* Romano, una Técnica Constructiva Olvidada," in *Actas del Séptimo Congreso Nacional de Historia de la Construcción: Santiago de Compostela*, ed. S. H. Fernandez (Madrid: Instituto Juan de Herrera 2011), 1:699-708.

[24]Laumain and Sabater, "Roman *Opus Craticium*," 1214.

[25]Vitruvius, *De Architectura* 2.8.20: "As for 'wattle and daub' I could wish that it had never been invented. The more it saves in time and gains in space, the greater and the more general is the disaster that it may cause; for it is made to catch fire, like torches. It seems better, therefore, to spend on walls of burnt brick, and be at expense, than to save with "wattle and daub," and be in danger." *Vitruvius: The Ten Books on Architecture*, trans. Morris Hicky Morgan (Cambridge: Harvard University Press, 1914), 57.

[26]Stefania Stellacci and Vasco Rato, "Timber-Framing Construction in Herculaneum Archaeological Site: Characterisation and Main Reasons for its Diffusion," *International Journal of Architectural Heritage* (2019): 1.

and scrap lumber. In the cities of Vesuvius, light volcanic rocks were common materials. Well-preserved examples have been preserved by the volcanic ash at Pompeii and Herculaneum, and these examples demonstrate that the use of *opus craticium* was not just for the poor.[27] The light weight of *opus craticium* walls made it a desirable technique for multistoried structures. Of course, the drawback was that it was not as structurally sound and was vulnerable to fire. Perhaps much of Vitruvius's displeasure with the technique was because of the fear of fire, to which Rome was particularly vulnerable with structures closely packed together in the city.

Figure 6.1. Casa a Graticcio, Herculaneum

Though not as widespread as the use of *opus craticium* in walls, Laumain documents entire structures constructed with lumber.[28] In order to prevent rotting from ground water, Vitruvius suggested laying a masonry base on which to place the timber posts.[29] Mortise and tenon joints and rivets were often used to connect the joints.[30] The Casa a Graticcio in Herculaneum was entirely constructed with wood, *opus craticium* walls,

[27]Laumain and Sabater, "Roman *Opus Craticium*," 1218-19; Laumain, "Nuevas Perspectivas," 706.
[28]Laumain and Sabater, "Roman *Opus Craticium*," 1218-19.
[29]Vitruvius, *De Architectura* 2.8.77.
[30]Stellacci and Rato, "Timber-Framing Construction," 9, 13-14.

and brick columns.[31] Laumain suggests that some "large buildings used timber framing not only as a partition and enclosure element, but also as supporting structure."[32] Temporary military camps commonly used wood for buildings since there was usually an ample supply of timber and the material was easy to use for construction.[33] Likewise, the civilian encampments that followed the legions (*canabae*) employed the same techniques.[34]

The Roman legionary fortress discovered at Inchtuthil is a good example of the kind of timber structures that could be produced.[35] Inchtuthil was a fortress established by Roman troops in Brittania around AD 83 and was abandoned and demolished around three years later.[36] The site covers approximately twenty-two hectares and was surrounded by an earthen bank and ditch. Buildings included headquarters, a hospital, sixty-six barracks, quarters for centurions and tribunes, six granaries, 170 storerooms, and other small buildings. None of the timber has survived, but it is understood that most of the structures were built with lumber. "Inchtuthil's buildings were almost exclusively of timber."[37] The excavators assume that oak was used, and the roof was probably terracotta tile. "Except for a massive nail hoard there are few finds."[38] The joints for the larger structures were probably mortise and tenon joints since most of the nails that have been discovered are not large enough for structural jointing. Elizabeth Shirley claims there are at least thirteen other associated forts. The presence of timber structures in the Roman period was clearly more common than what is generally assumed. The ability to study them, however, is uncommon.[39]

The problem with postulating a wooden church as the meeting place of the Council of Nicaea is, as we have already noted, that this theory is

[31]Laumain and Sabater, "Roman *Opus Craticium*," 1218; Laumain, "Nuevas Perspectivas," 706-7.

[32]Laumain, "The Roman Timber Framework," 2245.

[33]Laumain, "The Roman Timber Framework," 2244.

[34]Laumain, "The Roman Timber Framework," 2244-45, cites the study of Baudoux and Cantrelle (2006) of the *canabae* of Argentoratum.

[35]Elizabeth A. M. Shirley, "The Building of the Legionary Fortress at Inchtuthil," *Britannia* 27 (1996): 111-28.

[36]Shirley, "Legionary Fortress at Inchtuthil," 113.

[37]Shirley, "Legionary Fortress at Inchtuthil," 112.

[38]Shirley, "Legionary Fortress at Inchtuthil," 113.

[39]Over sixty structures from the first and second centuries have been excavated at Godmanchester in Britannia. Most of them were timber-framed structures. H. J. M. Green, "Domestic Buildings and Continuation into Anglo-Saxon Times," in *Durovigutum: Roman Godmanchester* (Oxford: Archaeopress, 2017), 155-64.

difficult to prove since wood will not survive for seventeen hundred years. Most of the examples that have survived, such as at Pompeii and Herculaneum, were preserved because of the rapid preservation conditions with the eruption of Vesuvius. If a wooden martyrion was first built around the tomb of Neophytos, then most of the lumber would have been removed when the masonry basilica replaced the earlier structure. Following the submersion of the basilica, any remaining wood quickly disappeared.

That brings us back to the two floors discovered in the prothesis of the submerged basilica. Other tombs, KM-1 through KM-5, are likewise located below the walls of the masonry basilica. The lower floor contained the tombs of people who wished to be buried near the martyr Neophytos. This structure could have been the earliest martyrion church of Neophytos that was constructed sometime after the Edict of Milan. The tombs were later added to the structure in the years following the construction of the martyrion church. It is impossible to determine the size of the martyrion. It may have begun as a small shrine marking the spot of the saint's execution or burial. Later, a larger church surrounded the shrine.

How large was the church? Eusebius's comments regarding the place of worship imply that the church was not large enough to comfortably accommodate some three hundred participants who squeezed into the structure. If the attendants who accompanied the bishops also attended, the number would have been higher. Was the late fourth-century masonry basilica built with the same dimensions as the earlier martyrion?

Let's look at the dimensions of the structure to see if it fits with Eusebius's description. The outside dimensions of the underwater basilica measure 59 by 134 feet. The walls of the basilica are around three feet thick, so the inside dimensions are 53 by 128 feet. We can assume that no one sat in the atrium during the proceedings, since they would not be able to see or hear the proceedings. Eliminating the space of the atrium (30 by 52 feet) cuts the space down to 98 by 53 feet. It is also questionable that the participants sat in the narthex (16 by 53 feet) since they also would have been marginally connected to the activity inside the basilica. Likewise, nobody sat in the two rooms flanking the apse (the prothesis and the diaconicon) and only one or two speakers probably addressed the assembly from the area of the apse. Thus, we can eliminate another 16 by 53 feet of space. That trims the internal space of the basilica to 53 by 66 feet, or roughly 3500 square feet. These calculations include all of the space in the nave and two aisles. Early sources recorded various numbers for the participants, but most reported between 250 and 300 churchmen from across the Mediterranean. This number does not include the priests and associates who traveled with the participants. That boils down to participants sitting wall to wall next to one another, inside the church in the space of little more than eleven square feet per person (three feet and four inches squared). If the earlier church was smaller, then the space would have been reduced even further. If the participants spilled out into a narthex and listened from afar, there could have been more space. Likewise, if the church had balconies, as many fourth-century churches did, there would have been more room to accommodate the bishops. In any case, these calculations may give us some perspectives regarding Eusebius's description of a house of prayer "as if expanded by God." Suffice it to say, the place would have been crowded.

Excavations in 2018 of an underwater well in the area of the atrium found pieces of wood and what are thought to be wooden girders.[40] These have not been dated, so they could be more recent pieces of lumber that have fallen into the well or, if they are older, perhaps pieces from the roof of the masonry basilica. Before the invention of flying buttresses, the early masonry churches used lighter roofs of lumber. It is remotely possible that the wooden pieces came from the earliest church, though the probability of surviving for 1700 years is unlikely. The debris covering the well may have provided the conditions for preserving the wood.[41]

An important result of the excavations at Nicaea is the discovery of many nails, both large and small. During excavations of the narthex seventeen nails were found[42] and during excavations of the atrium many more nails were unearthed.[43] The use of wood in the structure is evident with the discovery of these nails in the basilica. It has been mentioned above that the construction of large wooden structures generally employed mortise and tenon construction, sometimes with the use of

---

[40]Şahin, "Underwater Excavation at the Basilica Church," 73-74.

[41]The lumber of the well-known first-century boat currently on display at Nof Ginosar was preserved underwater by the mud that covered the boat.

[42]Şahin, "Neue Forschungen," 102.

[43]Şahin, "Underwater Excavation at the Basilica Church," 74, 76.

wooden pegs. Thus, one would not expect to find large numbers of nails. However, the large number and size of these nails is strong evidence that a wooden structure once existed at the site. Once the early wooden church was replaced with the masonry church, many of the nails from the early wooden structure would have been extracted and reused in other structures. Thus, the presence of so many nails from the excavation suggests that an early wooden church first existed at the site.

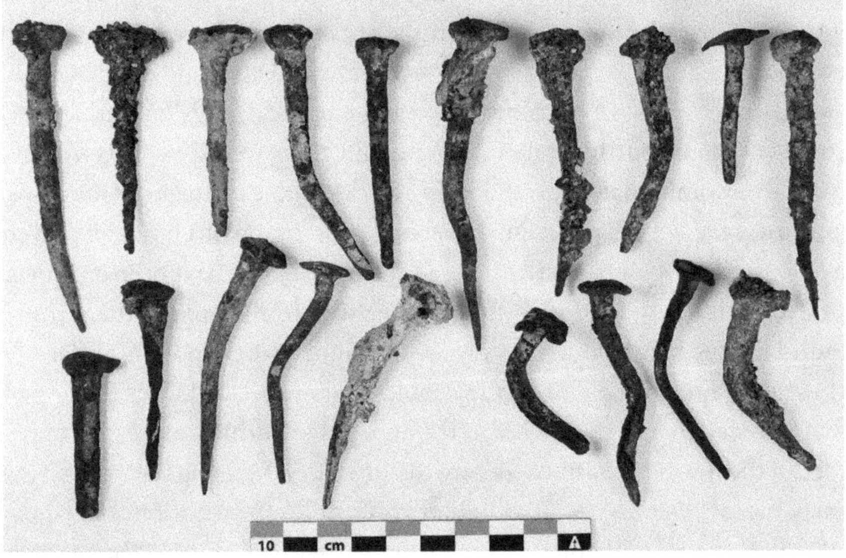

Figure 6.2. Nails from the submerged basilica

The martyrion of Thecla in Silifke may serve as a similar example of an early church that was later reconstructed on a larger scale. The martyrion and basilica of Thecla were constructed on three occasions with the later basilicas enlarging the earlier structures. The underground cave church measured 59 by 39 feet and was built during the third century. During the fourth century a basilica church was built above ground over the underground church. This basilica measured 108 by 85 feet. Later, during the fifth century the basilica was enlarged with another basilica surrounding the fourth century basilica and utilizing spolia from the basilica. This fifth century basilica measured 266 by 141 feet.[44]

[44]Stephen Hill, *The Early Byzantine Churches of Cilicia and Isauria*, Birmingham Byzantine and Ottoman Monographs 1 (Aldershot, UK: Variorum Ashgate, 1996), 208-25.

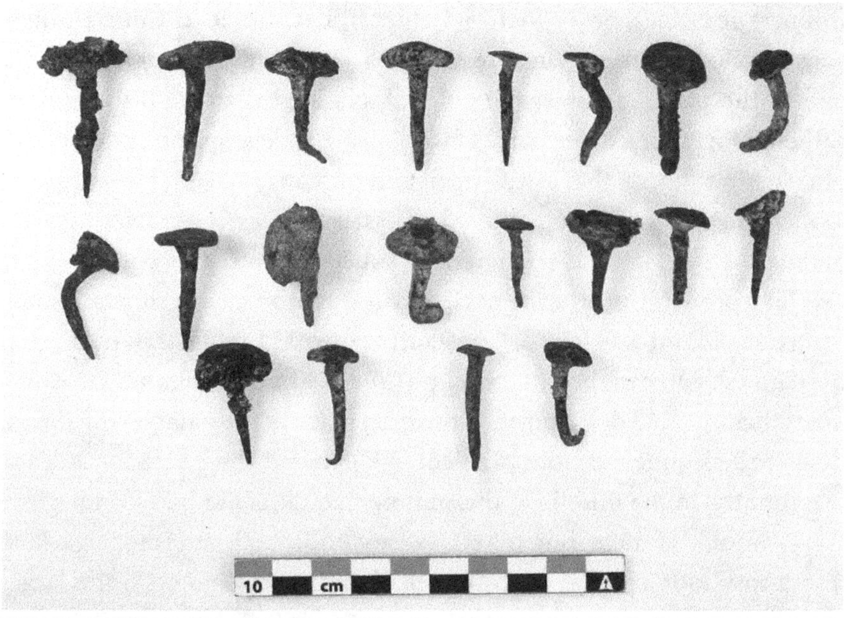

Figure 6.3. Nails from the submerged basilica

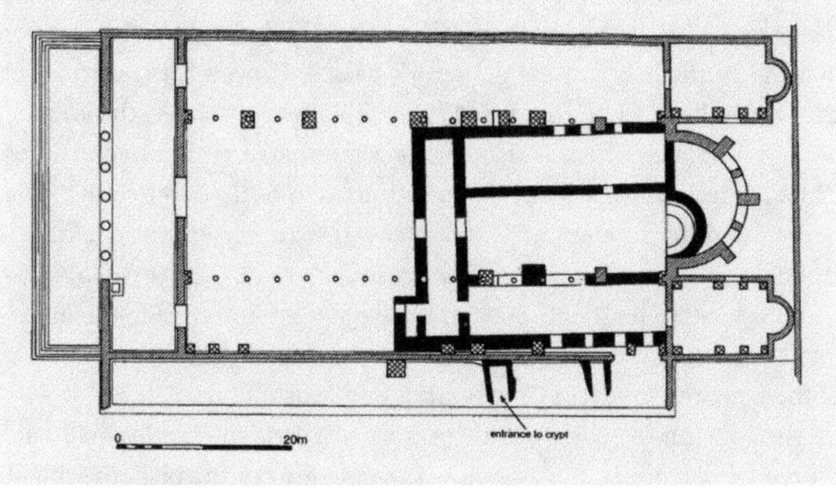

Figure 6.4. Diagram of Thecla Basilica, Silifke

SUMMARY

Contrary to the assumption of some scholars who claim that the First Council at Nicaea never met in a church, but rather in Constantine's palace, a close examination of the sources tells a different story. Eusebius, one of the participants at the council, claimed that the bishops first gathered together in "one place of worship." His description of that place of worship suggests that it was small and perhaps not suitable to accommodate all of those who gathered together at Nicaea. As necessity demanded, however, the participants squeezed into the church with overflow probably pressed into the narthex. It probably did not take long before a solution was found. Constantine offered his Nicaean palace for the council. Later in the same volume (*The Life of Constantine*) Eusebius notes that the final decision and vote took place in the palace, which was described as quite spacious. The council debated the issues for at least two months in the middle of the summer, and it is not hard to imagine that it would not take long for the sweaty bodies of the bishops packed into a modestly sized church to welcome the movement to the large, sumptuous palace.

The early eighth-century *Laudation of the 318 Fathers* further corroborates Eusebius's claim. Written for the church at Nicaea to commemorate what had happened earlier, the *Laudation* likewise testifies that the council met in the emperor's palace. However, the document cites an earlier source that listed the people who attended the council. What is important here is that the *Laudation* asserts that two bishops, Chrysanthus and Musonius, died over the two months of the council and were buried "in the church." Undoubtedly the church and the palace still stood when the *Laudation* was written and the tombs of the two bishops could still be seen. Today, none of the eighteen tombs inside the underwater basilica can be identified. But it is reasonable to assume that two of them are the tombs of Chrysanthus and Musonius.

Also, during the early eighth-century, the British traveler Willibald claimed to have seen the church with depictions of the bishops who attended the council. Later, the Byzantine historian Attaleiates claimed that the church was standing until the 1065 earthquake brought down its walls. It is hard to maintain that the council did not meet in a church when early literary evidence details the existence of a church at that time and Eusebius asserts that they first met in a "place of worship." As wonderful as Constantine's palace may have been, it would be an overstatement to call it a place of worship.

Archaeological evidence also suggests that the first church built at the site was constructed with lumber. Excavations in the prothesis have revealed another floor twenty-five inches below the floor of the current masonry basilica. The discovery of a large number of iron nails in the excavation also supports the same conclusion. The twelve years from the issue of the Edict of Milan to the convening of the Nicaean Council would have been ample time to build a church. In fact, we know that churches were hastily constructed shortly after the edict with the financial support of Constantine and the governors. There are many examples of early churches that were later expanded and rebuilt on a larger scale throughout Anatolia.

To summarize our findings, it is proposed that the First Council of Nicaea met in a relatively small wooden church that functioned as a martyrion for an unknown saint, perhaps Neophytos. This church was built shortly after the Edict of Milan and served as the initial meeting place for the council. In short order, however, Constantine offered his palace for a more comfortable meeting place. It was here in the palace that the final decision and vote took place. Nevertheless, the church at Nicaea still held a place of honor and was rebuilt near the end of the fourth century with a larger and more durable masonry basilica church. This church became a place of pilgrimage, not only as a martyrion but also as the place of the First Ecumenical Council for the newly legalized and imperially supported Christian world.

CHAPTER SEVEN

THE LEGACY OF NICAEA

Why has the Council of Nicaea assumed such a pivotal role in church history and in the role of Christianity throughout the world today? The Nicaean Creed, issued at the conclusion of the council, has been embraced as a foundational document by all of the major denominations of Christianity today, including all Protestant denominations, Roman Catholic, Eastern Orthodox, and Oriental Orthodox churches.

At the outset, it will be helpful to dispel a few myths regarding the Council of Nicaea. In popular thought and on uninformed websites it is common to hear the assertion that Nicaea created the myth of the Christian faith. Dan Brown's popular novel *The Da Vinci Code* promoted several Christian myths that furthered these and other fictions.

First, the council did not concoct the idea that Jesus was divine. All those who attended already believed Jesus was divine, including Arius. The christological question at stake was the preexistence of the divine Christ. Was Christ a created divine being? Second, the Council of Nicaea did not determine which books were to be included in Scripture. The issue of canonicity was not a topic addressed at the council. Debates on which books should be included in the New Testament had been ongoing throughout the first four centuries, but by the time of the Council of Nicaea, most Christians agreed on the bulk of the New Testament writings, but disagreed on some of the smaller and less well-known books that were eventually included in the canon. And third, the Council of Nicaea did not create the Trinity. Those who attended the council already believed in the triune God. Still, the Council of Nicaea had a profound impact on the church.

The Council of Nicaea was not the first gathering of church leaders to debate policies or to settle disputes. The gathering in Acts 15 to discuss the role of circumcision and the Torah is often called the Jerusalem Council, although Luke does not describe it as such. Thereafter, there were more than thirty gatherings of early church leaders to deal with the practical and theological issues that emerged during the first three centuries of the church's existence.[1] These are commonly called councils or synods of the church. All of these councils were local affairs generally attended by no more than a few dozen church leaders in the area. None of them had the impact of the Council of Nicaea.

Most of these councils dealt with disputes among the bishops, debates regarding false teachings (known as heresies), and the question of how to deal with the lapsed. During the periods of persecution, large numbers of Christians apostatized and denied their faith. Many of these lapsed Christians wished to return to the church when the persecutions ended. The questions confronting the leaders of the churches were, Should the church readmit the lapsed and under which conditions? Likewise, how should the church deal with bishops or teachers who formerly promoted heretical teachings but now repented? During this period there was no broad consensus among the churches throughout the Mediterranean realm regarding these issues.

For some, the legacy of the Council of Nicaea consists in the emergence of the church from rags to riches. That is, the transition from a vulnerable, defenseless, and persecuted religious movement that was forced to operate discreetly in the shadows of society to a religious movement that would quickly assume a position of power with imperial support. As Robert Grant claimed, Nicaea "marks the end of early church history and the dawning of the Middle Ages. There was a fundamental change in church-state relations."[2] Indeed, this transition had a profound impact on the spread of the faith, the construction of basilicas, the empowering of the clergy, and the imposition of Christianity on the culture

---

[1]MacMullen lists twenty councils from 253 until Nicaea in 325. Thompson goes back earlier and lists thirty-four councils from 200 to 325. Ramsay MacMullen, *Voting About God in Early Church Councils* (New Haven, CT: Yale University Press, 2006), 2-3; Thompson, "Early Christian Councils," Fourth Century Christianity, www.fourthcentury.com/councils-and-creeds/.

[2]Robert M. Grant, "Religion and Politics at the Council at Nicaea," *Journal of Religion* 55 (1975): 1-12.

of the Mediterranean world. The wealth and power of the church had both positive and negative consequences in the centuries that followed.

Christianity grew and paganism slowly died. The monastic movements, whose roots extended back earlier in time, expanded in the centuries after the Edict of Milan. The reclusive anchoritic monks and hermits had little contact with the broader society, yet their pious commitment reverberated throughout the nearby communities. The cenobitic monks, while still gathered together in monastic communities, were more involved with the broader society. Their outreach and care for the poor had a profound impact on the people. The monasteries were centers for learning and were instrumental in maintaining and expanding learning through the so-called Dark Ages.

Yet, the rise of Christianity to power had negative consequences. Clerics could use the faith as a cudgel to manipulate parishioners, and the fear of excommunication had both religious as well as social ramifications. As the emperors embraced the faith and Christianity became the official religion of the empire in 380, the distinction between religion and politics was blurred. The bulk of the Christian population had a genuine faith embedded in the convictions passed down by earlier Christians. However, a number of people found it expedient to convert for financial, social, or political gains. Christianity became a tool for personal advancement. The superficial faith of those in ecclesial and political leadership positions had a damaging effect on the trust that the population invested in their leaders.

Six more ecumenical councils followed the Council of Nicaea. In 381 a council convened at the basilica of Hagia Irene in Constantinople. This was followed by councils in Ephesus (431), Chalcedon (451), two more in Constantinople (553 and 680–681), and a second council at Nicaea (787). These councils ostensibly maintained the semblance of a united church, but increasingly political and ecclesiastical control as well as theological disputes led to a decisive split between the East and West. This is known as the Great Schism of 1054. Rome and Constantinople vied for control of the Christian world. The Pope, Leo IX, demanded that the Ecumenical Patriarch Michael I Cerularius recognize him as the head of all the churches. Cerularius refused to do so, and Leo IX excommunicated him.

At the same time, theological issues such as celibacy, the immaculate conception of Mary, and the *filioque* (does the Spirit proceed from the Father alone or from the Father and the Son?) were festering near the surface. This schism culminated in 1204 when Constantinople was sacked by the Crusaders during the fourth crusade. The split drove a wedge between the Eastern and Western churches that continues today.

Yet, with all of the detrimental developments that followed the Council of Nicaea, it is important that we not forget what made the council the centerpiece of our collective faith. The enduring legacy of the Council of Nicaea was that this council was the first attempt to bring together the collective wisdom of the entire church. Unlike the preceding local councils, the Council of Nicaea was truly ecumenical. Not all the invited guests attended the council. Those in the far western parts of the Mediterranean found it difficult to make the journey. However, the number and breadth of those who made the journey made this council unique.

Letters were sent out to all the known bishops and leaders of churches throughout the Mediterranean world, around 1,800 altogether. The response far exceeded the number of attendees at any of the former councils. Those who attended disproportionately came from the eastern Mediterranean churches. We can assume this was due to four factors. First, Christianity was disproportionately represented in the eastern Mediterranean with more churches and a larger Christian population at that time. Second, the distance for travel to Nicaea was much farther for attendees from the western Mediterranean. Depending on the location of the church, Western bishops would travel anywhere from two to six times the distance traveled by bishops in the East. Third, the chief issue addressed at the Council of Nicaea, the Arian controversy, was more pertinent in the eastern empire than in the West. The people and friends of Arius along with those who held similar positions and the opponents of these teachings all came from the eastern empire. Thus, the Christian communities in the west were more detached from the issue. Finally, by the early fourth century the churches in the West were looking more to Rome than to Constantinople for leadership. Even though Constantine moved the capital of the empire from Rome to Byzantium (Constantinople), the church in Rome had already assumed a leading role in the

West. Indeed, smaller councils were already held in Rome in 155, 193 and 313, and several others were held in Carthage. This struggle for the primacy of the sees continued in the centuries following Nicaea.

Constantine's purpose in calling the conference was to unite the church. In part, this was part of Constantine's program to unite the empire. No one at that time could foresee the fractures that eventually occurred in the future. Yet, to unite the church, it was necessary to set the boundaries of the faith.

Prior to the fourth century, Christianity had splintered into several manifestations of the faith. In fact, this was going on early in the first century. Most of the twenty-one letters in the New Testament were attempts to correct aberrant theology that was manifest throughout the newly established churches. In the early developmental years, with no trained clergy, no defined scripture, and the syncretistic influence of Greco-Roman culture, philosophy, and Judaism, the early Christians followed persuasive leaders who differed on what constituted the core of the faith.

Three of the biggest factions during the first three centuries were the Ebionites, the Montanists, and the Gnostics. The Ebionites clung to the Torah, believing that the Old Testament sacred law was still obligatory for Christians. We see an antecedent to this movement in Acts 15 and Paul's letter to the Galatians, where Christian converts from Pharisaism believed that circumcision and Torah compliance were required of not only Jewish converts but also Gentile converts. Some Ebionites, while maintaining the belief that Jesus was the Messiah, doubted the divinity of Jesus. Many of the Jewish-Christians who fled to Pella at the time of the first Jewish war abandoned their Jewish practices and joined the mainstream church. The Ebionites largely faded in the second century after the two Jewish-Roman wars.

In the late second century a Christian named Montanus started a movement in Phrygia that emphasized the role of the Holy Spirit and promoted new prophetic revelations. Montanus and his followers supported the basic beliefs of the broader church but differed in their belief regarding new prophecy. The movement was widely denounced in the church. Yet, in the early third century Montanism was defended by the

Christian apologist Tertullian, and the belief was never officially or universally condemned. Nevertheless, at the beginning of the fourth century Montanism dwindled in popularity outside of Phrygia, although pockets of so-called Montanists persisted until the sixth century.

Gnosticism became a bigger problem. Co-opting Neoplatonic philosophy along with elements of the mystery religions, Gnosticism offered a mysterious and appealing take on the teachings of Jesus. The heresy began in the first century, but it exploded in popularity in the second century with the teachings of Basilides and Valentinus. The primary teaching of the Gnostics was that salvation was obtained through wisdom and knowledge, rather than through the sacrifice of Jesus on the cross. The Gnostics wrote gospels and treatises that they adopted as scripture.

In the late second century Irenaeus of Lugdunum (modern Lyon) wrote several volumes titled *Against Heresies*. Irenaeus's polemic was chiefly directed against the Gnostics, though he briefly mentioned other heretical groups. Irenaeus's writings represent the most ambitious attempt to suppress false teaching in the church up to that point. However persuasive Irenaeus's words may have been, they lacked the rigor of imperial backing. A more forceful approach was taken at the Council of Nicaea.

Constantine had the foresight to recognize the damaging effects of divisions within the church and the empire. To remedy the problem, he did what he could to encourage broad participation from across the empire. The council was originally planned to meet at Ancyra (today's Ankara), but the emperor moved it to Nicaea. The site of Nicaea provided easier access for those coming from the west who had the greatest distance to travel. Nicaea also made it easier for the emperor to engage in the proceedings. To encourage participation Constantine offered to pay all the travel expenses for the bishop and his traveling entourage. Earlier attempts to deal with the issue were more localized and unsuccessful, but Constantine's hope was that broader representation from church leaders across the Mediterranean would resolve the issue once for all.

Almost three centuries earlier, Paul wrote to the Corinthians to address a problem of divisions within the church. "I appeal to you, brothers and sisters, in the name of our Lord Jesus Christ, that all of you agree with one another in what you say and that there be no divisions among you, but that you be perfectly united in mind and thought. My brothers and sisters, some from Chloe's household have informed me that there are quarrels among you. What I mean is this: One of you says, 'I follow Paul'; another, 'I follow Apollos'; another, 'I follow Cephas'; still another, 'I follow Christ.' Is Christ divided?" (1 Cor 1:10-13). Paul addressed the issue of divisions throughout his letters to the Corinthians. He even rebuked them for divisions during the Eucharist (1 Cor 11:18).

During the first century, the city of Corinth was the largest city in Achaia and its most cosmopolitan. This was reflected in the composition of the church. Probably more than any other church, the Corinthian church was divided by race, culture, gender, status, education, and money. Paul ministered in the city for eighteen months on his so-called second mission. There were dozens of Christian congregations in Corinth when Paul wrote his letters to them, and they seemed to be heading in different directions. Yet, the apostle addressed them with the singular term *church* rather than as plural *churches* (1 Cor 1:2; 2 Cor 1:1).

For the church to function well, it had to function as a body. Recognizing that people had different positions in society and possessed distinct abilities (or "gifts"), Paul drew on the human body as an example (1 Cor 12). Acknowledging that hands differ in appearance and function from feet and that eyes and ears lack any resemblance to one another, Paul argued that each appendage was not only acceptable, but actually necessary for the well-being of the body.

Paul's words were appropriate for what was happening at the time of the council, but the situation in the fourth century was exacerbated by accusations of heresy. Just as in Paul's day, many leaders in the early fourth century were following the persuasive teachings of prominent theologians. The issues were not clearly defined in Scripture even though those debating the issues on both sides appealed to Scripture. These positions became entrenched with pride and prestige. Prominent participants such as Eusebius of Caesarea and the emperor himself were swayed in both directions before finally casting their votes.

The question is, What constitutes heresy as opposed to variations of theology? What unites Christian churches of all denominations is a core of beliefs that function as the defining doctrines for Christianity.

Surrounding that core is a circle of beliefs that are important, yet peripheral to the core. Church teachings regarding the mode of baptism, the understanding of the Eucharist, church organization, the practice of the gifts of the Spirit, eschatological beliefs, worship styles, and music have separated theologians and churches over the years and have created the heterogeneous denominations today. However, within that complex of denominations, most Christians concur that other denominations are within the fold of Christendom. To be Christian is to hold and affirm the core of the faith.

Despite Saint Paul's emphasis on unity within and among the churches, the apostle still argued vehemently against heresy. Some of Paul's opponents in Corinth were singled out as false apostles and agents of Satan (2 Cor 11:13-15). The first letter to Timothy denounced Hymenaeus and Alexander who had "suffered shipwreck with regard to the faith" and whom Paul handed over to Satan so that they would not blaspheme (1 Tim 1:19-20). Other New Testament authors also condemned teachings and teachers they considered heterodox, such as John's description of the false prophets whom he called antichrists (1 John 4:1-3) and Jude's reference to ungodly persons who were headed for condemnation (Jude 4).

The legacy of Nicaea must be traced back to Constantine's intention in calling the council. Like Paul, Constantine's intention was not to create division but rather to unite the church. Lines had to be drawn to define the parameters of the faith, but the call to the faithful was a challenge to galvanize the church in a common profession. All who attended the Nicaean Council were invited to embrace the creed that was generated. At the beginning, twenty-two bishops supported Arius. In the end, the overwhelming majority signed on to the creed. Many of those who formerly supported Arius capitulated, perhaps due to the pressure of the majority and the threat of exile. Three ultimately refused: Arius, Theonas of Marmarica, and Secundus of Ptolemais. Three others, Eusebius of Nicomedia, Theognis of Nicaea, and Maris of Chalcedon, reluctantly signed. Theonas and Secundus were later accepted back into communion with Constantine's further attempts to unite the church.

Deeply embedded issues do not die easily, and the Arian problem continued to fester in the decades that followed. Constantine's successor,

Constantius II, and the later Emperor Valens both had Arian sympathies, so the issue continued to circulate in small circles. However, the issue was finally laid to rest when Valens's successor, Theodosius I, called a Second Ecumenical Council at the Hagia Irene in Constantinople in 381. Here Arianism was condemned, the Nicaean Creed was reaffirmed, and the issue slowly dissipated.

Paul and Constantine's efforts to unite the church ultimately collapsed. The eleventh century schism divided the Eastern church from the Western church. This was followed by the Protestant Reformation, which in turn resulted in the further splintering of churches and denominations. It is estimated that there are more than 45,000 Christian denominations worldwide. Though there is a great deal of cooperation among many churches for social and community projects, there remain sharp disagreements that hinder a truly united church.

Theological disputes over peripheral issues should never separate us from fellowship with other Christian believers. As individuals we interpret Scripture through separate eyes, apply Scripture diversely, and arrive at different theological positions. We can never bring all Christians under the same theological umbrella. The faith that was handed down to us from the apostles does not clearly delineate answers to all the theological questions we ask. It is too much to ask everyone to arrive at the same place. Yet in spite of our differences and various perspectives, our common faith, upheld and passed on by generations of spiritual ancestors, unites us in a common bond. The Nicaean Creed, which denominations generally affirm and which many congregations repeat on Sunday mornings, is the thread that binds us together. Nicaea takes us back to a time when we could still think of one united church.

CHAPTER EIGHT

CONCLUSION

An archaeologist's task is not finished with the unearthing of buried artifacts. Back at the lab, the discoveries must be numbered, cataloged, measured, analyzed, dated, and compared with similar finds elsewhere. Even then, the task is not done. The archaeologist is expected to interpret the finds, that is, to reconstruct structures and recreate the function and life of the communities that built and used the artifacts.

Led by Mustafa Şahin, the archaeological team working at the underwater basilica in Nicaea has done a thorough job of excavating the basilica and the surrounding area, carefully working in the difficult conditions presented by operating underwater in a structure that is offshore by some 150 feet. Employing the latest technology to explore the site and to analyze the finds, they have demonstrated a high level of care and expertise by examining even the smallest details of the basilica. While Şahin still argues for the lost temple of Apollo, I've suggested an alternative approach to understanding the ruins in Nicaea.

The structure began as a martyrion, perhaps dedicated to Neophytos, who was executed during the persecutions of Diocletian. An illuminated menologion currently in the Vatican Libraries depicts the martyrdom on the shores of the lake and describes the life of the saint. In the years following the execution, the site was celebrated as a memorial tomb for Neophytos. This may have consisted of little more than the tomb of Neophytos and small tokens of remembrance placed at the site by the early Christian community at Nicaea. Over the years, the site may have grown into a more elaborate open-air shrine for the saint. At some point the remains of Neophytos were placed in a sarcophagus. In time, a small structure may have enclosed the sarcophagus of Neophytos. It is likely that at this time, other Christians buried their loved ones near the tomb of the martyr.

Following the Edict of Milan, evidence suggests that the shrine was enclosed within an early wooden church, constructed in the early fourth century. Of the fifteen early churches discovered in Iznik, this is the earliest by at least one hundred years. It is believed that this church was relatively small in size, yet large enough to accommodate the Christian community in Nicaea. It is impossible to determine whether the church followed the basilical pattern adopted by many early churches or if the church took on some other shape. Christian burials continued in and around the church. Thirty-six tombs have been discovered around the structure, many of them inside the church. This is consistent with the early Christian practice of burials surrounding notable saints.

Later in the fourth century, a larger masonry basilica was constructed, enclosing and replacing the earlier wooden church. Some of the tombs lie underneath the late fourth-century masonry basilica, indicating that their occupants were buried before the masonry church was constructed. The masonry church was not only larger, but also more structurally sound than the wooden church. This masonry church followed the basilica pattern of most early churches. A central nave was flanked by two aisles. On the east, an apse was surrounded by a prothesis on the north and a diaconicon on the south. The sarcophagus containing the remains or relics of Neophytos were enclosed in the diaconicon of the church. Perhaps the church was constructed around an earlier structure that enclosed the sarcophagus of Neophytos. This left the martyrion of Neophytos undisturbed, and it became the diaconicon of the church. On the western end of the basilica, a narthex was preceded by an atrium.

The site of Iznik is located along the Northern Anatolian Fault, a series of seismic faults that follow the southern shore of the Black Sea. These faults have caused significant seismic movement over the past two thousand years, and it is possible that the seismic activity has resulted in the submergence of the basilica. A retaining wall was constructed to keep the waters at bay, but the battle was eventually lost, and the basilica was abandoned.

Nicaea is well-known for the First Ecumenical Council that met there. However, the precise location of the Council of Nicaea is disputed. Fourteen other Byzantine churches have been discovered in Iznik but none of them date as far back as the fourth century. The discovery and early date of the submerged basilica brings this question to the front. Could this basilica have been the site where the Council of Nicaea met?

After examining early written sources that described the First Council of Nicaea, along with the archaeological remains from the site, evidence leads us to the conclusion that an earlier wooden church existed at the site. This was the place where the council first met. Eusebius described the inaugural meeting in Nicaea at a "house of prayer," suggesting that they met in a church. His account also indicated that the attendees squeezed into the structure. Two months later the council concluded. This time, however, the meeting place was at Constantine's palace rather than the house of prayer. Additionally, Eusebius recounted a spacious palace in distinction to the small space where they first met. Due to the confined space in the church, it seems that Constantine offered a solution, and the proceedings were later moved to the emperor's palace. The *Laudation of the 318 Fathers*, written in the early eighth century to commemorate the council, referred to Constantine's palace, claiming that the palace was celebrated and preserved as the site of the Council of Nicaea. However, the *Laudation* also mentioned a separate structure, a church. The document stated that two of the participants at the Nicaean Council passed away and were buried in the church. I suspect that two of the tombs currently located in the submerged basilica were those mentioned by the *Laudation*.

Picking up on the references to the palace, it is common for scholars to assume that the First Council of Nicaea was held exclusively in the palace. The location of the palace is not known anywhere in Iznik. Likewise, prior to the discovery of the underwater basilica, no known church in Iznik could be dated to the fourth century. Some have concluded that no permanent Christian structure (church) existed in Nicaea during the fourth century. Some have even suggested that the so-called palace of Constantine was little more than a villa that the emperor appropriated for the meetings. The 2014 discovery of the submerged basilica in Lake Iznik and the subsequent excavations have seemingly supplied answers to one of those questions.

The First Council of Nicaea concluded with the issue of the Nicaean Creed, one of the earliest foundational theological documents of the early church. The monumental achievement of gathering some three hundred bishops from across the Mediterranean world was a remarkable point in time for Christian history. Nicaea became a pilgrimage site while the basilica was still visible. However, once the structure disappeared beneath the lake, there was nothing more to see. Thus, the site was almost forgotten. Few pilgrims came to the city. But the events surrounding the council were never forgotten. The discovery and excavation of the submerged basilica is an exciting development.

Today, Christians of all denominations look to Nicaea as a beginning of Christian theology. It was a beginning, not because Christians never thought about theology in the preceding three centuries, but because the work at Nicaea was a consensus of theology, a truly ecumenical moment for the church. With its magnificent city walls, fascinating ancient gates and numerous Byzantine churches, the Turkish city of Iznik is now complete with the discovery of the underwater basilica. The pilgrims can now return to ancient Nicaea.

GLOSSARY

acropolis—the "high city" generally containing the residence of the king and chief deities
agora—the Greek commercial center, generally an open area in the center of a city
aisle—two longitudinal areas flanking the nave of a basilica, often reserved for seating
ambo—a stepped speaker's podium, usually located in the center of the basilica
apse—the semicircular area generally at the front of a basilica, often with an altar
aqueduct—a water system conducting water from a source into a city
arcosolium—an arched burial niche cut into a structure or rock
atrium—an open area, surrounded by walls or columns, located outside the narthex of a basilica
basilica—a structure originally designed by the Romans for public gatherings; adopted as the plan for large churches
bouleuterion—shaped like a small theater, a structure where the civic officials (*boulē*) met
Byzantine period—time from Constantine up until the Muslim conquests (AD 325–1453)
***cappuccina* tomb**—a tomb consisting of terracotta roofing tiles surrounding the deceased
Cardo Maximus—the main north-south street in a Roman city
cavea—the seating area of the theater shaped as a semicircular bowl
cella—the inner room of a temple, the house of the deity containing the cult statue
chi-rho—the first two Greek letters for Christ, a typical Byzantine symbol of Christianity
column drum—a cylindrical section of a column, several of which constitute the entire column
colymbion—a basin in a church, usually located in the narthex, to dispense holy water or oil
crepidoma—the flat platform on which a temple rests, generally consisting of three steps

Decumanus Maximus—the main east-west street in a Roman city
diaconicon—a section of the pastophoria located to the right of the apse
entablature—the horizonal architectural pieces supported by columns
forum—an open-air square, the political center of a Roman city, similar to the Greek agora
frieze—a section of the entablature, usually decorated with reliefs depicting a story
gymnasium—a Greek school, including intellectual as well as physical instruction
Hellenistic period—time from Alexander the Great extending to the Roman period (300–50 BC)
in antis—columns set back from the front of a structure
in situ—a term used by archaeologists indicating remains as they were found "in place"
martyrion—a structure constructed over the site of a martyr's execution or burial
menorah—the seven-branched candelabrum, the distinctive symbol of Judaism
narthex—the outer entrance of a basilica, usually located in the west, prior to the nave
nave—the center section of a basilica where most of the congregants were seated
necropolis—the "city of the dead," the ancient cemetery
nymphaeum—a decorative fountain
opus sectile—an expensive floor consisting of geometric marble tiles
pastophoria—the rooms flanking the central apse of a basilica, used for sacred objects
pediment—the triangular gable supporting the roof of a temple
peripteral—a temple surrounded by columns
peristyle—a structure, commonly a temple, surrounded by columns
prothesis—a section of the pastophoria located to the left of the apse of a basilica
radiocarbon dating—the use of an isotope of carbon-14 to date carboniferous remains
Roman imperial period—time from first Roman emperors until Constantine (50 BC–AD 325)
sarcophagus—a large limestone tomb
shards—broken pottery or lamps
spolia—architectural materials reused in later structures
stratigraphy—the study of layers of soil and debris that accumulate over time
stylobate—the top step of the crepidoma, on which the columns and temple rest
synthronon—a tiered, semicircular seating area in the apse of a basilica
temenos—the sacred area surrounding a temple, sometimes enclosed with a wall
terracotta—fired clay, commonly used for lamps and pottery
theater—a semicircular structure designed for theatrical and musical productions
tholos—a circular structure, commonly colonnaded, used as a temple or honorific tomb

BIBLIOGRAPHY

Achtemeier, Paul. *1 Peter: A Commentary on First Peter.* Hermeneia. Philadelphia: Fortress, 1996.

Anatolios, Khaled. *Retrieving Nicaea: The Development and Meaning of Trinitarian Doctrine*. Grand Rapids, MI: Baker, 2011.

Attaleiates Michael. *The History*. Translated by Anthony Kaldellis and Dimitris Krallis. Cambridge, MA: Harvard University Press, 2012.

Aydın, Ayşe. "Hıristiyan Dinindeki Martir-Aziz ve Rölik Kültünün Kilikya-Isaurya Bölgesi Hıristiyanlığına Yansımaları (Märtyrer, Heilige und Reliquienkult im Kilikisch-Isaurischen Raum)," *Olba* 17 (2009): 63-82.

Ayres, Lewis. *Nicaea and Its Legacy: An Approach to Fourth-Century Trinitarian Theology*. New York: Oxford University Press, 2006.

Barry, Jennifer. *Bishops in Flight: Exile and Displacement in Late Antiquity.* Oakland: University of California Press, 2019.

Bayliss, Richard. "Provincial Cilicia and the Archaeology of Temple Conversion." 2 vols. PhD diss., University of Newcastle upon Tyne, 2001.

Beard, Mary, John North, and Simon Price. *Religions of Rome*. Vol. 1. Cambridge: Cambridge University Press, 1996.

Benjelloun, Yacine, J. de Sigoyer, H. Dessales, L. Baillet, P. Gueguen, and M. Şahin. "Historical Earthquake Scenarios for the Middle Strand of the North Anatolian Fault Deduced from Archeo-Damage Inventory and Building Deformation Modeling." *Seismological Society of America* 92 (2021): 583-98.

Benjelloun, Yacine, J. de Sigoyer, S. Garambois, J. Carcaillet, and Y. Klinger. "Segmentation and Holocene Behavior of the Middle Strand of the North Anatolian Fault (NW Turkey)." *Tectonics* 40 (2021): 1-32.

Benjelloun, Yacine, Mustafa Şahin, et al. "Construction History of the Aqueduct of Nicaea (Iznik, NW Turkey) and Its On-fault Deformation Viewed from Archaeological and Geophysical Investigations." *Journal of Archaeological Science* 21 (2018): 389-400.

Boero, Dina. "The Cultural Biography of a Pilgrimage Token: From Hagiographical to Archaeological Evidence." *Archiv für Religionsgeschichte* 21 (2020): 155-76.

Brent, Liana. "Disturbed, Damaged and Disarticulated: Grave Reuse in Roman Italy." In *TRAC 2016 Proceedings of the Twenty-Sixth Theoretical Roman Archaeology Conference*. Rome: Edizioni Quasar, 2017.

Brook, Eric. "Hagiography, Modern Historiography and Historical Representation." *Fides et Historia* 42.2 (2010): 1-26.

Brown, Peter R. L. *The Cult of the Saints: Its Rise and Function in Latin Christianity.* Chicago: University Chicago, 1982.

Buckler, W. H., and W. M. Calder, eds. *Monumenta Asiae Minoris Antiqua*. Vol. 6, *Monuments and Documents from Phrygia and Caria*. Manchester: Manchester University Press, 1939.

Calder, W. M. "Early Christian Epitaphs from Phrygia." *Anatolian Studies* 5 (1955): 25-38.

Camerlenghi, Nicola. *St. Paul's Outside the Walls: A Roman Basilica, from Antiquity to the Modern Era*. Cambridge: Cambridge University Press, 2018.

Cameron, Alan. *The Last Pagans of Rome*. New York: Oxford, 2010.

Cameron, Averil, and Stuart G. Hall, eds. *Life of Constantine: Introduction, Translation and Commentary*. Clarendon Ancient History Series. Oxford: Clarendon, 1999.

Carrier, Richard. "The Prospect of a Christian Interpolation in Tacitus, 'Annals' 15.44." *Vigiliae Christianae* 68, no. 3 (2014): 264-83.

Çetinkaya, Halük. "Byzantine Churches of Nicaea." *Nis and Byzantium* 19 (2020): 55-76.

Chiricat, Edouard. "The 'Crypto-Christian' Inscriptions of Phrygia." In *Roman Phrygia*, 198-214. Cambridge: Cambridge University Press, 2013.

Çınar, H. E., A. Y. Turgal, A. E. Erginal, O. Erenoğlu, E. U. Ulugergerli, and R. C. Erenoğlu. "Is Submergence of the Saint Neophytos Basilica (Lake İznik, NW Turkey) Caused by AD 740 Earthquake or Climate Change? Discussion of Geoelectrical Data." *International Conference on Science and Technology (ICONST)* (2019): 1-9.

Coleman-Norton, P. R. *Roman State and Christian Church: A Collection of Legal Documents to A.D. 535*. 3 vols. London: SPCK, 1966.

Crowley, Roger. *1453: The Holy War for Constantinople and the Clash of Islam and the West*. New York: Hyperion, 2005.

Currid, John D. *Doing Archaeology in the Land of the Bible: A Basic Guide*. Grand Rapids, MI: Baker, 1999.

Dindorf, Ludwig August, ed. *Chronicon Paschale*. Vol. 1. *Corpus Scriptorum Historiae Byzantinae*. Bonn: Weberi, 1832.

Downey, G. *The Shrines of St. Babylas at Antioch and Daphne*. In *Antioch On-the-Orontes II*, edited by R. Stillwell, 45-48. Princeton, NJ: Princeton University Press, 1938.

Dunn, James D. G. *Beginning from Jerusalem*. Vol. 2 of *Christianity in the Making*. Grand Rapids: Eerdmans, 2009.

Duval, Yvette. *Aupres des Saints Corps et Ame: L'inhumation "ad Sanctos" dans la Chretiente d'Orient et d'Occident du IIIe au VIIe siècle*. Paris: Etudes Augustiniennes, 1988.

Erginal, A. E., R. C. Erenoğlu, C. Yıldırım, H. H. Selim, N. G. Kıyak, O. Erenoğlu, E. Ulugergerli, and M. Karabıyıkoğlu. "Co-sesmic Beachrock Deformation of 8th Century AD Earthquake in Middle Strand of North Anatolian Fault, Lake İznik, NW Turkey." *Tectonophysics* 799 (2021): 1-8.

Ermiş, Ü. Melda. "İznik Sarayı Çevresindeki Kiliseler." In *The Proceeding of the International Workshop: Localisation of the 1st Council Palace in Nicaea*, edited by Mustafa Şahin and İbrahim Mert, 79-103. Bursa: Uludağ Universitesi, 2011.

Fine, Steven, and Leonard Rutgers. "New Light on Judaism in Asia Minor During Late Antiquity: Two Recently Identified Inscribed Menorahs." *JSQ* 3 (1996): 1-23.

Foss, Clive. *Nicaea: A Byzantine Capital and Its Praises.* Brookline, MA: Hellenic College, 1996.

Gastineau, R., J. de Sigoyer, P. Sabatier, S. C. Fabbri, F. S. Anselmetti, A. L. Develle, M. Şahin, S. Gündüz, F. Niessen, and A.C. Gebhardt. "Active Subaquatic Fault Segments in Lake Iznik Along the Middle Strand of the North Anatolian Fault, NW Turkey." *Tectonics, American Geophysical Union (AGU)* 40 (2021): 1-38.

Giannakopoulis, Nikos. "Groups and Associations in Bithynia and Pontus: Interaction with Prominent Statesmen and Provincial Governors." In *Sencer Şahin, Anısına Yazılar.* Istanbul: Kuzgun Yayınevi, 2016.

Gibbon, Guy. *Critically Reading the Theory and Methods of Archaeology: An Introductory Guide.* New York: Altamira, 2014.

Gibson, Elsa. *The "Christians for Christians" Inscriptions of Phrygia: Greek Texts, Translation and Commentary.* Harvard Theological Studies 32. Missoula, MT: Scholars Press, 1978.

Goldman, Andrew L. "New Evidence for Non-elite Burial Patterns in Central Turkey." In *Life and Death in Asia Minor in Hellenistic, Roman and Byzantine Times.* Edited by J. Rasmus Brandt et al. Oxford: Oxbow, 2017.

Grant, Robert M. "Religion and Politics at the Council of Nicaea." *Journal of Religion* 53, no. 1 (1975): 1-12.

Green, Bernard. *Christianity in Ancient Rome: The First Three Centuries.* London: T&T Clark, 2010.

Green, H. J. M. "Domestic Buildings and Continuation into Anglo-Saxon Times." In *Durovigutum: Roman Godmanchester*, 155-64. Oxford: Archaeopress, 2017.

Guarducci, Margherita. *The Tomb of St. Peter: The New Discoveries in the Sacred Grottoes of the Vatican.* New York: Hawthorn, 1960.

Güngördü, Sedat. "İznik Koimesis Kilisesi ve Önemi." Master's thesis, Uludağ Universitesi, 2019.

Gwynn, D. M. "Reconstructing the Council of Nicaea." In *The Cambridge Companion to the Council of Nicaea*, edited by Young Richard Kim, 90-110. Cambridge: Cambridge University Press, 2021.

Hanson, R. P. C. "The Transformation of Pagan Temples into Churches in the Early Christian Centuries." *Journal of Semitic Studies* 23 (1978): 257-67.

Hicks, Benjamin. "Pliny the Younger and the Role of the Governor in Imperial Communication." Paper from the 109th Annual Meeting of the Classical Association of the Middle West and South. Iowa City, IA, 2013.

Hill, Stephen. *The Early Byzantine Churches of Cilicia and Isauria*. Birmingham Byzantine and Ottoman Monographs 1. Aldershot, UK: Variorum Ashgate, 1996.

———. "Matronianus, 'Comes Isauriae:' An Inscription from an Early Byzantine Basilica at Yanıkhan, Rough Cilicia." *Anatolian Studies* 35 (1985): 93-97.

Instone-Brewer, David. "The Eighteen Benedictions and the Minim Before 70 C.E." *Journal of Theological Studies* 54 (2003): 25–55.

Jacobs, Ine. "Hosting the Council in Nicaea." In *The Cambridge Companion to the Council of Nicaea*, edited by Young Richard Kim, 65-85. Cambridge: Cambridge University Press, 2021.

Jaeschke, Verena. "The Roman Civic Center Under Maxentius (AD 306–312)—Buildings for a New Concept of Sovereignty." In *History Takes Place: Rome. Dynamics of Urban Change*, edited by Anna Hofmann and Martin Zimmermann. Berlin: Jovis Verlag, 2017.

Janin, Raymond. *La geographie ecclesiasatique de l'Empire Byzantin. Premiere Partie: Le siege de Constantinople et le Partiarcat Oecumenique*. Tome III. Paris: Les eglises et les monasteres 2, 1969.

———. *Les Eglises et les Monasteres des Grands Centres Byzantins (Bithynie, Hellespont, Latros, Galesios, Trebizonde, Athenes, Thessalonique)*. Paris: Institut Francais D'Etudes Byzantines, 1975.

Jeffers, James S. *The Greco-Roman World of the New Testament Era: Exploring the Background of Early Christianity*. Downers Grove, IL: InterVarsity Press, 1999.

Keil, Josef, and Adolf Wilhelm. *Denkmäler aus dem Rauhen Kilikien*. MAMA 3. Manchester: Manchester University Press, 1931.

Kim, Y. R., ed. *The Cambridge Companion to the Council of Nicaea*. Cambridge: Cambridge University Press, 2021.

Krautheimer, Richard. "The Constantinian Basilica." *Dumbarton Oaks Papers* 21 (1967): 115-40.

Lampe, Peter. "Traces of Peter Veneration in Roman Archaeology." In *Peter in Early Christianity*, edited by H. K. Bond and L. W. Hurtado, 273-317. Grand Rapids, MI: Eerdmans, 2015.

Lane, William L. "Social Perspectives on Roman Christianity During the Formative Years from Nero to Nerva: Romans, Hebrews, 1 Clement." In *Judaism and Christi-*

anity in First-Century Rome, edited by. K. P. Donfried and P. Richardson, 196-244. Grand Rapids, MI: Eerdmans, 1998.

Laumain, Xavier. "Nuevas Perspectivas sobre el *Opus Craticium* Romano, una Técnica Constructiva Olvidada." In *Actas del Séptimo Congreso Nacional de Historia de la Construcción: Santiago de Compostela*, edited by S. H. Fernandez, vol. 1 (2011): 699-708.

———. "The Roman Timber Framework: A Neglected Construction Method." *Structures and Architecture: Concepts, Applications and Challenges*, edited by P. J. S. Cruz, 2240-47. London: CRC Press, 2013.

Laumain, Xavier, and Angela Lopez Sabater. "Roman *Opus Craticuium*: A Rediscovered Construction Technology." In *International Conference on Structural Analysis of Historical Constructions*, edited by Jerzy Jasienko, 1213-19. Wroclaw, Poland: DWE, 2012.

Mackay, Christopher S. *Ancient Rome: A Military and Political History*. Cambridge: Cambridge University Press, 2004.

MacMullen, Ramsay. *Christianizing the Roman Empire, A.D. 100–400*. New Haven, CT: Yale University Press, 1984.

———. *Voting About God in Early Church Councils*. New Haven, CT: Yale University Press, 2006.

Mango, Cyril. "The Date of the Narthex Mosaics of the Church of the Dormition at Nicaea." *Dumbarton Oaks Papers* 13 (1959): 245.

———. "The Meeting-Place of the First Ecumenical Council and the Church of the Holy Fathers at Nicaea." *Δελτίον της Χριστιανικής Αρχαιολογικής Εταιρείας* 26 (2011).

Mayer, Wendy. "The Late Antique Church at Qausiyeh Reconsidered: Memory and Martyr Burial in Syrian Antioch." In *Martyrdom and Persecution in Late Antique Christianity*, edited by J. Leemans. Leuven: Uitgeverij Peeters, 2010.

Mayor, Adrienne. *The Poison King: The Life and Legend of Mithridates, Rome's Deadliest Enemy*. Princeton, NJ: Princeton University Press, 2010.

McKechnie, Paul. *Christianizing Asia Minor: Conversion, Communities, and Social Change in the Pre-Constantinian Era*. Cambridge: Cambridge University Press, 2019.

Meeks, Wayne A. *The First Urban Christians: The Social World of the Apostle Paul*. New Haven, CT: Yale University Press, 1983.

Mert, İbrahim Hakan. "Nikaia (İznik) Kent Plani Tipolojisi." In *The Proceeding of the International Workshop: Localisation of the 1st Council Palace in Nicaea*, edited by Mustafa Şahin and İbrahim Mert, 171-82. Bursa: Uludağ Universitesi, 2011.

Öztürk, Hüseyin Sami. "Nıkaıa'dan Yeni Yazıtlar V." *Cedrus* 3 (2015): 257-67.

Pachoumi, Eleni. "An Invocation of Chrestos in Magic. The Question of the Orthographical Spelling of Chrestos and Interpretation Issues in PGM XIII.288-95." *Hermethena* 188 (2010): 29-54.

Perczel, István. “Hagiography as a Historiographic Genre: From Eusebius to Cyril of Scythopolis, and Eustratius of Constantinople.” In *Christian Historiography Between Empires (4th–8th Centuries)*. Late Antique History and Religion 23. Leuven: Peeters, 2021.

Peschlow, Urs. “Nicaea.” In *The Archaeology of Byzantine Anatolia: From the End of Late Antiquity Until the Coming of the Turks*. Edited by Philipp Niewönhner. Oxford: Oxford University Press, 2017.

Pharr, Clyde. *The Theodosian Code and Novels and the Sirmondian Constitutions*. Princeton, NJ: Princeton University Press, 1952.

Puddu, Mauro. “Connecting the Dots: Between Sulci, Masullas and Karales.” In *Funerary Archaeology and Changing Identities: Community Practices in Roman-Period Sardinia*, 113-22. Oxford: Archaeopress, 2018.

Ramsay, William M. *The Letters to the Seven Churches of Asia and Their Place in the Plan of the Apocalypse*. 4th ed. London: Hodder and Stoughton, 1904.

Reed, Jonathan L. *The HarperCollins Visual Guide to the New Testament: What Archaeology Reveals About the First Christians*. New York: HarperCollins, 2007.

Ronchetta, Donatell. “The South-East Necropolis in Hierapolis in Phrygia: Planning, Typologies, and Construction Techniques.” In *Life and Death in Asia Minor in Hellenistic, Roman and Byzantine Times*, edited by J. Rasmus Brandt et al. Oxford: Oxbow, 2017.

Roth, Leland M. *Understanding Architecture: Its Elements, History and Meaning*. Boulder, CO: Westview Press, 1993.

Şahin, Mustafa. “Hava Fotoğrafları ve Arkeoloji Biliminde Yeni Bir Keşif: İznik Gölü Bazilikası.” *Yüksek Öğretim Dergisi* (Nov. 2018): 79-81.

———. “İznik Gölü Bazilika KalıntısıSualtı Yüzey Araştırması—2015.” *TINA Denizcilik Arkeoloji Dergisi* 4 (2015): 32-51.

———. “İznik Gölü Bazilika Kazıları—2016.” *TINA Denizcilik Arkeolojisi Dergisi* 6 (2016): 64-79.

———. “İznik Gölü Bazilika Kazıları 2017-2018.” *TINA Denizcilik Arkeolojisi Dergisi* 10 (2018): 116-26.

———. “Neue Forschungen und Ausgrabungen in Der Basilica des İznik Sees.” In *Imperial Residence and Site of Councils: The Metropolitan Region of Nicaea / Nicomedia*, 93-106. Asia Minor Studien, Imperial Residence and Site of Councils 96. Bonn: Rudolf Habelt, 2020.

———. “Nikaia’nın Kayıp Apollon Tapınağı.” *Bursa’da Zaman* (July 2017): 52-53.

———. “Underwater Excavation at the Basilica Church in İznik Lake—2019.” *International Journal of Environment and Geoinformatics (IJEGEO)* 9 (2022): 71-80.

Şahin, Mustafa, and Ahmet Bilir. “Underwater Survey in Lake Iznik—2015.” In *North Meets East 3: Aktuelle Forschungen zu antiken Häfen*, edited by M. Seifert and L. Ziemer, 75-84. Aachen: Shaker, 2016.

Şahin, Mustafa, and Mark Fairchild. "Nicea's Underwater Basilica." *Biblical Archaeology Review* 44, no. 6 (November–December 2018): 30-37, 61.

Şahin, Sencer. *Katalog der antiken Inschriften des Museums von Iznik (Nikaia) / İznik Müzesi Antik Yazıtlar Kataloğu*. Vol. 10.3. Bonn: Rudolf Habelt, 1987.

Schneemelcher, Wilhelm, ed. "The Acts of Andrew," In *New Testament Apocrypha*. Vol. 2, *Writings Related to the Apostles; Apocalypses and Related Subjects*, 101-51. Rev. ed. Louisville, KY: Westminster John Knox, 1989.

Schneider, Alfons M. *Die römischen und byzantinishchen Denkmäler von Iznik-Nicaea*. Istanbuler Forschungen, 16. Berlin: Deutsches archäologisches Institut, 1943.

Schneider, Eugenia Equini. *Elaiussa Sebaste: An Archaeological Guide*. Istanbul: Homer, 2008.

Schuddeboom, Feyo. "The Conversion of Temples in Rome." *Journal of Late Antiquity* 10 (2017): 166-86.

Sevcenko, Nancy Patterson. "The Walters 'Imperial' Menologion." *Journal of the Walters Art Gallery* 51 (1993): 43-64.

Shepardson, Christine. "Rewriting Julian's Legacy: John Chrysostom's On Babylas and Libanius's Oration 24." *Journal of Late Antiquity* 2, no. 1 (2009): 99-115.

Shirley, Elizabeth A. M. "The Building of the Legionary Fortress at Inchtuthil." *Britannia* 27 (1996): 111-28.

Stellacci, Stefania, and Vasco Rato. "Timber-Framing Construction in Herculaneum Archaeological Site: Characterisation and Main Reasons for Its Diffusion." *International Journal of Architectural Heritage* (2019): 1.

Strabo, *Geography*. In *The Geography of Strabo: An English Translation, with Introduction and Notes*, translated by Duane W. Roller. Cambridge: Cambridge University Press, 2014.

Stark, Rodney. *Cities of God: The Real Story of How Christianity Became an Urban Movement and Conquered Rome*. New York: Harper Collins, 2006.

Tabbernee, William. *Montanist Inscriptions and Testimonia: Epigraphic Sources Illustrating the History of Montanism*. PMS 16. Macon, GA: Mercer University Press, 1997.

Talloen, Peter, and Lies Vercauteren. "The Fate of Temples in Late Antique Anatolia." In *The Archaeology of Late Antique "Paganism."* Leiden: Brill, 2011.

Thompson, Leonard L. *The Book of Revelation: Apocalypse and Empire*. New York: Oxford University Press, 1990.

White, Ellen. *Layer by Layer: A Primer on Biblical Archaeology*. Winona, MN: Anselm, 2019.

Wilken, Robert Louis. *The Christians as the Romans Saw Them*. New Haven, CT: Yale University Press, 2003.

Wisniewski, Robert. *The Beginnings of the Cult of Relics*. New York: Oxford, 2018.

Wulff, Oskar. *Die Koimesiskirche in Nicäa und ihre Mozaiken nebst den verwandten kirchlichen Baudenkmälern*. Strassburg: Heitz and Mündel, 1903.

IMAGE CREDITS

FIGURE CREDITS

Figure I.1. Map of ancient Anatolia, Macedonia, and Greece © Tutku Educational Travel

Figure I.2. Map of Roman provinces of Bithynia and Phrygia © Tutku Educational Travel

Figure 1.1. Roman bridge crossing the Sangarius River near Osmaneli © Fairchild

Figure 1.2. Masonry jutting out into Lake Iznik, north of the submerged basilica © Fairchild

Figure 1.3. Aurelia Theodote Diogenes funerary inscription, Nicaea Museum © Fairchild

Figure 1.4. Aurelius Chrestos funerary inscription, Nicaea Museum © Fairchild

Figure 1.5. Emperor Constantine, Museo Capitoline, Rome © Fairchild

Figure 2.1. House church, Laodicea © Fairchild

Figure 2.2. Yanikhan martyrion basilica © Fairchild

Figure 2.3. Sardis, indirect temple-church conversion © Fairchild

Figure 2.4. St. John Basilica, utilizing spolia from Artemission, Ephesus © Fairchild

Figure 3.1. Submerged basilica suction tube tray, Nicaea © Fairchild

Figure 3.2. February 2023 earthquake remains at Antakya © Fairchild

Figure 3.3. Fault lines at Lake Iznik © Tutku Educational Travel

Figure 3.4. Map of Byzantine Nicaea ©Tutku Educational Travel

Figure 3.5. Yenişehir Gate, Nicaea © Fairchild

Figure 3.6. Nave of Hagia Sophia, Nicaea © Fairchild

Figure 3.7. Synthronon of Hagia Sophia, Nicaea © Fairchild

Figure 3.8. Diaconicon of Hagia Sophia, Nicaea © Fairchild

Figure 3.9. Remains from the Koimesis basilica, Nicaea © Fairchild

Figure 3.10. Excavations at the Roman theater, Nicaea © Fairchild

Figure 3.11. C. Cassius Philiscus obelisk, Nicaea © Fairchild

Figure 3.12. Berber Kaya tomb, Nicaea © Fairchild

Figure 3.13. Nicaea north walls, near the Istanbul Gate © Fairchild

Figure 4.1. Apollo temple, phase 1. Drawing provided by Professor Mustafa Şahin
Figure 4.2. Apollo temple, phase 2. Drawing provided by Professor Mustafa Şahin
Figure 4.3. Temple-basilica conversion, phase 3. Drawing provided by Professor Mustafa Şahin
Figure 4.4. Converted basilica, phase 4. Drawing provided by Professor Mustafa Şahin
Figure 4.5. Joint of narthex wall and southern nave wall © Fairchild
Figure 4.6. Diagram of tombs in submerged basilica. Drawing provided by Professor Mustafa Şahin
Figure 4.7. *Cappuccina* tombs near the Yenisehir Gate, Nicaea © Fairchild
Figure 4.8. *Cappuccina* tombs partially buried under wall. Photo provided by Professor Mustafa Şahin
Figure 4.9. Erotic oil lamp, Nicaea. Photo provided by Professor Mustafa Şahin
Figure 5.1. Codex Sinaiticus, St. Catherine's Monastery, Egypt © Fairchild
Figure 5.2. Christ Pantocrator. Photo provided by Professor Mustafa Şahin
Figure 5.3. Diocaesarea martyrion, northern necropolis © Fairchild
Figure 5.4. Elaiussa Sebaste west martyrion, Cilicia © Fairchild
Figure 5.5. Elaiussa Sebaste east martyrion, Cilicia © Fairchild
Figure 5.6. Papylos martyrion basilica, Kanytelis, Cilicia © Fairchild
Figure 5.7. Thecla basilica, Silifke, Cilicia © Fairchild
Figure 5.8. Yanikhan martyrion arcosolium, Cilicia © Fairchild
Figure 5.9. Koimesis ambo, Nicaea Museum © Fairchild
Figure 6.1. Casa a Graticcio, Herculaneum © Fairchild
Figure 6.2. Nails from the submerged basilica. Photo provided by Professor Mustafa Şahin
Figure 6.3. Nails from the submerged basilica. Photo provided by Professor Mustafa Şahin
Figure 6.4. Diagram of Thecla Basilica, Silifke, from Stephen Hill, *The Early Byzantine Churches of Cilicia and Isauria*, figure 43.

PLATE FIGURE CREDITS

Plate 1. Submerged basilica at Nicaea © Fairchild
Plate 2. The ancient walls and one of 114 towers encircling Nicaea © Fairchild
Plate 3. Underground pool and menorah, east of the Koimesis Church, Nicaea © Fairchild
Plate 4. Flavia Prisca, Christians for Christians funerary inscription, Kutahya Museum © Fairchild
Plate 5. Boteris funerary inscription, Nicaea Museum © Fairchild
Plate 6. Christians for Christians, Bursa Museum © Fairchild
Plate 7. Alexandros Martyr funerary inscription, Kutahya Museum © Fairchild
Plate 8. Christians for Christians funerary inscription, Kutahya Museum © Fairchild

Plate 9. Menologion of Neophytos, Vatican Library © Fairchild
Plate 10. Laodicea pavement chi-rho, alpha-omega graffiti © Fairchild
Plate 11. Laodicea step graffiti—a church with eight crosses © Fairchild
Plate 12. Zeus temple—direct conversion to a basilica, Diocaesarea, Cilicia © Fairchild
Plate 13. Submerged Byzantine basilica at Cenchreae, Greece © Fairchild
Plate 14. Hagia Sophia, Nicaea © Fairchild
Plate 15. Istanbul Gate, Nicaea © Fairchild
Plate 16. Marcus Plancius Varus, Lefke Gate, Nicaea © Fairchild
Plate 17. Roman theater, Nicaea © Fairchild
Plate 18. Lake Iznik ruins, Nicaea © Fairchild
Plate 19. Atrium well and column pieces © Fairchild
Plate 20. Valens and Valentinian coins. Photo provided by Professor Mustafa Şahin
Plate 21. Joint of narthex wall and southern nave wall © Fairchild
Plate 22. Submerged *cappuccina* tombs. Photo provided by Professor Mustafa Şahin
Plate 23. Skeletal remains. Photo provided by Professor Mustafa Şahin
Plate 24. Atrium well © Fairchild
Plate 25. Diaconicon sarcophagus remains © Fairchild
Plate 26. Yanikhan martyrion, Cilicia © Fairchild
Plate 27. Neophytos sacrophagus panel, Nicaea Museum © Fairchild
Plate 28. Inside Neophytos sarcophagus panel, Nicaea Museum © Fairchild
Plate 29. Remains of submerged sarcophagus. Photo provided by Professor Mustafa Şahin

GENERAL INDEX

Aberkios of Hierapolis, 32
Acts of Andrew, 18-19
Adana, 59
Aizanoi, 66
Alexander bishop of Alexandria, 44, 46
Alexandros martyr, 34
Ambrose, 63
Anatolian Plate, 74, 76-77
Anatolius of Gangra, 27
Antakya, 74-75
Anthimus of Nicomedia, 27
Antigonus Monophthalmus, 12
Aperlai, 77
Aphrodisias, 66
Apollo Temple (Apollonion), 8, 9, 94, 96, 98, 100-101, 106, 108-13
Aquila, 52, 67
Arabian Plate, 74
Archampoli, 77
Arius, 44-47, 136, 152, 155, 159
Athanasius, 45-47, 136
Atrium, 8-9, 58, 72, 74, 96, 98-99, 102, 108-9, 122, 129, 146-47, 162
Ascania, 5, 69
Augustine, 104, 114
Aurelius Trophimus, 33-34
Aydın, Ayşe, 59
Babylas, 100, 101
Bactyanus, 98
Basil II, 35, 37, 80, 114
Basilica of Saint John, 65
Basilica of Maxentius, 142
Basilica Porcia, 57
Bayliss, Richard, 63-66, 99-101
Benjelloun, Yacine, 77-78, 83
Berber Rock, 90
birkat ha-Minim, 49
Bithynia, 7, 12-19, 21, 24, 28, 34, 37-38, 47, 49, 83-84, 90, 98
Böcek Ayazma, 87
Boero, Dina, 119-20
Boyalıca Fault, 78
Brook, Eric, 39
Bursa, 3, 5, 70
Bursa Museum, 34
Çanakkale Onsekiz Mart University, 79
Cappuccina tomb, 71, 82, 92, 104-5, 141
Cardo Maximus, 81
Cenchrea, 77
ceramics, 6, 108
Çetinkaya, Halük, 82, 84-85, 87-89, 131
Chalcedon, 14, 154, 159
chi-rho, 4, 31, 43
Chrestos, 30-32
Christ Pantocrator, 119
Christians for Christians inscriptions, 31, 33-35
Chronicon Paschale, 8, 94, 96, 98, 111, 113
Chrysanthus, 139, 150
Claros, 109, 111
Claudius Gothicus, 13-14, 17, 31
Claudius II Gothicus, 83
Çınar, H. E., 79-80
Codex, 31, 62, 67, 99
Collegia, 60
Colymbion, 74, 109, 122
Commodus, 8, 94, 96, 98
Constantine, 2, 4, 8-9, 14, 34, 40-48, 53, 57, 62-63, 68, 90, 99, 136-38, 140, 142, 150-51, 155-57, 159-60, 163
Constantinople, 8, 14-15, 26, 35, 47, 78, 90, 139, 154-55, 160
Constantius I, 41
Constantius II, 160
Corasion, 59, 121-22, 130
Corinth, 109, 158-59

Corycos, 59, 121-22, 130
Council of Nicaea, 3, 4, 7, 9, 40, 47-48, 74, 79, 120, 139-42, 145, 151-57, 163-64
Currid, John, 69
Daphne, 100-101
Decius, 26, 37-38, 63, 85, 114
Delos, 109, 111
Decumanus Maximus, 82, 91
Diaconicon, 57, 71-73, 93, 115, 124, 129, 131, 133, 135, 146, 162,
Didache, 51
Didyma, 66, 111
Dikilitaş, 90
Dio Cassius, 14, 61
Dio Chrysostom, 61
Diocaesarea, 59, 66, 112, 121-22, 130
Diocletian, 26-27, 37, 41, 59, 62, 95, 98, 161
Diotrephes, 50
Diomedes of Tarsus, 27
Domitian, 17, 19, 21-22, 61
Dorymedon, 34
Downey, G., 100
Dunn, James, 50, 52
Dura-Europos, 55
earthquake, 7, 74-80, 85, 87, 93, 131, 139, 150,
Ebionites, 156
Ecumenical Council, 2, 5, 10, 14, 41, 45, 47, 85, 131, 151, 154, 160, 163
Edict of Milan, 4, 7, 9, 27-30, 37, 43, 48-49, 56, 58, 62-63, 67-68, 95-96, 98-99, 102, 104, 112, 115, 121, 135-36, 139-42, 146, 151, 154, 162
Edict of Serdica (Toleration), 30, 43
Edicts, 8, 27-28, 37, 60, 62-63, 68, 102
Elaiussa Sebaste, 59
Elbeyli, 90, 115
Electrical Resistivity, 79, 108
Ephesus, 15, 16, 20, 50, 52, 65, 67, 154
Epistle to Diognetus, 53
Eumeneian Formula, 29, 33
Eurasian Plate, 74
Eusebius of Caesarea, 4, 16, 20, 31, 38, 41-46, 57, 62, 137-42, 146-47, 150-51, 158, 163
Eusebius of Nicomedia, 46-47, 159
Eustathios of Gangra, 27
Eutychos, 35
Fault, 7, 74-79, 93, 162
Foss, Clive, 14-15, 26, 87, 89
Funerary inscription, 7, 28-31, 33, 35, 48
Galerius, 30, 41, 43, 62
Gastineau, R., 77, 78
Gibbon, Guy, 69
Gibson, Elsa, 33-34
Gnosticism, 50, 157
Goths, 14, 80-81
Great Schism, 154
Güngördü, Sedat, 132
Grant, Robert, 46, 136-37, 140, 153
Gymnasium, 13, 16, 82, 84, 91
Hadrian, 13, 83
Hagia Irene, 47, 154, 160
Hagia Sophia, 82, 85
Hanson, R.P.C., 66-67, 101
Helena, 4, 41
Herculaneum, 144, 146
Hill, Stephen, 121-23, 127, 129-30, 148
home (house) church, 50-52, 54-56, 67, 141
homoiousios, 47
homoousios, 46-47
Hosios of Cordoba, 44-45
Ichthus, 33, 53
Ignatius, 20-21
Illyricum, 46
Imperial Decrees, 26-27, 29, 46, 60, 62-63, 67, 142
Inchtuthil, 145
Instone-Brewer, David, 49
Irenaeus, 157
Isauria, 59
Istanbul Gate, 6, 13, 82-84, 91, 140
İznik Fault, 78
Jacobs, Ine, 45, 137, 140
Jeffers, James, 51
John, 20, 50-52, 65, 67, 116, 159
Julian, 47, 62, 100-101
Justinian, 26, 83-84, 140
Juvenal, 61
Kanytelis, 59, 121, 126, 131
Kekova, 77
Koimesis Church, 18, 87, 89, 131-32, 134-35
Krautheimer, Richard, 142
Kutahya Museum, 34-35
Kyaneai, 65
Kyzikos, 78-79
Lactantius, 41
Lake Ascania, 13, 47-48, 77, 80, 87, 109, 112, 114
Laodicea, 30, 56, 67
Laskarsis, 87
Lateran Basilica, 142
Laudation of the 318 Fathers, 137-38, 150, 163
Laumain, Xavier, 143-45
Lefke Gate, 6, 13, 83, 90, 115
Letoon, 65
lex iulia, 60
Lucian, 44

Lucinius, 4
Lysimachus, 12
McKechnie, Paul, 29, 57
MacMullen, Ramsay, 28, 54, 57, 61, 153
Mango, Cyril, 87, 138-40
Manzikert, 14
Markos Iulios Eugenios, 29
Maris of Chalcedon, 159
Martial, 61
martyr, 7, 9, 25-28, 34, 36, 38, 40, 44, 48, 58-59, 68, 85, 89, 95, 98-100, 104, 112-17, 119, 121-22, 124, 126, 129-35, 146, 162
martyrion, 6, 7, 9, 26, 58-59, 68, 73, 93, 100, 101, 104, 113-16, 119, 121-35, 141, 146, 148, 151, 161-62
Martyrium Ignatii, 20
Mayer, Wendy, 100
Maximian, 27, 37, 41
Maximinus II, 43
Meeks, Wayne A, 51
Menologion, 35-36, 80, 114, 161
menorah, 18, 88
Mert, İbrahim, 91
Michael Attaleiates, 78-79, 139
Miletus, 111
Milvian Bridge, 4, 41
Mithridates VI, 12-13
Montanus, 51, 156
Murawiew, 132, 134
Musonius, 139, 150
Nails, 10, 73, 108, 145-48, 151
Narthex, 58, 71-74, 87, 96, 98-99, 102, 108-10, 122, 124, 128-32, 142, 146-47, 150, 162
Necropolis, 58-59, 88, 104, 115-16, 122-23, 126, 134-35, 140
Nicaean Creed, 5, 152, 160, 164
Nicholas of Myra, 46
Nicomedes I, 12
Nicomedes IV, 12-13
Nicomedia, 12-14, 18, 21, 24-27, 37, 41, 43, 46-47, 77, 90, 159
Nikephoros III Botaneiates, 14
Neophytos, 7, 9, 27, 35-40, 48, 79, 87, 95, 98-101, 107, 112-16, 119-20, 131-35, 141, 146, 151, 161-62
North Anatolian Fault, 7, 76-78, 93
Nympha, 67
oil lamp, 73, 74, 98, 107-8
Öküzlü, 59
opus craticium, 143-44
Öztürk, Hüseyin, 30
Pachoumi, Eleni, 31
Patricus Nikephoros, 132
Paul, 10, 15-18, 31-33, 47, 50, 52, 67, 100, 115, 156-60
PBS, *Secrets of the Dead*, 80
Pepuza, 51
Perczel, István, 38
Pergamon, 14, 18, 66
Persecution, 3, 4, 7, 17, 19, 22, 24-30, 34, 43, 48, 52-63, 68, 85, 95, 98, 100, 114, 119, 121, 153, 161
Peschlow, Urs, 115, 140
Peter, 16-18, 24, 31, 47, 115
Philemon, 52, 67
Philostorgius, 46
Philostratus, 61
Phrygia, 7, 16, 28, 31-35, 51, 56, 57, 156-57
Plancius Varus, 83
Plate, 74, 76, 77
Pliny the Younger, 13, 19, 21, 52, 53, 61, 84
Pneumatomachians, 47
Pompeii, 57, 108, 144, 146
Prisca, 67
Prothesis, 57, 71, 72, 73, 93, 99, 108, 124, 129, 131, 141, 146, 151, 162
Quintilian, 61
Radiocarbon, 105
Ramsay, William, 34
Reed, Jonathan L, 52, 55
Rome, 12-13, 16-17, 20, 31-33, 43, 55, 63-64, 67, 80, 104, 115, 142, 144, 154-56
Rough Cilicia, 9, 58, 121, 124, 135
Sabbatius, 34
Şahin, Mustafa, ix, 2, 3, 7, 8, 69-74, 80, 91-101, 107-10, 115, 119, 139, 141, 147, 161
Sagalassos, 65-66
Sangarius River, 11
Sarcophagus, 29, 30, 32, 40, 71-73, 82-83, 87, 93, 105, 115, 122, 130-35, 161-62
Schneider, Eugenia, 126
School of Tyrannus, 16, 50
Schuddeboom, Feyo, 99
Secundus of Ptomemais, 46
Seismologist, 77, 80, 93, 108
Seleucia ad Calycadnum, 59, 121, 127
Sevcenko, Nancy, 35
Shirley, Elizabeth, 145
Selge, 66
Severos, bishop of Laodicea Katakekaumene, 30
Severus, 98
Side, 65
Silifke, 59, 127, 148
Simena, 77

Şimşek, 56
Smintheon, 109
Socrates Scolasticus, 100
Sozomen, 100
Spolia, 64-65, 82-83, 110, 124, 126-27, 148
Stark, Rodney, 40
Statius, 61
Stellacci, Stefania, 143-44
Strabo, 13, 81, 84, 91
Suetonius, 19, 31, 61
Symeon Metaphrastes, 35
Synagogue, 16, 18, 49, 55
Synod at Tyre, 46-47
Tabbernee, William, 29, 30, 34, 35
Talloen, 64-65, 67, 101, 107
Taşucu, 59
Temenos church, 64-65
Temple Conversions, 64-68, 101, 112
Temple-church, 66
Temple of Domitian, 16
Temple-Spolia-Church, 64-65
Tertullian, 53-55, 157
Theater, 6, 54, 82, 84, 88, 93, 124
Theimussa, 77
Theodoret, 100
Theodosius I, 47, 62-63, 73, 99, 160
Theodosius II, 67
Theodote of Nicaea, 27, 31
Theognis of Nicaea, 46, 159
Theonas of Marmarica, 46, 159
Thespesius of Gangra, 27
Thessalonica, 43, 63
Thompson, Glen, x, 44, 61, 153
Thompson, Leonard, 60-61
Timber Construction, 142-45
Tischendorf, Constantin, 118
Titus, 17, 82
Token, 63, 119, 120, 135, 161
towers, 6, 81, 83, 93
Trajan, 13, 17, 19-25, 47, 52
Trophimos martyr from Synnada, 34
Tryphon of Nicaea, 26, 85
Uludağ University, ix, 3, 6, 70, 92
Valens, 47, 72, 99, 105, 141, 160
Valentinian, 62, 72, 99, 105, 141
Van, 74-76
Vatican, 35-37, 48, 55, 80, 94, 114, 161
Vercauteren, 64-65, 67, 101
Vespasian, 13-14, 17, 82-83
Victorinus, 96
Villa Quintiliorum, 55
Vitruvius, 143-44
Walls, 6, 8, 10, 14-15, 36, 56, 66, 79-82, 85, 87-89, 93-99, 101, 102, 106, 110-13, 115-16, 119, 126, 134-35, 140, 143-44, 146, 150, 164
well, 9, 72, 74, 96-99, 108-9, 147
White, Ellen, 69
Willibald, 74, 108, 109, 139, 150
Wood, 10, 72-74, 108, 110, 122, 123, 141, 143-48, 151, 162, 163
Wulff, Oskar, 132, 133
Yanıkhan, 59, 121, 129
Yenişehir Gate, 3, 6, 13, 83, 89, 105